{The Concise Guide to}

DNS AND BIND

Nicolai Langfeldt

 201 W 103rd Street
Indianapolis, IN 46290

Nicolai Langfeldt

The Concise Guide to DNS and BIND

International Standard Book Number: 0-7897-2273-9

Library of Congress Catalog Card Number: 00-107094

Printed in the United States of America

First Printing: November 2000

03 02 01 00   4   3   2   1

Trademarks

Warning and Disclaimer

Associate Publishers
Tracy Dunkelberger
Jeff Koch

Acquisitions Editor
Kathryn Purdum

Development Editor
Maureen A. McDaniel

Technical Editor
John Traenkenschuh

Managing Editor
Thomas F. Hayes

Senior Editor
Susan Ross Moore

Copy Editor
Megan Wade

Indexer
Deborah Hittel

Proofreaders
Jeanne Clark
Kay Hoskin

Team Coordinator
Vicki Harding

Interior Designer
Trina Wurst

Cover Designer
Radar Design

About the Author

Nicolai Langfeldt is a senior UNIX and network services consultant, working professionally in the field since 1992. Having discovered the Internet in 1988, he took a few years to learn the ropes and has since contributed some back. In 1995, he wrote, and has since maintained and supported, the DNS HOWTO of the Linux Documentation Project. He also has since added the NFS HOWTO to the LDP. In addition, he maintains various free UNIX software that are available on the Net. He and some friends founded Linux Norge in 1996, a central starting point for Norwegians interested in Linux. He lives and works in Oslo, Norway.

About the Technical Editor

John Traenkenschuh is a cubicle dweller who has worked on many corporate network infrastructures and operating system roll-out projects at two major corporations. His current job activities have him transitioning from DNS to LDAP design and support, and he is a Certified Checkpoint Security Engineer (CCSE). While not an Alpha Geek, he is working on his Beta credentials through studying Ancient Mysteries of the Universe, proper UNIX administration, and Star Trek episodes 1 through 14. In his spare time he works at his hobbies, which include woodworking and learning more about Red Hat Linux. He has an avid interest in computer security, having worked as a security analyst for more than five years, and has a future goal of writing a book on computer security for corporations that want "to get it right."

Dedication

To Anne Line, who did half the work on this book and with whom I will enjoy sharing the fruits of it.

Acknowledgments

Thanks to...

...Jens Thomassen, Arnt Gulbrandsen, Steinar Haug, and Thorkild Stray for their help with DNS from my first meeting with the beast, the LDP DNS HOWTO, and this book.

...the ISC and the BIND Internet community for existing and for corresponding with me about BIND and DNS. Also thanks to all the readers of the DNS HOWTO for giving me feedback and encouragement.

...Peter Gabriel, Lamb, The Eurythmics, Lisa Ekdahl, Bel Canto, Leonard Cohen, Marie Brennan, Björk, The Beatles, The Lars Bremnes Band, Anneli Drecker, Mammarazi, Kaliber, Kate Bush, Kari Bremnes, Loreena McKennitt, Hedningarna, Simon and Garfunkel, and Ym Stammen.

...Glen Turner of the University of Adelaide for graciously providing information about AARNet2.

Contents

Introduction **1**
About This Book **1**
The Internet Before DNS **1**
DNS to the Rescue **2**
The Versions of BIND **2**
If It's Worth Doing, It's Worth Doing Right **3**

I Basic DNS

1 DNS Concepts **7**
DNS Is a Hierarchic, Distributed Database **7**
What Is a Domain? **8**
    The Importance of Caching **9**
    Subdomains **9**
Zones and Delegation **9**
Reverse Zones **11**
Duplication and Distribution of Zones **11**
How Resolution Works **12**
    A Records **13**
    Recursion **13**
    NS Records **15**
    CNAME Records **18**
    PTR Records **18**
    A Reverse Lookup **18**
DNS as a Tree **19**

2 DNS in Practice **21**
The BIND Software **21**
    ISC **21**
    Where to Get BIND **22**
    Compiling BIND **22**

Configuring BIND **23**

    `named.conf` **23**

    `root.hints` **24**

    `pz/127.0.0` **25**

Testing It All **26**

    `ndc`: *Starting, Restarting, and Reloading BIND* **26**

    Testing the Zone Files **27**

    The Details of DNS Caching **29**

Resolver Setup **30**

    `/etc/resolv.conf` **31**

    Other Files **32**

    Client Resolver **34**

A Zone **34**

    A Forward Zone **34**

    A Reverse Zone **41**

    Another Zone **42**

Subdomains and Delegation **46**

Reverse Delegations for Classless Nets **47**

Secondary Servers **49**

    Adding a Slave Server **49**

    Stealth Servers **50**

    NOTIFY **50**

3 Maintenance and Enhancements **53**

More Practical Details **53**

Maintaining and Changing Zones **53**

    How SOA Records Controls DNS **53**

DNS Round Robin and Load Distribution **57**

The Trouble with CNAME Records **59**

Wildcard Records **60**

    Restrictions on Wildcards **61**

    The Problem with Wildcards **62**

Logs and Debugging **62**

    BINDs Start, Reload, and Reconfig Logging **62**

    Logging Channels **63**

Logging Categories **64**

BINDs Default Logging Configuration **65**

Controlling Debug Logging **66**

Adding More Domains **67**

Contingency Planning **67**

Internal Redundance **68**

External Redundance **69**

Extended Outages **69**

Practical Uses of Forwarding **70**

The Australian Academic and Research Network **70**

Forwarding in Your Network **71**

Maintaining the root.hints File **72**

4 Getting a Domain **75**

Top-Level Domains and Their Owners **75**

Finding the TLD Owners **76**

Finding the Reverse Zone Owners **76**

The whois Database **76**

Getting the Domain **80**

Slave Servers **80**

When Your Domain Is Taken **80**

Paying for Everything **81**

II Advanced DNS

5 Using Dig and nslookup **85**

Dig **85**

Query Type **86**

Query Options **87**

Dig Options **88**

Dig Batch Files **89**

Dig's Output **90**

Using Dig **92**

nslookup **92**

Tell Us What You Think!

As the reader of this book, *you* are our most important critic and commentator. We value your opinion and want to know what we're doing right, what we could do better, what areas you'd like to see us publish in, and any other words of wisdom you're willing to pass our way.

As an Associate Publisher for Que, I welcome your comments. You can fax, email, or write me directly to let me know what you did or didn't like about this book—as well as what we can do to make our books stronger.

Please note that I cannot help you with technical problems related to the topic of this book, and that due to the high volume of mail I receive, I might not be able to reply to every message.

When you write, please be sure to include this book's title and author as well as your name and phone or fax number. I will carefully review your comments and share them with the author and editors who worked on the book.

Fax: 317-581-4666

Email: opsys@mcp.com

Mail: Associate Publisher
Que Corporation
201 West 103rd Street
Indianapolis, IN 46290 USA

INTRODUCTION

About This Book

This is a book about DNS implemented with BIND, the most widespread implementation of DNS. This book specifically covers BIND 8, the latest production version of BIND, which runs on UNIX and NT. For several good reasons, this is the version of BIND that should be used by every BIND user.

Throughout the book you will find listings of configuration files. These files can be downloaded from the Internet at `http://www.macmillanusa.com/que/concise/bind/` or `http://langfeldt.net/dns/`, where you also can find an errata, should any errors be discovered in this book.

Also, note that in all computer dialog listings in this book, the dollar sign ($) and hash symbol (#) both indicate a shell command-line prompt, as is traditional in UNIX texts.

The Internet Before DNS

In the beginning, before the Internet got big or was even called the Internet, each computer on it needed to know only about a handful of other computers on the Net and a list of all the important Internet hosts that was kept in one file called the `hosts.txt` file. This file was very similar to the

/etc/hosts file on UNIX machines and the lmhosts file on Windows machines. In addition, it was maintained by a central authority, the *InterNIC*, from which computers would periodically transfer it. Site administrators would mail changes to the InterNIC, which would then incorporate the changes. Then, as time progressed, computers would pick up the latest version and get the updated information. Eventually, the change would be known all over the Net.

There is a problem with this simple scheme, though. It does not scale; as the file and Net grow, the maintenance and distribution of a single file from a single point become intractable. In 1983, long before the World Wide Web was even a glimmer in Tim Berens Lee's eye, the Internet was growing quite quickly, and the inadequacy of the hosts.txt file was obvious. It had grown large and cumbersome, and it was easy to see that one central file was not a future-proof solution.

DNS to the Rescue

So, the Net.gods discussed the problem and came up with a plan for a new and better system that could deal with huge numbers of computers. It would have no single administration or distribution bottleneck like the InterNIC—or even any distribution bottleneck—which would enable changes to be distributed in a timely manner. As you read this book, it will become clear, I hope, that DNS is all these things. DNS is quite simply a distributed database with delegation of responsibilities (administration and distribution), which together with one rather important detail—caching of query answers—makes for a pretty good name service for today's Internet.

The Versions of BIND

BIND is an acronym for Berkeley Internet Name Daemon. BIND implements this distributed database. For many years, BIND 4 was the one and only implementation, but it grew old and rusty and was replaced by BIND 8. In addition, BIND 4 had many security problems that have been fixed in BIND 8. At any time, the latest version of BIND 8 is *the* recommended version of BIND, especially for security-conscious sites. However, many sites still use some variant of BIND 4.

A good reason for still using BIND 4 is that most UNIX vendors still ship BIND 4 as their supported version. They have probably also modified it relative to the original version of BIND 4 that they used. On some sites, vendor support is important, so they use BIND 4.

If you use BIND 4 for some other reason, you should be sure you run the latest available version of BIND 4. Some of the most important and pressing security problems of BIND 4 have been fixed in the latest version. Also, if you use BIND 8, you should at all times use the latest available version of it. Chapter 15, "Compiling and Maintaining BIND," covers where to find the latest BIND version and how to get announce mails when new versions are published.

If It's Worth Doing, It's Worth Doing Right

...and this goes doubly for DNS. DNS glues the Internet together (along with several other things of course), and if you mix glue the wrong way, it won't be glue—it will be goo. If you set up DNS incorrectly, a likely outcome will be service disruptions for your users, your customers, and anyone else your organization has relationships with via the Internet. And, let's face it, things such as service disruptions get noticed by users because they create unpleasant situations. The really treacherous part is that DNS problems can blindside you a week, or even *weeks*, after you made some unrelated change to your network.

So, pay attention to all your DNS-related work. DNS is a simple design, but many of the details in its running can foul up everything.

Together, Chapter 2, "DNS in Practice," and Chapter 3, "Maintenance and Enhancements," are the core of this book, and in one way are all you will ever need to know about DNS and BIND. However, in reality, there is a lot more to it than that, which is why this is not a 100-page booklet.

## PART I

BASIC DNS

1 DNS Concepts

2 DNS in Practice

3 Maintenance and Enhancements

4 Getting a Domain

1

DNS Concepts

DNS Is a Hierarchic, Distributed Database

DNS's hierarchy is the result of two things. The most obvious is the domain names, such as www.amazon.com. This is a hierarchic name that is read from left to right. Rightmost is com, which is one of the many hundreds of *top-level domains*, or *TLDs*. Of these TLDs, com, edu, and org are the most well-known, but many, many others exist—one for each nation and territory on the planet. The International Standards Organization (ISO) has a standard for two-letter country codes called ISO-3166. The Internet authorities simply adopted these codes as names for these national domains. Under each TLD several more domains exist, such as amazon in our example. In addition, within the amazon domain, you find several more domain names, including the name of a machine (or several machines sharing one name), such as www. Together, the domain names make up www.amazon.com, which is called a *fully qualified domain name* (*FQDN*) because no part of the name is left out. Both TLD and FQDN are acronyms often found in technical discussions on the Internet.

However, the hierarchy also comes from one other thing, which is linked with the distribution. *Distribution* is the way in which the contents of the DNS database are dispensed among servers on the Net. These make a hierarchy, almost in direct relation to the domain name structure. Authorities on the Net, called *registrars*, have authority over com and the other TLDs.

They give, or delegate, authority over subdomains to the people who manage those subdomains. For instance, people employed by Amazon manage the amazon.com part of the database with their own set of DNS servers that have authority over the amazon.com domain. It is even possible for Amazon, or any other entity, to have several subdomains with delegated authority. This delegation of authority from com to amazon is a very important feature because it distributes both the administrative and technical responsibilities of managing DNS throughout the Net. Herein lies the point of DNS and the reason it can keep growing while the hosts.txt file could not. The delegation of authority over subdomains ensures that DNS is scalable; no single part of DNS will be bogged down by the weight of its responsibilities.

What Is a Domain?

DNS is a hierarchic database. A good analog in computing is a tree data structure as used in programming. Similar to a tree data structure, DNS has a root node, edges, and leaf nodes. Because it's a database, it also has lookup keys and values found by these keys by traversing the tree structure.

If you examine a DNS name such as www.amazon.com, you'll see that all these parts are represented in the name. But first, it's important to realize that in reality the DNS name is www.amazon.com. (with the trailing period). The period is not normally typed, but it is there and is significant. It represents the root node of DNS. Just as in programming, you *must* know where the root node is because it cannot be found automatically. However, after you know where the root of the tree is, everything else can be found. The root is also called the *root domain*. It and each part of the domain name represent a domain, or subdomain, depending on how you look at it. To get between the nodes, which are *nameservers*, edges are necessary, and DNS has edges. In fact, the contents of the DNS database are all edges.

In DNS, each server has a root.hints file that tells it where to look for rootservers (see Figure 1.1).

Figure 1.1   After a DNS server knows where the rootservers are, the rest is a given.

To find the address of a host such as www.amazon.com, your DNS asks the rootservers whether they know its address. They won't know it, but they'll help your DNS on its way by telling it the address of the servers of the com TLD. This pointer represents an edge in the tree structure and points to the next DNS server your DNS needs to talk to. Again, your DNS asks for www.amazon.com, and again the server does not know it. But, it knows the address of the DNS server at amazon.com and tells it to your DNS, which means your DNS has found another edge, taking it to another node and another nameserver. And again, your DNS asks for the address of www.amazon.com. This time, however, because it has finally reached a nameserver that knows this address, the correct record is returned from the database.

The Importance of Caching

All the information gathered while finding the address of www.amazon.com is cached by your DNS so it does not need to ask again. The next time someone asks for the address of www.macmillanusa.com (Macmillan USA), it already knows the address of the com servers so it need not bother the rootservers again. This caching is another key to why DNS works. If the servers never cached the answers they got, the rootservers would be flooded, nay, *devastated*, by queries—one for each domain name lookup done all over the Net. Instead, the local DNS servers need only to establish the server for each TLD and each subdomain that is requested once. So, instead of the load on the rootservers being linear with the number of queries performed on the Net, the load becomes drastically smaller. The caching reduces the load on the root and TLD servers from an amount under which they could not function at all to one under which they can quickly and competently perform their work. The first server setup we will look at is a caching-only nameserver, meaning it performs only caching and is not a server of any particular domains.

Subdomains

Domain names, then, are stacked up—you can have domain within domain within domain, ad nauseum. You might have noticed that in some places they are not stacked any deeper than the typical com case. In the United Kingdom, however, several national subdomains exist, such as co.uk for commercial enterprises and ac.uk for academic endeavors. The Amazon site in the U.K., therefore, is called www.amazon.co.uk.

The distinction between a domain and a subdomain is not fixed. A domain—any domain—might have a subdomain, but it also is a subdomain of another domain, possibly a TLD. So, amazon.com is a subdomain of the com domain, and the com domain is a subdomain of the root domain.

Zones and Delegation

Although DNS appears to be working with domains and subdomains, the boundary of the authority of domains is not drawn between a domain and a subdomain. It is drawn between *zones*, with which DNS works. The line between what is a zone and what is a domain is a bit arbitrary. One thing is sure, though: If a division of authority exists then separate zones exist. When a domain is delegated to you, you set up a zone file for the domain. If the zone has subdomains that other people maintain, you delegate those domains to them, and they will set up zones for them. If the zone has subdomains that you maintain then the zone can contain both the domain and the subdomains.

A good example of this is the university I attended, the University of Oslo. Its domain name is uio.no, as in Universitetet i Oslo. It has several subdomains. One is ifi.uio.no, which is the institute where I took my informatics, or computer science, courses. Another, math.uio.no, is the math department where I later found my first job as a computer administrator.

ifi.uio.no is a separate zone. The computer science department has its own network that it manages, from network cabling up to DNS. Therefore, the domain is managed by people different from the people who manage uio.no, so the authority of the domain ifi.uio.no has been delegated and a separate zone set up. The people at ifi.uio.no can then manage their own zone without consulting with the people at uio.no (see Figure 1.2).

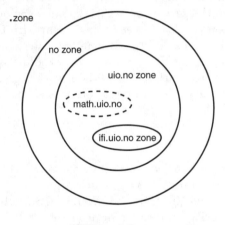

.zone

no zone

uio.no zone

math.uio.no

ifi.uio.no zone

Solid lines circle zones;
stippled lines circle subdomains

Figure 1.2   All zones are administratively independent of each other, whereas subdomains are not.

On the other hand, math.uio.no is not a separate zone. The math department network at the university is managed by the computing center—the same people who manage uio.no. Therefore, the two domains are kept in the same zone. In theory, the computing center could have created a separate zone for math.uio.no and then delegated the authority of it to themselves, but they chose not to.

The importance of the distinction between a domain and a zone is perhaps still a bit unclear, but it will get clearer as you read the book.

Reverse Zones

When a computer is contacted by another computer, the IP stack can supply only the IP number of the originating computer. If the destination computer needs to know the name of the originating computer, for whatever reason, it must find a way to get this information. This also is DNS's job.

To make a reverse lookup possible, you must be able to look up the address and get a name back. In IPv4, this is done with a rather straightforward mechanism. If you have the address of a peer host on the network, such as 129.240.222.66, you look up the name 66.22.240.129. in-addr.arpa in DNS and get the name gilgamesj.uio.no back.

The name is simply the IP address with each address octet in reverse order, with the domain name .in-addr.arpa appended. The in-addr.arpa domain is a special domain that is used only for reverse lookups. The in-addr part stands for *Internet address*, and the arpa comes from the old name of the Internet, the ARPAnet. Therefore, you look up the internet addresses of the ARPAnet in it.

The reverse order of the IP number is a nuisance to write out, and it would also be easier to read it if the IP number was not reversed. However, that would not work. Because IP numbers are also hierarchic, but from left to right, the octets need to be reversed so they are hierarchic from right to left, just as DNS is. Other than that, the in-addr.arpa domain is, technically, just like the other, more familiar, forward domains.

Duplication and Distribution of Zones

DNS is distributed in one other way. Because DNS is so vital to the Internet, it has been designed to be redundant. For each zone, several servers exist. When one server breaks down, the other servers for that domain will still be capable of answering queries about that zone on their own. All a subdomain's authoritative servers are listed in the domain above it. When your computer tries to find an address from a name, it has many alternative servers to query at each step in the process. If one server fails to answer within a set timeout, another will be queried. If they all fail then the query will fail and not return any result. The redundancy not only ensures robustness against failures, it also provides load distribution between the servers that are authoritative for a domain.

It is the responsibility of you, the zone owner, to design and implement the redundancy and robustness you need from DNS. Most TLD authorities require at least two working name-servers for a zone before they will delegate authority over it to the zone owner.

The rootservers are redundant, too. This serves both to distribute load and to be robust against any failure in one, or several, of them.

If you examine where on the Internet the rootservers are located, you discover another important characteristic—they are located in widely different networks in different parts of the world. If the two required nameservers of a zone were located in the same computer room, a single fuse, router, or network switch failure could wipe out name service. Even if they are in separate rooms of the same building, they are still liable to become unavailable to the outside if a single access router, line driver, or power line fails. If two companies share name service, they both must be without network connectivity before name service becomes unavailable. If the two companies are also located in separate cities and use separate Internet providers then they are pretty safe from one single failure taking out their name service.

The rootservers are the most important servers on the entire Internet, which is why they are very redundant. Right now, 13 root nameservers exist on different networks and on different continents. It's pretty unlikely that DNS will fail due to a rootserver failure.

The redundancy necessitates a zone duplication mechanism, a way to copy the zones from a master server to all the redundant slave servers of that zone. Until recently, these servers were usually called *primary* and *secondary* servers, not *master* and *slave*. You will still find this old usage in a lot of documents and discussions on the Net.

In any case, DNS has a duplication mechanism called *zone transfer*. When, as a DNS administrator, you make changes and updates in the zone file on the master server, the slave server will either act on a notification of the update, or if the notification is lost, notice that a long time has elapsed since it last heard from the master server. It will then check whether there are any updates available. If the check fails, it will be repeated quite often until the master answers, making the duplication mechanism more robust against network failures. If the slave server has been incapable of contacting the master server for a long time, usually a week, it will not give up. Instead, it will stop serving queries from the old data it has stored. Serving old data masquerading as correct data can very well be worse than serving no data at all.

How Resolution Works

After you have divided DNS into zones forward and reverse, and they all are redundant and working well, you need a way to get from one zone to another. This mechanism is vital to DNS, and it is vital that you understand it and how important it is because it will help you solve many of the DNS problems you encounter. Several of the questions found in Internet forums about DNS stem from not understanding this linkage and the importance of it being all there and working.

As mentioned earlier, DNS is similar to a tree data structure as used in programs. It has a root node and edges that are used to descend the tree from the root to other nodes and find the data requested.

When a piece of software requests a piece of information from DNS, it specifies two things: the RR (or *resource record*) type, which is the kind of information it needs, and the domain name of the record, which in database language is the *lookup key*.

A Records

To find the address of www.amazon.com, it specifies that it wants the A (address) record for www.amazon.com. Software tools are available to perform such lookups on the command line and display the results. I will use dig, which is a very powerful DNS tool. Unfortunately, dig is not ubiquitous, but it is the best tool I know for this task. If your system lacks dig, see Chapter 15, "Compiling and Maintaining BIND," for instructions on how to compile and install BIND. When you have installed a new BIND, you will also have dig.

First, use dig to find the A record for www.amazon.com:

```
$ dig www.amazon.com A

; <<>> DiG 8.2 <<>> www.amazon.com A
;; res options: init recurs defnam dnsrch
;; got answer:
;; ->>HEADER<<- opcode: QUERY, status: NOERROR, id: 4
;; flags: qr aa rd ra; QUERY: 1, ANSWER: 1, AUTHORITY: 1, ADDITIONAL: 0
;; QUERY SECTION:
;;       www.amazon.com, type = A, class = IN

;; ANSWER SECTION:
www.amazon.com.         1M IN A         208.216.182.15

;; AUTHORITY SECTION:
www.amazon.com.         1S IN NS        ns-10.amazon.com.

;; Total query time: 5248 msec
;; FROM: roke.uio.no to SERVER: default -- 127.0.0.1
;; WHEN: Tue Feb 29 20:50:22 2000
;; MSG SIZE  sent: 32  rcvd: 78
```

If you look through all that verbiage, you will find what we asked for. In the ANSWER SECTION, you see that www.amazon.com has an A record that says the address is 208.216.182.15.

Recursion

When I issued the previous query, another important thing was done for me. The DNS server I contacted recursed through the domain levels for me, hopping from server to server and caching all the results as it got them. Finally, it returned the A record I asked for, as well as another record, which we'll discuss momentarily.

To see how recursion really works, you need to tell dig to not issue recursive queries. The DNS server dig talks to will then simply give the best answer it has available. By adding +norec to the dig command, you turn off recursion:

```
$ dig www.amazon.com A +norec

; <<>> DiG 8.2 <<>> www.amazon.com A +norec
;; res options: init defnam dnsrch
;; got answer:
;; ->>HEADER<<- opcode: QUERY, status: NOERROR, id: 45249
;; flags: qr ra; QUERY: 1, ANSWER: 1, AUTHORITY: 4, ADDITIONAL: 4
;; QUERY SECTION:
;;      www.amazon.com, type = A, class = IN

;; ANSWER SECTION:
www.amazon.com.         11S IN A        208.216.181.15

;; AUTHORITY SECTION:
AMAZON.COM.             1d23h59m11s IN NS   AUTH00.NS.UU.NET.
AMAZON.COM.             1d23h59m11s IN NS   NS2.PNAP.NET.
AMAZON.COM.             1d23h59m11s IN NS   NS1.PNAP.NET.
AMAZON.COM.             1d23h59m11s IN NS   NS-1.AMAZON.COM.

;; ADDITIONAL SECTION:
AUTH00.NS.UU.NET.       1d23h59m15s IN A  198.6.1.65
NS2.PNAP.NET.           1d23h59m11s IN A  206.253.194.97
NS1.PNAP.NET.           1d23h59m11s IN A  206.253.194.65
NS-1.AMAZON.COM.        1d23h59m11s IN A  209.191.164.20

;; Total query time: 6 msec
;; FROM: roke.uio.no to SERVER: default -- 127.0.0.1
;; WHEN: Tue Feb 29 20:51:11 2000
;; MSG SIZE  sent: 32  rcvd: 212
```

But, something went wrong here! You were supposed to get the best answer, not the right answer. The answer from the previous query was cached, so you got the A record straight away this time. We'll have to use another example:

```
$ dig www.math.uio.no A +norec

; <<>> DiG 8.2 <<>> www.math.uio.no A +norec
;; res options: init defnam dnsrch
;; got answer:
;; ->>HEADER<<- opcode: QUERY, status: NOERROR, id: 31338
;; flags: qr ra; QUERY: 1, ANSWER: 0, AUTHORITY: 13, ADDITIONAL: 13
;; QUERY SECTION:
;;      www.math.uio.no, type = A, class = IN

;; AUTHORITY SECTION:
.                       5d23h57m29s IN NS  G.ROOT-SERVERS.NET.
.                       5d23h57m29s IN NS  F.ROOT-SERVERS.NET.
```

```
.                   5d23h57m29s IN NS  B.ROOT-SERVERS.NET.
.                   5d23h57m29s IN NS  J.ROOT-SERVERS.NET.
.                   5d23h57m29s IN NS  K.ROOT-SERVERS.NET.
.                   5d23h57m29s IN NS  L.ROOT-SERVERS.NET.
.                   5d23h57m29s IN NS  M.ROOT-SERVERS.NET.
.                   5d23h57m29s IN NS  I.ROOT-SERVERS.NET.
.                   5d23h57m29s IN NS  E.ROOT-SERVERS.NET.
.                   5d23h57m29s IN NS  D.ROOT-SERVERS.NET.
.                   5d23h57m29s IN NS  A.ROOT-SERVERS.NET.
.                   5d23h57m29s IN NS  H.ROOT-SERVERS.NET.
.                   5d23h57m29s IN NS  C.ROOT-SERVERS.NET.

;; ADDITIONAL SECTION:
G.ROOT-SERVERS.NET.   6d23h57m29s IN A  192.112.36.4
F.ROOT-SERVERS.NET.   6d23h57m29s IN A  192.5.5.241
B.ROOT-SERVERS.NET.   6d23h57m29s IN A  128.9.0.107
J.ROOT-SERVERS.NET.   6d23h57m29s IN A  198.41.0.10
K.ROOT-SERVERS.NET.   6d23h57m29s IN A  193.0.14.129
L.ROOT-SERVERS.NET.   6d23h57m29s IN A  198.32.64.12
M.ROOT-SERVERS.NET.   6d23h57m29s IN A  202.12.27.33
I.ROOT-SERVERS.NET.   6d23h57m29s IN A  192.36.148.17
E.ROOT-SERVERS.NET.   6d23h57m29s IN A  192.203.230.10
D.ROOT-SERVERS.NET.   6d23h57m29s IN A  128.8.10.90
A.ROOT-SERVERS.NET.   6d23h57m29s IN A  198.41.0.4
H.ROOT-SERVERS.NET.   6d23h57m29s IN A  128.63.2.53
C.ROOT-SERVERS.NET.   6d23h57m29s IN A  192.33.4.12

;; Total query time: 15 msec
;; FROM: roke.uio.no to SERVER: default -- 127.0.0.1
;; WHEN: Tue Feb 29 20:51:32 2000
;; MSG SIZE  sent: 33  rcvd: 452
```

In the previous code, the nameserver says it does not know the answer and to ask one of the listed servers for the answer.

NS Records

The previous listing shows two kinds of records. First, it shows *NS* records, which specify the names of the nameservers for a zone. All zones have NS records indicating which servers to ask for information about that zone. Each zone with a subzone must have NS records for the subzone so that interested parties can find the servers of the subzone. These NS records make up the edges in the DNS tree structure.

One obvious problem with the NS records exists, though. To query one of the nameservers, you need its address as well. Luckily, the addresses were also supplied by the server you asked so you don't need to ask for them before you can proceed. This is also good because, if you had to ask for the addresses for each partially answered query as well, the query would literally explode into numerous subqueries to find the addresses of the nameservers of this and then to find the addresses of the nameservers of them again.

As you can see, they are all rootservers. Therefore, you can ask one of them, m.root-servers.net, whether it can help you by adding @m.root-servers.net to the command line:

```
$ dig @m.root-servers.net. www.math.uio.no A +norec

; <<>> DiG 8.2 <<>> @m.root-servers.net. www.math.uio.no A +norec
; (1 server found)
;; res options: init defnam dnsrch
;; got answer:
;; ->>HEADER<<- opcode: QUERY, status: NOERROR, id: 16796
;; flags: qr; QUERY: 1, ANSWER: 0, AUTHORITY: 5, ADDITIONAL: 5
;; QUERY SECTION:
;;      www.math.uio.no, type = A, class = IN

;; AUTHORITY SECTION:
NO.                     2D IN NS        IFI.UIO.NO.
NO.                     2D IN NS        NAC.NO.
NO.                     2D IN NS        NN.UNINETT.NO.
NO.                     2D IN NS        NS.EU.NET.
NO.                     2D IN NS        NS.UU.NET.

;; ADDITIONAL SECTION:
IFI.UIO.NO.             2D IN A         129.240.64.2
NAC.NO.                 2D IN A         129.240.2.40
NN.UNINETT.NO.          2D IN A         158.38.0.181
NS.EU.NET.              2D IN A         192.16.202.11
NS.UU.NET.              2D IN A         137.39.1.3

;; Total query time: 369 msec
;; FROM: roke.uio.no to SERVER: m.root-servers.net.  202.12.27.33
;; WHEN: Tue Feb 29 20:52:05 2000
;; MSG SIZE  sent: 33  rcvd: 223
```

The rootserver did not know the address you asked for, but it told you who might know. Next, ask nac.no:

```
$ dig @nac.no. www.math.uio.no A +norec

; <<>> DiG 8.2 <<>> @nac.no. www.math.uio.no A +norec
; (1 server found)
;; res options: init defnam dnsrch
;; got answer:
;; ->>HEADER<<- opcode: QUERY, status: NOERROR, id: 26737
;; flags: qr ra; QUERY: 1, ANSWER: 0, AUTHORITY: 3, ADDITIONAL: 3
;; QUERY SECTION:
;;      www.math.uio.no, type = A, class = IN

;; AUTHORITY SECTION:
uio.no.                 1D IN NS        nissen.uio.no.
```

```
uio.no.                 1D IN NS        ifi.uio.no.
uio.no.                 1D IN NS        nn.uninett.no.

;; ADDITIONAL SECTION:
nissen.uio.no.          1D IN A         129.240.2.3
ifi.uio.no.             1D IN A         129.240.64.2
nn.uninett.no.          1D IN A         158.38.0.181

;; Total query time: 45 msec
;; FROM: roke.uio.no to SERVER: nac.no.  129.240.2.40
;; WHEN: Tue Feb 29 20:52:21 2000
;; MSG SIZE  sent: 33  rcvd: 151
```

You're getting closer because now you know the addresses of the servers of the uio.no zone. So, you should next ask one of them:

```
$ dig @ifi.uio.no www.math.uio.no A +norec

; <<>> DiG 8.2 <<>> @ifi.uio.no. www.math.uio.no A +norec
; (1 server found)
;; res options: init defnam dnsrch
;; got answer:
;; ->>HEADER<<- opcode: QUERY, status: NOERROR, id: 26176
;; flags: qr aa ra; QUERY: 1, ANSWER: 2, AUTHORITY: 3, ADDITIONAL: 3
;; QUERY SECTION:
;;      www.math.uio.no, type = A, class = IN

;; ANSWER SECTION:
www.math.uio.no.        1D IN CNAME     mnemosyne.uio.no.
mnemosyne.uio.no.       1D IN A         129.240.222.126

;; AUTHORITY SECTION:
uio.no.                 1D IN NS        nissen.uio.no.
uio.no.                 1D IN NS        ifi.uio.no.
uio.no.                 1D IN NS        nn.uninett.no.

;; ADDITIONAL SECTION:
nissen.uio.no.          1D IN A         129.240.2.3
ifi.uio.no.             1D IN A         129.240.64.2
nn.uninett.no.          1D IN A         158.38.0.181

;; Total query time: 57 msec
;; FROM: roke.uio.no to SERVER: ifi.uio.no.  129.240.64.2
;; WHEN: Tue Feb 29 20:52:37 2000
;; MSG SIZE  sent: 33  rcvd: 191
```

Finally, you found what you were looking for—the A record of www.math.uio.no. Notice how ifi.uio.no was capable of answering right away? That was because it knew the answer to the question and did not have to refer you on to another server to find it.

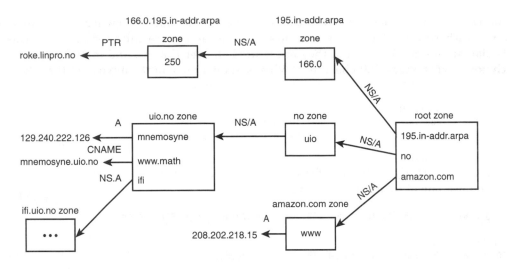

Figure 1.3 Nodes and edges in a DNS tree.

When a DNS server must find an RR that goes with a domain name, it first checks its own cache to see whether it has a match or how good a match it has. It might already know the nameserver for the zone or a zone closer to the root even if it doesn't have the answer. If nothing is found then a root server is queried. Each NS record returned leads you toward the server that knows the answer, and when queried, that server will in turn either answer the query or give you another NS record to pursue. The important linkage between zones, domains, and subdomains is the delegations, in the form of NS records. If they are not in place for a domain, the resolution of that domain will simply not work.

In some cases, such as `www.math.uio.no`, a CNAME record is returned instead of what you asked for, causing a detour to the name to which the CNAME points to ultimately find the information you asked for.

## 2

DNS IN PRACTICE

The BIND Software

BIND can be used to implement DNS on UNIX and Windows NT. The most interesting component is called the *name daemon*.

This chapter takes you through some experiments in DNS configuration. The first time you set up DNS, you should be sure you do so on a machine on which you can perform tests. In addition, you should make sure you have root access to this machine. I urge you to set up your test nameserver with the same configurations I use here and to perform the same tests I demonstrate. Also, if you change any existing files, be sure you back them up first.

ISC

The ISC (Internet Software Consortium) maintains BIND and provides it to you free of charge, with a minimal obligation from you. The following is the essence of the LICENSE file in the BIND distribution:

```
Permission to use, copy, modify, and distribute this software for any
purpose with or without fee is hereby granted, provided that the above
copyright notice and this permission notice appear in all copies.
```

Then follows a standard disclaimer of pretty much everything.

UNIX vendors provide BIND as part of their OS offering, usually in a network services package. As explained in the Introduction, different versions of BIND exist, and you should run the latest version of it to get the best security. Additionally, running BIND version 4 should be avoided if at all possible. One way to know whether you have BIND 4 is if your BIND wants to read a file called named.boot that contains lines with keywords such as secondary. You can check this in the named(1) man page on your system.

The merits of using a vendor-supported BIND versus those of using the latest BIND is a subject for debate, and you might have to yield to company policies. But the reasons for using the latest version are very good. First, the latest version of BIND will always be more secure than any version of BIND 4. Plus, through the BIND 8 series, many enhancements and improvements in security have been added. Quite simply, the latest version is likely to be the best choice at any given time. The community support for BIND is good, but the ISC also offers support contracts, so check its Web site. Your friendly neighborhood UNIX consultants also might be able to support BIND to your and your company's satisfaction. I highly recommend using the latest version of BIND with the support with which you and your superiors feel comfortable.

Where to Get BIND

ISC's FTP site address is ftp://ftp.isc.org/. BIND, however, resides in the /isc/bind/src subdirectory, where you always will find the latest release version of BIND. The latest available release also is announced on the Web page at http://www.isc.org/. You will want all three packages in the directory of the current release: src, doc, and contrib.

A few OS vendors, including most Linux and BSD vendors, will supply you with an easy-to-install package with the latest version of BIND. On the other hand, your computer already might have a recent version of BIND installed. But, you might find an updated package on your OS vendor's FTP or Web site as a replacement package or a patch to install. I recommend checking for and getting and installing the latest version or patch that has been created, unless you decide to compile and install BIND yourself.

Compiling BIND

You might want to compile, configure, test, and play with BIND for the first time on a machine not in your production environment.

If you need to, or want to, compile BIND yourself, you'll be faced with the usual tasks of compiling well-maintained free software. BIND works on almost all platforms, but if your platform is not among those on which the ISC tests BIND, compiling it yourself could involve a lot of work. On the other hand, if you use a tested platform, compiling and installing BIND should be easy. The documentation files in the src package provide details about compilation.

In Chapter 15, "Compiling and Maintaining BIND," you will find more specific information about fetching, compiling, and maintaining BIND. Installing the latest and greatest version of BIND provides no guarantees. BIND *must* be maintained to be kept secure—both to avoid break-ins on your DNS servers and to avoid the more subtle problems that a buggy DNS can cause. You also will find in Chapter 15 information on how to keep up with developments in BIND and DNS and how to find discussion forums for everything from how to solve various problems to how DNS will develop in the next few years.

Configuring BIND

Now that you have a current version of BIND installed, you're ready to begin configuration. The name daemon, named, is configured with one main file, depending on how it was installed. This file is usually called /etc/named.conf or /usr/local/etc/named.conf; however, it might be called something else if it was configured differently. In this file, you perform the basic config-uration of your named as well as enumerate the zones you are going to serve and the files in which they are contained.

Before you can proceed, four files must be set up. First, you'll need to set up a caching-only nameserver. This is good to have if you are on the wrong end of a slow network connection with no other nameservers on your network.

The files discussed in the following sections can be found on this book's Web site in the caching.tar.gz or caching.zip file.

named.conf

named.conf is the main configuration file. You need to place it in the right location, so use the following commands:

```
// Config file for caching-only nameserver

options {
        directory "/var/named";

        // Uncommenting this might help if you have to go through a
        // firewall and things are not working out:

        // query-source port 53;
};

zone "." {
        type hint;
```

```
        file "root.hints";
};

zone "0.0.127.in-addr.arpa" {
        type master;
        file "pz/127.0.0";
};
```

In the previous code, the `directory` command names the directory in `named.conf` in which `named` will look for the filenames. Because no default directory exists, `named` will look for the files in the current directory if you do not name a directory. `/var/named`, `/usr/named`, and `/usr/local/named` are all used, among others. Find a name that fits your partitioning scheme. The other sections in the file load files you will examine soon.

One other point I should make is that `named.conf` is similar to a computer program, with BIND acting as the compiler. If you make even the smallest syntax error, the file will be void and invalid.

root.hints

As you will recall from Chapter 1, "DNS Concepts," you need to know where to find the root nodes of DNS, which are called the *root nameservers*. You can use the `root.hints` file to do so. You place it in the directory you named in `named.conf`:

```
;
; There might be opening comments here if you already have this file.
; If not, don't worry.
;
.                       6D  IN  NS      G.ROOT-SERVERS.NET.
.                       6D  IN  NS      J.ROOT-SERVERS.NET.
.                       6D  IN  NS      K.ROOT-SERVERS.NET.
.                       6D  IN  NS      L.ROOT-SERVERS.NET.
.                       6D  IN  NS      M.ROOT-SERVERS.NET.
.                       6D  IN  NS      A.ROOT-SERVERS.NET.
.                       6D  IN  NS      H.ROOT-SERVERS.NET.
.                       6D  IN  NS      B.ROOT-SERVERS.NET.
.                       6D  IN  NS      C.ROOT-SERVERS.NET.
.                       6D  IN  NS      D.ROOT-SERVERS.NET.
.                       6D  IN  NS      E.ROOT-SERVERS.NET.
.                       6D  IN  NS      I.ROOT-SERVERS.NET.
.                       6D  IN  NS      F.ROOT-SERVERS.NET.

G.ROOT-SERVERS.NET.     5w6d16h IN  A   192.112.36.4
J.ROOT-SERVERS.NET.     5w6d16h IN  A   198.41.0.10
K.ROOT-SERVERS.NET.     5w6d16h IN  A   193.0.14.129
L.ROOT-SERVERS.NET.     5w6d16h IN  A   198.32.64.12
M.ROOT-SERVERS.NET.     5w6d16h IN  A   202.12.27.33
A.ROOT-SERVERS.NET.     5w6d16h IN  A   198.41.0.4
H.ROOT-SERVERS.NET.     5w6d16h IN  A   128.63.2.53
```

```
B.ROOT-SERVERS.NET.        5w6d16h IN A    128.9.0.107
C.ROOT-SERVERS.NET.        5w6d16h IN A    192.33.4.12
D.ROOT-SERVERS.NET.        5w6d16h IN A    128.8.10.90
E.ROOT-SERVERS.NET.        5w6d16h IN A    192.203.230.10
I.ROOT-SERVERS.NET.        5w6d16h IN A    192.36.148.17
F.ROOT-SERVERS.NET.        5w6d16h IN A    192.5.5.241
```

This file simply enumerates the rootservers and their addresses with standard NS and A records. The file is called hints because its contents are not taken as gospel; everything in it is simply a hint. Your named will check for itself how things really are and then develop a preference for one nameserver based on its track record for response time.

However, the file needs to be maintained so that, after several years of neglect, it does not fall completely out of sync with reality and no longer provides a usable starting point for your named file to resolve queries. For more information, see Chapter 3, "Maintenance and Enhancements."

pz/127.0.0

This file is required for the simple reason that some software, especially the popular DNS program nslookup, will not work unless it can perform a reverse lookup of the nameserver's address. The pz part of the filename is a directory name, meaning the file resides in the subdirectory pz. This subdirectory is so named because *primary zone* used to be the name of what is now known as a *master zone*. Some DNS administrators like to organize their zone files into separate directories—master zones, and *slave*, or secondary, zones. Zone files have several different naming conventions. If you are exploring an existing BIND installation while reading this, you might find a completely different naming convention in use. If so, you might want to continue using the naming convention currently in use at your site.

As shown in the previous named.conf file, a master zone exists. Using the naming convention I prefer, it would be placed in the pz directory and given the name of the network in which it resolves hosts: 127.0.0. The following is an example:

```
;
$ORIGIN 0.0.127.in-addr.arpa.
$TTL 1D
;
@               IN      SOA     ns.penguin.bv. hostmaster.penguin.bv. (
                                1       ; Serial
                                8H      ; Refresh
                                2H      ; Retry
                                1W      ; Expire
                                1D)     ; Minimum TTL
                NS      ns.penguin.bv.
1               PTR     localhost.
```

```
;; QUERY SECTION:
;;      1.0.0.127.in-addr.arpa, type = PTR, class = IN

;; ANSWER SECTION:
1.0.0.127.in-addr.arpa.  1D IN PTR   localhost.

;; AUTHORITY SECTION:
0.0.127.in-addr.arpa.   1D IN NS       ns.penguin.bv.

;; Total query time: 51 msec
;; FROM: lookfar to SERVER: 127.0.0.1
;; WHEN: Tue Mar 28 21:47:37 2000
;; MSG SIZE  sent: 40  rcvd: 111
```

As you see, it returns the PTR record I asked for, and as expected, it points to localhost. If you received a different result, please go back and check the 127.0.0 zone file for typos.

I can ask for one other thing from the 127.0.0 zone file:

$ dig @127.0.0.1 0.0.127.in-addr.arpa SOA

```
; <<>> DiG 8.2 <<>> @127.0.0.1 0.0.127.in-addr.arpa SOA
; (1 server found)
;; res options: init recurs defnam dnsrch
;; got answer:
;; ->>HEADER<<- opcode: QUERY, status: NOERROR, id: 6
;; flags: qr aa rd ra; QUERY: 1, ANSWER: 1, AUTHORITY: 1, ADDITIONAL: 0
;; QUERY SECTION:
;;      0.0.127.in-addr.arpa, type = SOA, class = IN

;; ANSWER SECTION:
0.0.127.in-addr.arpa.    1D IN SOA        ns.penguin.bv. hostmaster.penguin.bv. (
                                          1              ; serial
                                          8H             ; refresh
                                          2H             ; retry
                                          1W             ; expiry
                                          1D )           ; minimum


;; AUTHORITY SECTION:
0.0.127.in-addr.arpa.    1D IN NS         ns.penguin.bv.

;; Total query time: 60 msec
;; FROM: lookfar to SERVER: 127.0.0.1
;; WHEN: Tue Mar 28 21:55:13 2000
;; MSG SIZE  sent: 38  rcvd: 112
```

Again, the returned data is as expected. If you get something different, go back and check for typos in the zone file.

Now for something more exciting. If you're using a dial-up connection to the Internet, now is the time to get it up and running. To see whether the caching name daemon can resolve names for you, ask it to resolve www.amazon.com:

```
$ dig @127.0.0.1 www.amazon.com

; <<>> DiG 8.2 <<>> @127.0.0.1 www.amazon.com
; (1 server found)
;; res options: init recurs defnam dnsrch
;; got answer:
;; ->>HEADER<<- opcode: QUERY, status: NOERROR, id: 6
;; flags: qr rd ra; QUERY: 1, ANSWER: 1, AUTHORITY: 2, ADDITIONAL: 2
;; QUERY SECTION:
;;      www.amazon.com, type = A, class = IN

;; ANSWER SECTION:
www.amazon.com.          42S IN A        208.216.182.15

;; AUTHORITY SECTION:
www.amazon.com.          1D IN NS        ns-20.amazon.com.
www.amazon.com.          1D IN NS        ns-10.amazon.com.

;; ADDITIONAL SECTION:
ns-20.amazon.com.        1D IN A         208.33.216.20
ns-10.amazon.com.        1D IN A         208.192.211.10

;; Total query time: 3743 msec
;; FROM: lookfar to SERVER: 127.0.0.1
;; WHEN: Tue Mar 28 22:00:28 2000
;; MSG SIZE  sent: 32  rcvd: 130
```

As the previous code shows, the nameserver does its job.

If your nameserver does not return an A record for www.amazon.com, you have some kind of problem you need to find. Are you inside a firewall, for example? If you are, look in named.conf. One solution might be to uncomment the query-source line and restart named. However, if you are inside a firewall, you might not be allowed to access the Internet at all, and this test will fail miserably. Other solutions are using some host outside a firewall to experiment; getting a hole in the firewall for your DNS server; and reading Chapter 3, which discusses forwarding. You might be able to forward DNS queries to a DNS server on the inside of the firewall, which will presumably have Internet access.

The Details of DNS Caching

A caching DNS server is a simple thing to administrate. In addition, it will save you waiting time whenever you try to resolve hostnames because it caches the hostnames you look up for later use. This is especially useful in situations where you're on the wrong end of a slow network link.

A caching DNS server's job is to resolve hostnames. It does so in the manner described in Chapter 1. It saves in its memory pool each and every answer it receives upon sending queries to other DNS servers. The answers stay in the memory pool until they expire. Their expiration time is specified by the TTL of the RR, with each DNS query answer having an associated TTL that tells caching servers how long to cache the answer. If you look at the previous www.amazon.com query answer, the TTL is just 42 seconds. That's hardly any time at all. More typical TTLs are in hours, or perhaps even days, but several Web server addresses have very low TTLs. This enables the Web service administrators to make changes in the service on very short notice because DNS caches won't be out there hanging onto the query answer forever. A low TTL does have one disadvantage, though—it can cause an increased load on the network and nameservers. For instance, in the case of www.amazon.com, the record must be re-resolved every 42 seconds. If you have many thousands, or millions, of users, this represents a significant load increase compared to if the TTL was 24 hours.

Some people wonder whether they can control how large the cache will grow, or whether the cache can be saved to disk, enabling it to be persistent across reboots or named restarts. In general, the answer to both these questions is no. However, for more information on controlling how large the cache will grow, see Chapter 8, "Security Concerns."

Resolver Setup

Now that your caching nameserver is working, it's time to tackle the other half of DNS: the resolver. As seen in Chapter 1, when a name lookup is required, a resolver performs the steps necessary to resolve the query. The details of the resolution will be taken care of by a nameserver, but your host OS needs a way to talk to the nameserver.

The OS resolver is not part of DNS, but it does use DNS for resolving hostnames. However, it also uses other sources. Chief among the other sources is the local /etc/hosts file and NIS (formerly known as YP). If the resolver configuration indicates that DNS should be used for hostname resolution, a local recursive DNS server is contacted and it performs the actual resolution described in Chapter 1. The OS resolver merely sends the initial query, say for the A record of www.amazon.com, to the local DNS server. The caching nameserver we set up just now is just such a local and recursive DNS server. The relationship between the resolver, DNS, and other name services is shown in Figure 2.1.

Under UNIX, the OS resolver is part of the standard C library. Newer versions of this library do not need any configuration if a nameserver is available locally. Older versions, on the other hand, do require it. If the nameserver is not available locally, you will need it, so we will set it up.

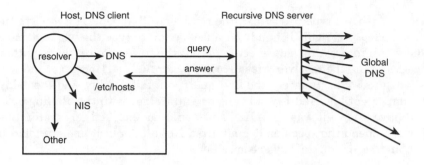

Host, DNS client   Recursive DNS server

Figure 2.1   The relationship between the resolver, DNS, and other name services.

The UNIX resolver is configured in one, or sometimes two, files. All UNIX systems share this file: /etc/resolv.conf. Vendor variations exist in the contents allowed in this file. I will not go into the differences each vendor allows and the extensions they have made here. For more information, see the OS man page for this file, which is often called resolver(5) rather than resolv.conf(5).

/etc/resolv.conf

If the OS resolver is to use DNS, it consults /etc/resolv.conf to find out how to communicate with DNS, as well as some other necessary specifics.

Nameserver

You can define as many as three nameservers in the file. You do it by entering lines such as the following:

```
nameserver 127.0.0.1
nameserver 192.168.0.1
```

In this code, I defined two nameservers. The first one is 127.0.0.1, which is the local host on which we now have a working nameserver. The second one is 192.168.0.1, which is the IP number of a DNS server internal to the network to which my computer is attached. If the first nameserver fails for some reason, the second one will be tried. The timeout for a query to be seen as failed is quite long, though, so if it fails, you will notice long pauses as the resolver waits for the timeout to occur.

Domain

You also can define a domain within which your resolver will look for hostnames unless you specify an FQDN, with the trailing dot, as in the following example:

```
domain linpro.no
```

This specifies that, when I type `telnet cat`, the resolver will append `linpro.no` to the name and try to resolve `cat.linpro.no`. This is handy because having to type the whole name every time would be tedious. An interesting side effect in all but the newest of resolvers is that when I type `telnet math.uio.no`, the resolver tries to look up `math.uio.no.linpro.no`, and when that fails, it tries `math.uio.no`. Fortunately, the first query will fail quickly, and the delay will in most cases be imperceptible. Had I typed `telnet math.uio.no.` with the trailing dot, the resolver would have known it was an FQDN and would have looked up `math.uio.no` at once, without trying to append the specified domain first. Not all applications are tolerant of the trailing dot, though, so it can't always be specified.

The newest resolvers will not append the domain name if a dot is in the name given it to look up. However, this behavior is configurable. See the man page for more information.

Search

Newer resolvers support another directive as well—search. In the search directive, you can list the domains in which you want your resolver to search, as in the following:

```
search linpro.no uio.no ifi.uio.no
```

This specifies that the three domains `linpro.no`, `uio.no`, and `ifi.uio.no` are to be appended to the given name in turn until the lookup succeeds. When `ssh gram` is executed, the resolver first looks for `gram.linpro.no`, which does not exist; then `gram.uio.no`, which does not exist, either; and finally `gram.ifi.uio.no`, which will succeed because it does exist.

How many domains, totaling how many characters, you specify varies some; check the man page.

Search and domain are mutually exclusive, so if both are found, the last one will prevail.

Other Things

Some vendors have extended `/etc/resolv.conf` to configure more aspects of resolving than just DNS. SGIs IRIX enables you to specify the order in which name services such as DNS, NIS (formerly YP), and the `/etc/hosts` file are queried. This too is discussed in the man page.

Other Files

Quite a few UNIX systems use an additional file to configure the resolver. Whereas `/etc/resolv.conf` enables you to set up DNS resolution, you also might need to specify that DNS is to be queried at all. Some OSes, including older AIX, take the mere presence of a `/etc/resolv.conf` file as an indicator that DNS is to be queried. In contrast, Solaris, Linux, and most new versions of UNIX do not. They require additional configuration to query DNS.

/etc/nsswitch.conf

Several UNIX systems, including Solaris, Linux, and so on, use /etc/nsswitch.conf to configure which name services the resolver should use. If your system has a man page for this file, it should use it. If you look in it, you will find a line starting with hosts:. This specifies which services will be queried for hostnames. Most UNIX systems support dns, nis, and files for /etc/hosts. They also might support other name services such as nisplus.

Most times you will want just files and dns in some order that suits you. The following is one possibility:

```
hosts:  files dns
```

The previous code enables me to override DNS by entering things in /etc/hosts. This can be helpful when I do development work and want to connect to development servers instead of production servers without changing the code, or configuration files, on which I'm working.

/etc/host.conf

On some versions of some OSes, the /etc/host.conf file specifies the resolution service order. If so, a single line similar to the following will specify the same order as shown in the previous nsswitch.conf file:

```
order hosts,bind
```

This code specifies that the /etc/hosts file comes first, and then BIND and DNS.

And So On...

Some UNIX systems, especially older versions, use other files to specify name service order. On newer resolvers, the resolv.conf file doesn't even need to be present because, when nsswitch.conf specifies DNS and no resolv.conf exists, 127.0.0.1 is queried. On some UNIX systems, though, the presence of a resolv.conf file is required because DNS won't be queried without it.

As time passes, more and more UNIX systems are switching to resolv.conf and nsswitch.conf. Luckily, this makes the system administrator's task easier, eliminating the need to remember how the various UNIX systems differ.

In any case, after the resolv.conf file—and possibly one other file—has been set up, any network software on your computer, such as telnet, ssh, and Netscape, should be capable of using domain names from DNS. Try it.

Client Resolver

After you know your name daemon works and that it can resolve hostnames for the host on which it runs, it is time to configure all the clients who are going to use the nameserver. You must configure the resolver on each of them as well, just as you set it up on the server, configuring /etc/resolv.conf and any other files as needed. Windows, Macintosh, and other OSes will also be able to use your BIND-based name daemon without problems. Configuration methods vary even more wildly than on UNIX, though.

A Zone

So, you have a domain registered, or you're going to register one (see Chapter 4, "Getting a Domain"), and you want to set up DNS for your domain and network. As an example, I will set up zone files for the company Penguin AS, which owns the domain penguin.bv. bv is the TLD for Bouvet Island, a south Atlantic island that is a property of Norway (the choice of company name is a subliminal message about what OS the author likes). I have assigned the 192.168.55.0/255.255.255.0 subnet to the company. This is a private, internal network according to RFC 1597, so I can use it freely.

NORID, which administrates bv, has decided not to assign any domains within the bv TLD. Therefore, I will appropriate it in examples because no one will be looking for bv domains and be confused if an RR escapes from their nameservers into DNS.

The NORID policy has caused some lamentations from Dutch companies; "bv" is similar to the American "Inc." in Holland, and is therefore a highly desirable TLD to be under.

The zone files for penguin.bv can be found on the book Web page in the penguin.tar.gz or penguin.zip file.

A Forward Zone

Let's first look at some theory. The general format of a DNS record is as follows:

```
name    ttl     class   type    data
```

In the previous code, *name* is the DNS name to which the record belongs. In the next code listing, the DNS names are ns, mail, www, ftp, rms, esr, and so on. Note the special name @ used for the SOA record—it is used for the zone origin penguin.bv in this case. If you look back at the 127.0.0 zone shown previously, you can see @ is also used there instead of 0.0.127.in-addr.arpa. You also can see that several lines do not have a name; for example, none of the HINFO records have names. If the name is left out, it defaults to the last seen name. Thus, the @ at the SOA is used as the default name for all the opening NS and MX records that follow the SOA record.

ttl controls caching, which I will explain later when I explain the SOA record.

BIND supports different classes of records, but we will concern ourselves only with the IN, or InterNet, class. The IN class is the default class for zones and doesn't need to be specified. Therefore, I won't bother specifying it here, which will save me some typing. The other classes of records are used for other kinds of networks, and in one case called Hesiod, which is an MIT project, they're used for user authentication data. This is similar to NIS, but it uses BIND as the database.

type must be one of the known RR types. So far, I have used SOA, NS, A, and PTR. HINFO and MX will be introduced shortly. Others do exist, though—see Chapter 13, "Resource Records," for a complete list.

For the previous code, *data* depends on the type of record you're looking at. Some types, such as the SOA record, have many data fields; however, most types have only one data field. HINFO and MX are among those that have two data fields.

penguin.bv is a small company, even though its products are used all over the world, so it doesn't have many machines. We're going to set up a zone with a Web server, an FTP server, a combined mail and nameserver, and some machines it uses internally. Starting with the configuration files from the caching nameserver, we first add the forward zone file pz/penguin.bv:

```
 1  ;
 2  ; penguin.bv zone
 3  ;
 4  $TTL 804800      ; 7 days
 5  ;
 6  @       3600     SOA     ns.penguin.bv.  hostmaster.penguin.bv. (
 7                   2000041300      ; serial
 8                   86400           ; refresh, 24h
 9                   7200            ; retry, 2h
10                   3600000         ; expire, 1000h
11                   172800          ; minimum, 2 days
12                   )
13                   NS      ns
14                   NS      ns.herring.bv.
```

As you can see from the previous code, three mandatory bits exist in a zone file—the $TTL line, the SOA RR, and the NS RR for the zone.

The first line of the SOA RR (line 6) contains two important things. The first is the name of the zone origin server, namely ns.penguin.bv. This should be the name of the primary nameserver, not the zone name itself, unless they are the same. Secondly, it holds the email address of the contact person for the zone, which for our example is hostmaster.penguin.bv. This name should be taken to mean hostmaster@penguin.bv, replacing the first period (.) with the at sign (@). It is recommended that you maintain a hostmaster@*domain* email address, alias, or list so you always have a traditional contact address for DNS issues. In any case, email to the address you put here *must* be read because it is used to report bad DNS data, as well as security problems. You should be careful to avoid contact email addresses with periods in the username because of the "first period becomes @" rule.

The next lines of the code contain several important values. The serial number, at line 7, must be changed every time you update the zone file, by incrementing the it. When slave servers want to check whether they are up to date, they retrieve the SOA record and compare the serial number of the zone file they have cached to the one on the primary server. If the serial number of the master is higher than that on the slave, a zone transfer is triggered and the updated zone is copied from the master to the slave. A popular, and useful, convention is to keep the serial number in YYYYMMDDNN format, in which the first eight digits denote the date of the last change and NN denotes the number of the change within that day. On the other hand, some software will maintain the number as a strict serial number, incrementing it by one for each edit.

At line 8, the refresh interval is set to 24 hours. This is the interval between each time a slave server will check whether the master server has been updated. So, in this case, it might take up to 24 hours before the slave server checks whether the master has been updated. After these 24 hours have passed, the slave will check whether it is updated as described previously. If the zone changes often and the changes are important, this value should be lower. Zone transfers are a bit resource-demanding, so if you house very many zones, the cumulative load might be noticeable. On small nameservers, though, it is hardly noticeable and is nothing to worry about.

The retry interval becomes relevant only if the slave server fails to raise the master server when the refresh interval has passed. If it fails to get the SOA record, it will retry after waiting out the retry interval, which in this case is two hours.

If the SOA record query and zone transfer fail after the retry interval, the zone transfer will be retried repeatedly. But, after the expire interval has passed without contact with the master server, the zone will expire on the secondary. It will be removed from the slave server and will not answer queries for the zone anymore. This could be problematic, so the expire interval should be long enough that the zone will not expire in the case of a catastrophe that takes the primary DNS server site out for a long time. One thousand hours, which is 41 days or roughly 5 weeks, is usually sufficient. Often, though, one or two weeks is used, but that has repeatedly proven to be too short a time to restore the primary nameserver.

You can use one other method to cause a zone to expire: If you make a typo when updating a zone file or the configuration file, the zone you edited, or even several zones, might be rejected out of hand by named. Unless you catch the typo, the zones will expire no matter how carefully you choose your expiry time.

This chapter has already discussed the last value and the $TTL value. It is used to control the caching of records in the zone. Traditionally, the minimum ttl field of the SOA record was the default TTL value for all records in the zone. Recently, though, a transition has started, and has not yet ended at the time of this writing. The SOA TTL is the time to cache negative answers, meaning when a query fails, the fact is cached for that length of time. Enter $TTL. It specifies the default TTL of the records in the zone. Thus, a cache server will cache answers from the penguin.bv zone for seven days. If it does not get an answer for a penguin.bv name, that fact is cached for two days. Negative caching is described in detail in RFC 2308.

You can override the TTL for each record, though. Above the SOA record, TTL has been over-ridden to 3,600 seconds, or one hour.

The values used here are recommended in http://www.ripe.net/docs/ripe-203.html, which is an informative document that I recommend you read. These values are well suited for a zone that does not change often. However, if your zone—or some specific records in the zone—changes often, or if it is important that changes be known quickly when they are made, you should use other values. If you do use other values, remember that they can be overridden for selected records and that lower TTLs and refresh intervals are therefore necessary.

Line 13 shows the third required bit—the NS record for the zone. At least one NS record is required. We have two in our example, as we should because our friends at Herring Co. are hosting a secondary nameserver for us. You can't specify the server addresses in NS records; instead you must specify hostnames and then give the A records of the hosts that are within, or under, the current zone. The address of ns.penguin.bv is provided on line 19, shown later in this section. No address is given for ns.herring.bv within this zone, though, because its address can be found by other means. In addition, modern BINDs ignore records that do not belong in the zone file in which they occur. Thus, you are unable to specify the address of ns.herring.bv within the penguin.bv zone. If, on the other hand, a nameserver exists in the zones domain or in a subdomain of the zone, an A record must be supplied. This is because all lookups must go through the domain for which we're writing a zone file, and no other way is available to find the address of the nameserver.

Configuring these three mandatory items correctly is important to ensure that lookups for your domain don't fail. So get it right!

Now that you've gotten past all this red tape—however important—you can get on with the purpose of this file. Let's take a look at some more RRs. The two MX records for the domain are first, however:

```
15                  MX      10 mail
16                  MX      20 mail.herring.bv.
```

MX records specify the Mail Exchangers for the zone. *Mail Exchangers* are the servers to which mail software sends mail for the domain, which in our example is penguin.bv. The MX record requires two data fields: the priority field and the name field for the mail server. Mail software attempts to deliver mail through the server with the lowest priority value first and then, if that fails, to the others sorted by priority. In other words, mail.penguin.bv is the primary mail server, and mail.herring.bv is the secondary mail server. Having many redundant mail servers is not a very high priority because the originating mail server saves mail for several days before the delivery fails. Three days is the norm for saving mail, so remember that in case something breaks and mail can't be delivered to the listed servers.

The localhost line exists for a combination of reasons:

```
17  localhost     A      127.0.0.1
```

UNIX software and users frequently refer to the localhost as localhost. Because of the name search heuristics you configure in resolv.conf, the name localhost is looked for in the domains listed to search. So, in the likely case of penguin.bv being in the search list on the penguin.bv machines, the name localhost.penguin.bv will be looked up.

Next, you can start defining the first actual machine; ns.penguin.bv is defined to have the address 192.168.55.2:

```
18  ; Nameserver
19  ns            A      192.168.55.2
20
21  ; Mailserver, same machine.
22  mail          A      192.168.55.2
23                MX     10 mail
24                MX     20 mail.herring.bv.
25                HINFO  PC Tunes
```

The next A record is for mail.penguin.bv, and it gives the same address. The mail server is also listed with MX records in case someone is trying to send mail to a user at @mail.penguin.bv. Again, the secondary is at mail.herring.bv. A new type of record, a HINFO record, is sometimes included. Some people, including me, like to use it, whereas others don't, arguing that these records don't provide many benefits and can possibly cause harm. HINFO records can pose a security threat, telling crackers what kind of OS a machine runs, which enables them to try only the break-in procedures known to work on that particular OS. The HINFO record carries two data fields as well, CPU and OS. CPU is often taken to mean what kind of computer rather than the specific CPU model, as it is here. Common CPU fields for PCs are x86, i386, and so on. A Sun Sparc Server 20 might be shown as Sun or SPARC or perhaps even Sun4, SS20, or any of the various names the computer or its architecture is known as. As you will see, I've been very consistent about how (un)specific I am in the CPU field; "SUN" is about as unspecific as "PC". The OS, on the other hand, is sometimes just an OS name, but sometimes also the version. If you want to include the version, the OS field must be quoted because a space is the field separator:

```
lbt             HINFO  PC "Linux 2.3"
```

The following continues our example:

```
27  ; WEB, both http://www.penguin.bv/ and
28  ; http://penguin.bv/ with A records
```

```
29
30  www             A         192.168.55.3
31  ; People often send mail to webmaster@www.domain
32                  MX        10 mail
33                  MX        20 mail.herring.bv.
34                  HINFO     PC Tunes
35  @               A         192.168.55.3
```

With these A records, the Penguin Web server can be accessed as both `http://www.penguin.bv/` and `http://penguin.bv/`. The HTTP protocol merely needs an A record for the server to which you want to connect. So, you simply give HTTP the address of the computer to which to connect:

```
37  ; FTP server
38
39  ftp             A         192.168.55.4
40                  HINFO     PC BSD
41
42  ; The firewall/router:
43
44  gw              A         192.168.55.1
45                  A         192.168.55.129
```

Line 44 shows one host with two A records. Routers, gateways, and firewalls often have several network interfaces. DNS supports listing them all under the same hostname, but some people prefer to give each interface a separate name.

The rest of the zone is as follows:

```
47  ; Internal hosts
48
49  rms             A         192.168.55.130
50                  HINFO     PC HURD
51
52  esr             A         192.168.55.131
53                  HINFO     PC Linux
54
55  lbt             A         192.168.55.132
56                  HINFO     PC Linux
57
58  jkh             A         192.168.55.134
59                  HINFO     PC BSD
60
61  dek             A         192.168.55.135
62                  HINFO     SUN Solaris
63
64  tolk            A         192.168.55.136
65                  HINFO     PCP PalmOS
66
67  laser           A         192.168.55.137
68                  HINFO     Printer Postscript
```

That concludes pz/penguin.bv. The following, however, is a small addition to the named.conf file:

```
zone "penguin.bv" {
        type master;
        file "pz/penguin.bv";
};
```

That pretty much sums up what the zone is. The opening zone keyword takes one parameter, the zone's domain name or origin. If an $ORIGIN exists within the file, these must match. Because this is the master server, the zone goes in the file pz/penguin.bv. See the section "Secondary Servers" later in this chapter to find out how to set up secondary, or slave, servers for a zone.

Run ndc reconfig and inspect the zone with Dig:

```
$ dig mail.penguin.bv ANY

; <<>> DiG 8.2 <<>> mail.penguin.bv ANY
;; res options: init recurs defnam dnsrch
;; got answer:
;; ->>HEADER<<- opcode: QUERY, status: NOERROR, id: 4
;; flags: qr aa rd ra; QUERY: 1, ANSWER: 4, AUTHORITY: 2, ADDITIONAL: 2
;; QUERY SECTION:
;;      mail.penguin.bv, type = ANY, class = IN

;; ANSWER SECTION:
mail.penguin.bv.        1w2d7h33m20s IN HINFO  "PC" "Tunes"
mail.penguin.bv.        1w2d7h33m20s IN MX  10 mail.penguin.bv.
mail.penguin.bv.        1w2d7h33m20s IN MX  20 mail.herring.bv.
mail.penguin.bv.        1w2d7h33m20s IN A   192.168.55.2

;; AUTHORITY SECTION:
penguin.bv.            1w2d7h33m20s IN NS  ns.penguin.bv.
penguin.bv.            1w2d7h33m20s IN NS  ns.herring.bv.

;; ADDITIONAL SECTION:
mail.penguin.bv.       1w2d7h33m20s IN A  192.168.55.2
ns.penguin.bv.         1w2d7h33m20s IN A  192.168.55.2

;; Total query time: 16 msec
;; FROM: lookfar to SERVER: default -- 127.0.0.1
;; WHEN: Sat Apr 15 17:57:52 2000
;; MSG SIZE  sent: 33  rcvd: 191
```

This is exactly as expected. Now I'll insert a common typo in the zone file. Line 42 is changed to the following:

```
MX      20 mail.herring.bv
```

In other words, the trailing period is dropped on the second MX record for www.penguin.bv. After using the ndc reload command, dig provides the result:

```
$ dig www.penguin.bv MX
...
www.penguin.bv.          1w2d7h33m20s IN MX  10 mail.penguin.bv.
www.penguin.bv.          1w2d7h33m20s IN MX  20 mail.herring.bv.penguin.bv.
...
```

Most people make this error at one time or another, and the reason is simple. BIND considers all names to be relative to the zone origin, unless they are FQDNs by virtue of having a trailing period. When I removed the trailing period, the name mail.herring.bv was no longer seen as an FQDN and the zone origin penguin.bv was added to the end. The fix is trivial, of course—you can just add a period to the end of all FQDNs. Small bugs like these also are a good reason to always inspect the changes you make in zone files—for example, with dig—no matter how trivial the changes were. In addition, you should also read the log files when reloading the zones.

A Reverse Zone

Now let's look at the reverse zone. As you see in the following code, a *reverse* zone is simply an up-ended version of the forward zone:

```
$TTL 804800       ; ~7 days
;
@       3600    SOA     ns.penguin.bv. hostmaster.penguin.bv. (
                        2000041300      ; serial
                        86400           ; refresh, 24h
                        7200            ; retry, 2h
                        3600000         ; expire, 1000h
                        172800          ; minimum, 2 days
                        )
                NS      ns.penguin.bv.
                NS      ns.herring.bv.

; Externally available hosts:
1               PTR     gw.penguin.bv.
2               PTR     mail.penguin.bv.
3               PTR     www.penguin.bv.
4               PTR     ftp.penguin.bv.

; Internal hosts:
129             PTR     gw.penguin.bv.
130             PTR     rms.penguin.bv.
131             PTR     esr.penguin.bv.
132             PTR     lbt.penguin.bv.
134             PTR     jkh.penguin.bv.
135             PTR     dek.penguin.bv.
136             PTR     tolk.penguin.bv.
137             PTR     laser.penguin.bv.
```

Notice that all the machine names are typed out here. The origin of this file is 55.168.192. in-addr.arpa. On the other hand, the machine addresses are not typed out, so the records have names such as 1.55.168.192.in-addr.arpa, which is exactly what you want.

The following adds it to named.conf:

```
zone "55.168.192.in-addr.arpa" {
        type master;
        file "pz/192.168.55";
};
```

Here again the zone's domain name is on the zone line. Then, a closer description of the zone exists within the braces.

An ndc reconfig and dig can be used to examine it:

```
# dig 1.55.168.192.in-addr.arpa PTR

; <<>> DiG 8.2 <<>> 1.55.168.192.in-addr.arpa PTR
;; res options: init recurs defnam dnsrch
;; got answer:
;; ->>HEADER<<- opcode: QUERY, status: NOERROR, id: 4
;; flags: qr aa rd ra; QUERY: 1, ANSWER: 1, AUTHORITY: 2, ADDITIONAL: 1
;; QUERY SECTION:
;;      1.55.168.192.in-addr.arpa, type = PTR, class = IN

;; ANSWER SECTION:
1.55.168.192.in-addr.arpa.  1w2d7h33m20s IN PTR  gw.penguin.bv.

;; AUTHORITY SECTION:
55.168.192.in-addr.arpa.  1w2d7h33m20s IN NS  ns.penguin.bv.
55.168.192.in-addr.arpa.  1w2d7h33m20s IN NS  ns.herring.bv.

;; ADDITIONAL SECTION:
ns.penguin.bv.          1w2d7h33m20s IN A  192.168.55.2

;; Total query time: 36 msec
;; FROM: lookfar to SERVER: default -- 127.0.0.1
;; WHEN: Sat Apr 15 18:23:13 2000
;; MSG SIZE  sent: 43  rcvd: 151
```

As we already knew, 192.168.55.1 has the name gw.penguin.bv. But now we also know that the zone works.

Another Zone

Let's take a quick look at a real set of forward and reverse zones. This example, which is based on a real zone, wasn't created by me so it's different from how I would set it up.

zone/walrus.bv

As you see from the heading, this nameserver uses a slightly different naming convention. Instead of pz, the directory is called zone. The following are the file's contents:

```
$TTL 1D
@       IN      SOA     walrus.bv. root.walrus.bv. (
                        199609206       ; todays date + todays serial #
                        8H              ; refresh, seconds
                        2H              ; retry, seconds
                        1W              ; expire, seconds
                        1D )            ; minimum, seconds
                NS      walrus.bv.
                NS      ns2.psi.net.
                MX      10 walrus.bv.   ; Primary Mail Exchanger
                TXT     "goo goo g'joob."

localhost       A       127.0.0.1

router          A       206.6.177.1

walrus.bv.      A       206.6.177.2
ns              A       206.6.177.3
www             A       207.159.141.192

ftp             CNAME   walrus.bv.
mail            CNAME   walrus.bv.
news            CNAME   walrus.bv.
www             CNAME   walrus.bv.

funn            A       206.6.177.2

;
;       Workstations
;
ws-177200       A       206.6.177.200
                MX      10 walrus.bv.   ; Primary Mail Host
ws-177201       A       206.6.177.201
                MX      10 walrus.bv.   ; Primary Mail Host
ws-177202       A       206.6.177.202
                MX      10 walrus.bv.   ; Primary Mail Host
ws-177203       A       206.6.177.203
                MX      10 walrus.bv.   ; Primary Mail Host
ws-177204       A       206.6.177.204
                MX      10 walrus.bv.   ; Primary Mail Host
ws-177205       A       206.6.177.205
                MX      10 walrus.bv.   ; Primary Mail Host
...
ws-177250       A       206.6.177.250
                MX      10 walrus.bv.   ; Primary Mail Host
```

```
ws-177251      A       206.6.177.251
               MX      10 walrus.bv.   ; Primary Mail Host
ws-177252      A       206.6.177.252
               MX      10 walrus.bv.   ; Primary Mail Host
ws-177253      A       206.6.177.253
               MX      10 walrus.bv.   ; Primary Mail Host
ws-177254      A       206.6.177.254
               MX      10 walrus.bv.   ; Primary Mail Host
```

Notice that the times here are given with one-letter suffixes indicating hours, weeks, and days. This is a handy notation, eliminating the need to calculate how many seconds exist in a week, which can be time consuming. As you also can see, other values are used in the SOA record. The zone originates at walrus.bv, which is the name of the nameserver. Additionally, the zone contact is root@walrus.bv and the last update occurred on September 20, 1996. The secondaries will check with the master every 8 hours and retry every two hours if it fails. If it continues to fail, the secondaries will stop answering after one week. As stated earlier, one week might be too short in cases of emergency. The default ttl and minimum, negative caching ttl are one day. Also notice that only one digit is set aside for numbering the daily changes in the serial number. So, the zone file can be changed only 10 times per day. That might be sufficient for most people, but perhaps a tad too few if you're prone to mistakes and have to increment the serial number many times for each change you make. If that happens, you might run out on a given day.

Hostnames also are provided for each kind of service, such as FTP, mail, and news, with CNAME records pointing to the main host. Providing service names in a domain is a good policy because it enables you to use, for example, ftp for all FTP services. Then, if the FTP server is moved to another host, the CNAME record can simply be changed. Therefore, users of the FTP service never have to be retrained to use another hostname. After the Web became so popular, this kind of naming policy became more prevalent, with www.domain being the most obvious example of it. This practice is also described in RFC 2219.

In addition, each host has a name based on its IP number, instead of a "real" name. This often can be seen within large organizations. The idea here is that you always know what IP number a host is supposed to have, eliminating any confusion. Nowadays, the wide deployment of DHCP has made it less of a problem. Of course, some people prefer names for their machines and will feel like they're being treated as numbers, but you can't win 'em all.

You also should notice that Walrus has its secondary nameserver offsite at its ISP, psi.net. As I've mentioned a few times before, it is good practice to keep your secondary nameservers offsite.

zone/206.6.177

The following shows the reverse zone:

```
$TTL 1D
@               IN      SOA     walrus.bv. root.walrus.bv. (
                                199609206       ; Serial
                                28800    ; Refresh
                                7200     ; Retry
                                604800   ; Expire
                                86400)   ; Minimum TTL
                NS      walrus.bv.
                NS      ns2.psi.net.
;
;       Servers
;
1       PTR     router.walrus.bv.
2       PTR     walrus.bv.
2       PTR     funn.walrus.bv.
;
;       Workstations
;
200     PTR     ws-177200.walrus.bv.
201     PTR     ws-177201.walrus.bv.
202     PTR     ws-177202.walrus.bv.
203     PTR     ws-177203.walrus.bv.
204     PTR     ws-177204.walrus.bv.
205     PTR     ws-177205.walrus.bv.
...
250     PTR     ws-177250.walrus.bv.
251     PTR     ws-177251.walrus.bv.
252     PTR     ws-177252.walrus.bv.
253     PTR     ws-177253.walrus.bv.
254     PTR     ws-177254.walrus.bv.
```

The previous code contains no surprises. Here too we see an up-ended zone file and an offsite secondary nameserver.

To make these zones operative, simply add the following lines to your `named.conf` file:

```
zone "walrus.bv" {
        type master;
        file "zone/walrus.bv";
};

zone "177.6.206.in-addr.arpa" {
        type master;
        file "zone/206.6.177";
};
```

These sections are just as before; the only difference is the name of the directory in which the zone files are stored.

Subdomains and Delegation

In Chapter 1, I discussed the importance of delegation of domains from root server to TLD server to subdomain and possibly even subdomain of that again, as in the case of ifi.uio.no. In practice, delegation is quite simple.

penguin.bv wants to open new offices on the other side of the island, and it decides to delegate a DNS domain for that office. The domain will be called emperor.penguin.bv and reside on a DNS server at the Emperor office. The Emperor office has been assigned the net at 192.168.56.0 through 192.168.56.127 and the subnet mask is 255.255.255.128. This is called a *classless* net because it's divided not on an octet boundary as is customary, but within an octet. You can read more about the reasons for assigning classless nets in RFCs 1367 and 1467, as well as RFC 2050. RFC 2050 also provides a glimpse into how the Internet is governed and describes the Registry hierarchy from IANA down to the ISPs. The predecessors of RFC 2050—RFCs 1366 and 1466—discuss the motivations for this policy in more detail.

To make the domain delegation work, the hostmaster at Penguin AS simply adds two records in the penguin.bv zone:

```
emperor         NS      ns.emperor
                NS      ns.herring.bv.
ns.emperor      A       192.168.56.3
```

These two NS records, along with the matching A records, only implement the delegation. This adds an edge in the DNS tree so the new zone can be found (see Figure 2.2). As I've said before, the chain of NS/A pairs must be unbroken from the rootservers all the way to your servers so outside computers or users can find your domain. If anyone outside your domain can't find it, you should start debugging the delegation chain.

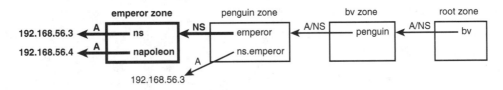

Figure 2.2   ns.emperor.penguin.bv, a new edge in the trees.

Other than the ability to add edges and delegate domains, the most important thing is the use of a glue record. While DNS can look up the address of ns.herring.bv without any problem, the only normal way to find the address of ns.emperor.penguin.bv is by asking the emperor.penguin.bv server about its address. Unfortunately, you don't know the address of the emperor.penguin.bv nameserver yet, so you can't. The A record for ns.emperor.penguin.bv is added to take care of this step, which is the glue record. In old DNS zones, glue records existed for practically all subdomain nameservers, whether they were in the subdomain or somewhere else entirely. This is not a recommended practice anymore, though, and in fact,

BIND 8 rejects glue records that are not for a subdomain of the zone in which they occur. However, the use of redundant glue records can cause a phenomenon known as DNS poisoning, in which several glue A records, if not well maintained, fall out of date over time. This usually isn't noticed though, because the other nameserver(s) still works. Unfortunately, the incorrect A records are cached and taken at face value, causing the wrong address to be used. If a DNS server has previous knowledge of all the nameservers of a domain and they're all incorrect, the domain will become impossible to look up.

After, or before, having the domain delegated, the administrator at `emperor.penguin.bv` sets up her own zones and has the people at Herring bring up a secondary server. This subdomain zone is just like every other zone.

Reverse Delegations for Classless Nets

The fact that `emperor.penguin.bv` was assigned a classless net complicates reverse lookups. DNS can delegate only zones at the dots (.) in the domain names. But a classless net is specifically not divided at a dot; instead, one or more bits are divided into one of the octets, probably the last one.

As explained in RFC 1466, the use of classless nets is necessary to keep the Internet functioning. However, because this scheme was devised after DNS's reverse lookup method was established, the reverse lookup method was not designed to cope with this situation.

The problem, restated, is that DNS can delegate only whole A, B, or C nets, which are all divided at octet boundaries. After someone is delegated a net smaller than C, administration of the reverse lookup zone can't be delegated because one zone can't be partitioned across several servers.

A fix—well, almost a fix—has been devised. RFC 2317 describes this fix. The trick is to let DNS follow its normal order of resolution, but once you get to the partitioned address octet, you insert a CNAME record instead of the expected NS/A or PTR records. The CNAME record gives an obfuscated name, which DNS then proceeds to resolve into a PTR record in the normal manner—though the name is a bit strange.

In the case of the Emperor office of Penguin AS, the ISP sets up a reverse zone for `192.168.56`, containing CNAME records. This is the contents, less the opening formalia, of the `56.168.192.in-addr.arpa` zone at the ISP:

```
; 0-127 subnet
1               CNAME   1.0-127.56.168.192.in-addr.arpa.
2               CNAME   2.0-127.56.168.192.in-addr.arpa.
...
126             CNAME   126.0.56.168.192.in-addr.arpa.
;
```

```
; 128-255 subnet
;
129             CNAME    129.128-255.56.168.192.in-addr.arpa.
130             CNAME    130.128-255.56.168.192.in-addr.arpa.
...
254             CNAME    254.128-255.56.168.192.in-addr.arpa.
;
0-127           NS       ns.emperor.penguin.bv.
0-127           NS       ns.herring.bv.
128-255         NS       ns.walruss.bv.
128-255         NS       ns2.psi.net.
```

In the course of resolving 1.56.168.129.in-addr.arpa, DNS will find a CNAME record pointing to 1.0-127.56.168.192.in-addr.arpa. DNS knows how to resolve that name even if it is odd-looking. As the zone shows, the 0-127.56.168.192.in-addr.arpa zone is delegated to the emperor nameservers.

Note that RFC 2317 uses a slash (/) of subnetting bitmasks for the CNAME record names. However, the use of a slash in domain names is not strictly allowed and it is now discouraged. The scheme shown in the previous code, start-end, is one of the legal alternatives.

On the emperor servers, a zone now must be set to resolve these addresses. This is part of the 0-127.56.168.192.in-addr.arpa zone:

```
1               PTR      gw.emperor.penguin.bv.
2               PTR      ftp.emperor.penguin.bv.
3               PTR      ns.emperor.penguin.bv.
...
```

I haven't shown you any forward zones for emperor.penguin.bv, but the contents of this reverse zone are quite unremarkable, only the name is a bit odd. At walruss.bv, an equally unremarkable corresponding zone will be set up for 128-255.56.168.192.in-addr.arpa.

The observant reader will notice that it is rather tedious to type in the 56.168.192.in-addr.arpa zone. The zone contains 256 records of mind-numbing likeness. Fortunately, BIND 8 has a cure for this. The zone shown previously could be written like the following, still less formalia:

```
$GENERATE 0-127          $    CNAME  $.0-127.56.168.192.in-addr.arpa.

$GENERATE 128-255        $    CNAME  $.128-255.56.168.192.in-addr.arpa.
```

This is a rather straightforward loop declaration. The first line says to loop from 1–126, and for each number to generate CNAME records with the given name replacing all occurrences of $ with the number. The second line does the same thing, but for 128–255 and a slightly different name.

Recalling the `walrus.bv` zone, a similar use of numbers exists there. It too can be replaced by `$GENERATE`:

```
$GENERATE 200-254      ws-177$         A       206.6.177.$
$GENERATE 200-254      ws-177$         MX 10   walrus.bv.
```

Is this cool or what? As you might have noticed, I believe in any device that can save typing. The same goes for Walrus's reverse zone:

```
$GENERATE 200-254         $            PTR     ws-177$.walrus.bv.
```

For an alternative discussion of this topic, please read RFC 2317.

Secondary Servers

Before a domain application is approved, at least one secondary server must be operative, as well as the master server. RFC 2182 describes how secondary DNS servers should be selected and operated. This RFC is even a BCP, Best Current Practice, so I recommend it. It discusses many diverse DNS server topics, from placement to firewalls to hidden nameservers to how many secondary servers you need.

It boils down to this: If you want your domain to operate reliably, and even in the face of failures wherever they occur, your DNS should operate reliably. To make it reliable, your DNS servers should be placed in diverse locations both geographically and network topologically. Separate your servers as widely as possible, measured overland and along the network, and they will be independent. If they share power lines, though, they are liable to all fail when the power fails. If they share a WAN or LAN, they also are liable to all fail if the WAN or LAN fails.

Adding a Slave Server

Now, when the good people at Herring AS set up secondaries for Penguin and Walrus AS, they insert something similar to the following into their `named.conf` files:

```
zone "penguin.bv" {
        type slave;
        file "sz/penguin.bv";
        masters {
                192.168.55.2;
        };
};

zone "55.168.192.in-addr.arpa" {
        type slave;
        file "sz/192.168.55";
```

```
masters {
        192.168.55.2;
};
```
    };

The `zone` lines are exactly as on the master; after all, they name the zone. The zone type is `slave`, which is correct. Additionally, the zone data is stored not in `pz` but in `sz`, for secondary zone. Inside the `masters` statement, you can list all the possible DNS servers from which to copy this zone. If you list all the other servers here, the secondary has a good chance of getting fresh copies of the zone from one of them. Recall that a zone will expire on the slave server if the slave has been unable to get updates for the zone's expire time.

If you want to list multiple servers, separate them with a semicolon (;).

You usually will want to list all your secondary servers in NS records for the zone in question.

Stealth Servers

Various reasons exist for setting nameservers for a zone that are not listed in the zone's NS records. These are sometimes called *stealth servers*.

Many unlisted servers are located on the inside of a company network, providing lookup and resolution service to all the hosts on the inside. If the server has the domain's zone files, it will be capable of answering queries for the zone directly from the zone file instead of having to resolve the names in the usual manner, which is more time consuming. This internal server often is unavailable from the Internet, and listing it in the NS records only causes DNS on the outside to spend time contacting a server that will never answer. The hosts on the inside do not need the listing; they will ask the servers anyway because their resolver was set up that way. Therefore, it is not listed.

Another reason for running an unlisted server is that the listed servers might be in some way impractical to log in to and work on, be it for security reasons or for any other reason. In that case, you can run an unlisted master server, on which it is convenient to work and from which the slaves will get updates.

NOTIFY

Originally, slave DNS servers would poll only the master server as set by the zone's `refresh` parameter. Some people have been unhappy with that, so the NOTIFY extension to the DNS protocol was defined in RFC 1996. Using this protocol, a zone's master can notify the zone's slaves of changes in the zone. So, instead of waiting for a few hours for a refresh cycle to start, the zone update propagates to the slave servers pretty quickly. I say "pretty quickly" because after a zone has been updated, your DNS server waits for a random number of seconds before sending the NOTIFY. This avoids being bombarded by SOA and zone transfer requests all at the same time, and the delay distributes the queries from the slaves in time.

A master server notifies all the nameservers listed in NS records that are not itself. If you have unlisted nameservers, you can use an `also-notify` declaration within the zone declaration:

```
zone "..." {
        ...
        also-notify { 192.168.57.5; };
};
```

The secondary nameservers will act on a NOTIFY only if they receive it from a declared master server. If your master server is multihomed or has interface aliases, it might be sending the NOTIFYs from the wrong address. You can override this within the global options declaration in `named.conf`:

```
options {
        ...
        query-source 192.168.55.2;
};
```

This causes BIND to use the given address as the source address for all traffic it originates.

3

Maintenance and Enhancements

More Practical Details

The things you can do once you have established your zone are legion. I will describe some of the more usual activities in this chapter. In my judgment these might not be day-to-day activities for most DNS admins; but, instead, they might be valuable things to have in the back of your mind and to look up when needed.

Maintaining and Changing Zones

As time passes you will need to make changes to your zones. Some of these changes will be mundane and no special attention is needed when they are made. Other changes, such as moving a much used service might need special attention to make the change known quickly to all your users.

How SOA Record Controls DNS

As explained in Chapter 1, "DNS Concepts," and Chapter 2, "DNS in Practice," the SOA record controls how fast updated zones propagate from the master to the slave servers and how long RRs are cached in caching servers before they are flushed. Both of these affect your ability to make instant changes in the zones you maintain.

I will consider two scenarios: moving a Web server and moving a DNS server. How quickly you need these changes to be made depends on how critical you consider the services to be. If you run DNS for an e-commerce site, everything is likely to be considered critical, even if the powers that be want everything to be done cheaply. You need to be able to tell these powers that be how things must be done to make it work with DNS.

Moving a Service

Let's consider the case of moving a Web server from one housing service to another. Depending on how many machines provide the service you might or might not be faced with the whole service being offline for a while, or perhaps by moving machines one by one you can maintain service during the whole moving period. In either case, you want DNS to serve the new address of the service as soon as it is up on the new site. I'll be moving www.penguin.bv. The following is an extract of the penguin.bv zone showing the records affected:

```
$TTL 804800     ; 7 days
;
@       3600    SOA     ns.penguin.bv. hostmaster.penguin.bv. (
                2000041300      ; serial
                86400           ; refresh, 24h
                7200            ; retry, 2h
                3600000         ; expire, 1000h
                172800          ; minimum, 2 days
                )
                NS      ns
                NS      ns.herring.bv.

; WEB, both http://www.penguin.bv/ and
; http://penguin.bv/ with A records

www             A       192.168.55.3
; People often send mail to webmaster@www.domain
                MX      10 mail
                MX      20 mail.herring.bv.
                HINFO   PC Tunes
@               A       192.168.55.3
```

Because the default TTL for the penguin.bv zone is seven days, I need to start the work more than seven days ahead of time. The first thing to do is to reduce the TTL for the Web server A records. How low should we set them? Remember, all cached RRs will stay in the cache for the duration of the TTL from the moment they are cached. When moving www.penguin.bv we'll be turning off the machine, dragging it into a car, driving for 10 minutes, and then getting it up on the new site with a new address. Let's say about 20–30 minutes. The zone will be updated with the new record just before the machine is turned off. So, within 20 minutes after that we want all the users to have the new address. A TTL between 5 and 10 minutes would seem appropriate. I'll use 10 minutes. So, at least seven days (the old TTL) before the machine is moved I set these values for the A records that have to do with the Web server:

```
www     600     A       192.168.55.3
...
@       600     A       192.168.55.3
```

Now they will expire after 10 minutes in the caches. Of course I changed the serial number as well. And then I reloaded the server and checked the logs, and so did you, right?

The second problem is that all the slave servers need to be updated immediately when the update is made, or they will continue serving the old records, and many of your clients will keep getting and caching the old updated A records, to their frustration, and not incidentally, yours too.

If you have full access to the slave servers this will not be a big a problem, a simple trick will solve it. You can log onto the slave server, remove the zone file for the updated zone and restart named. This will cause the named to immediately request the zone from the master, which solves the problem. If you do not control the slave servers, and this is probably much more common, you need to find another way to force the transfer.

Zone Transfer by NOTIFY

The trouble with the NOTIFY request is that it travels by UDP and can be dropped by the network. The U in UDP is not for Unreliable, although it might as well be. Additionally, if a slave does not support NOTIFY you're out of luck. Also, this is one case where the very sensible time delay of NOTIFY, which I described in Chapter 2, will be frustrating. You can't know if your server is still waiting out the delay or if the NOTIFY got lost. Fortunately you can enable more logging in named.conf so you can see everything that happens:

```
logging {
        channel my_log {
                file "/var/log/named.db";
                severity dynamic;
                print-category yes;
                print-severity yes;
        };
        category notify { my_log; };
        category xfer-out { my_log; };
};
```

Run "ndc restart" to pick up the configuration change. Update the zone serial number in the zone and run "ndc trace 3" and then "tail –f /var/log/named.db" to see what happens when you, finally, run "ndc reload" to load the updated zone:

```
29-Apr-2000 16:39:50.897 ns_notify(penguin.bv, IN, SOA):
                         ni 0x400bf728, zp 0x80e188c, delay 24
29-Apr-2000 16:40:14.899 sysnotify(penguin.bv, IN, SOA)
29-Apr-2000 16:40:14.901 Sent NOTIFY for "penguin.bv IN SOA"
                         (penguin.bv); 1 NS, 1 A
29-Apr-2000 16:40:14.916 Received NOTIFY answer from 192.168.226.3 for
                         "penguin.bv IN SOA"
29-Apr-2000 16:40:15.084 zone transfer (AXFR) of "penguin.bv" (IN)
                         to [192.168.226.3].8478
```

Actually there will be more unless you grep the tail output, but the interesting bits are shown above. First, we see that named decides that a NOTIFY is in order, and to delay it 24 seconds. Then, the time to send the notify arrives and it is sent. A response is promptly received, and in short order the zone is transfered by the slave. This is what is supposed to happen for each and every slave server. If it does not, it should suffice to do an "ndc restart," because named will issue NOTIFY requests when starting, just in case a zone changed since the last reload or restart. In this manner you should be able to get the slaves reloaded promptly.

Zone-Transfer by Other Methods

If all your slaves do not implement NOTIFY and you do not have full access, you need to get the slaves to check the zone for updates frequently so that the zone transfer happens fast enough. Controlling this is what the refresh value is for. If you would like to have the zone transfered within 10 minutes of an update, set the refresh period to 10 minutes. But be sure to do it more than one old refresh interval before the change takes place so that the new, decreased refresh interval is picked up in time. In cases such as the moving of an important server a refresh period of one minute would not be out of place. This is quite possibly the simplest way to accomplish this in any case. If you plan ahead. But increase it again afterwards.

The last technique is to call up the admins of the slave servers and arrange for them to be available when the move is made. Then phone around and get them to reload the zone by force, by removing the zone file from the slave servers and reloading as described earlier. This works best if there aren't many of them to call.

Moving a Nameserver

Moving a nameserver is probably easier technically, but involves more people than just the nameserver admin. It also involves all the servers that are slaves of it, and all the servers it is a slave for, as well as all those that delegate domains to it. If you count all that, you find a lot of things depend on that nameserver—both the function it performs and its IP address. Additionally, if the nameserver is used as a resolving, recursive nameserver by someone, all their resolv.conf files need to be fixed.

Actually, it's not as many as that. As discussed in Chapter 2 spurious glue records are now avoided, discouraged, and even handled as errors. This means that the number of glue records in need of change is small. It is probably one. It should be the one in the domain above yours that points to your nameserver inside your domain. If you recall the emperor zone within the penguin.bv zone, it contained these records:

```
emperor        NS      ns.emperor
               NS      ns.herring.bv.
ns.emperor     A       192.168.56.3
```

The people delegating name service to your nameserver will have a glue record analogous to that in their zone. In this case, the bv TLD admins will have something like this:

```
...
penguin        NS      ns.penguin.bv.
penguin        NS      ns.herring.bv.
ns.penguin     A       192.168.55.2
ns.herring     A       192.168.226.3
...
```

So, before moving a server you will need to notify the admins of the zone above you. It is quite likely, as is the case for penguin.bv, that this is a TLD registrar, and you have to cope with the registrar's forms and requirements, and processing time. Which means that you don't know when the registrar will change their glue record. But most registrars will not change the glue record unless there is a nameserver giving authoritative answers for the zone at the new address. This precludes you from just moving the name server ASAP after the registrar has changed the record. In addition, the TTL on a TLD is likely to be one day, but your superior zone might not be a TLD and in any case, the TTL might be a week, or more. More than a week might pass before all the world knows that your nameserver has moved. That's a long time. Plan ahead.

Whether you're right under a TLD or you admin a corporate sub-domain, a good course of action is to first set up a new server, change the NS records within the zone and then notify the domain above you of the change. Only when the glue record has been changed and has propagated to the slaves and expired from caches, should you disable the old server. If need be, you can do this by way of a third machine that acts as master temporarily while you move the real host.

Remember that the NS record must point to a domain name, and that domain name must point to an A record. It cannot point to a CNAME record. Whenever you move a nameserver play it straight—or run quickly to put things right.

DNS Round Robin and Load Distribution

In these days of exponential growth of Internet users any moderately successful Web site will receive more traffic than one machine can handle. There are many ways to cope with this, and

```
                7200              ; retry, 2h
                3600000           ; expire, 1000h
                172800            ; minimum, 2 days
                )
                NS      ns
                NS      ns.herring.bv.
                MX      10 mail
                MX      20 mail.herring.bv.

; Nameserver
ns              A       192.168.55.2

; Mailserver, same machine.
mail            A       192.168.55.2
                MX      10 mail
                MX      20 mail.herring.bv.
                HINFO   PC Tunes
```

When one host has several names, for whatever reason, CNAME records are often used. Modern BINDs restricts the use of CNAME records quite severely. The restrictions were in the RFCs from the beginning, but it was never enforced. BIND 8 enforces them. The main rule is that a name that has a CNAME record cannot have any other records. Additionally MX, NS, and SOA records cannot point to names that are CNAME records. If a CNAME record had been used for ns above:

```
ns              CNAME mail
```

it would have invalidated the SOA and NS records, which both point to `ns.penguin.bv`. If a CNAME record had been used for mail:

```
mail            CNAME ns
```

all the other records for mail would have been invalid. Thus, I used one A record for each instead.

There is an option you can set for each zone you have, <tt/multiple-cnames/, if you set it to <tt/yes/ BIND will give you more freedom to use CNAME records. As the BIND documentation says: "Allowing multiple CNAME records is against standards and is not recommended. Multiple CNAME support is available because previous versions of BIND allowed multiple CNAME records, and these records have been used for load balancing by a number of sites." This is a handy option to have in a transitional phase; it allows you to be master or slave server for zones that have not been transitioned to the stricter CNAME rules yet.

Wildcard Records

DNS has the concept of *wildcard records*. They are most often used for MX records. On first sight they seem useful enough, but they are counter intuitive and often used incorrectly.

In the `penguin.bv` zone mail could have been set up like this:

```
@               MX      10 mail
                MX      20 mail.herring.bv.
*               MX      10 mail
                MX      20 mail.herring.bv.
mail            MX      10 mail
                MX      20 mail.herring.bv.
rms             A       192.168.55.130
```

Which, by the way, is not the same as used to be in the penguin zone, and probably not what you, or I, want.

The proper name for the wildcard record is `"*.penguin.bv"`. Thus it will not match a query for a MX record for "penguin.bv." A query for that will instead match the "@" record. A query for "mail.penguin.bv" will match the explicit record for mail, any record occurring in the zone overrides the wildcard. But, almost any other query will match the wildcard record. In practice, the wildcard record will make names that are not in the zone appear to be defined. For example a query for "foobar.penguin.bv" will be answered with an answer for "foobar.penguin.bv," not "*.penguin.bv." This is known as *synthesizing* resource records— records are created on demand, from thin air. It is impossible to determine if a name in an answer is caused by a wildcard record or not.

Restrictions on Wildcards

In addition to not matching penguin.bv the wildcard record also does not match the name rms.penguin.bv. Wildcards does not match any name for which there is any data in the zone, even if the data present is not the kind the query requires. Explicit MX records must be set up for each name that occurs in the zone that is meant to have a MX record associated with it. This is a bit of a bummer as it restricts the usefulness of wildcards severely.

Wildcard RRs do not cross zone boundaries. The wildcard above does not affect the emperor.penguin.bv zone. The emperor.penguin.bv zone is searched for matches for queries within its scope. In the same manner wildcard records does not apply to subdomains within the same zone such as this setup:

```
*               MX      10 mail
                MX      20 mail.herring.bv.
sigurd.king     A       192.168.56.3
eirik.king      A       192.168.56.4
```

A query for a MX for sigurd.king.penguin.bv will not match the wildcard record. The wildcard "*.king.penguin.bv" must be added to take care of this. "*.*.penguin.bv" is not allowed, nor is "foobar.*.penguin.bv." Only one wildcard, and only at the left end of the domain name is allowed.

In addition to all this, you should be sure that the mail server on the receiving end of wildcard MX records is able to handle the rather unpredictable names it might be handed. Consider "i.hate.penguin.bv," and whatever else Internet users will be able to think of.

The Problem with Wildcards

If you consider all these restrictions, you will find that wildcard records only match names for which there are no other DNS entries. This is probably the opposite of what you wanted. You wanted MX records for all the names in DNS, not all the names not in DNS. This is counter intuitive enough that many people make errors when using wildcards and the resulting problems are enough that wildcards are considered harmful by quite a few people.

Logs and Debugging

BIND 8 has quite an advanced logging apparatus, and at first sight, it can also be incomprehensible. The logs are important and should be paid attention to, so you catch errors sooner rather than later.

All logging options must occur within one "logging" directive. If there are several logging directives the last one found takes precedence. To get the logging you want during the loading of zones, a good place to have the logging directive is at the very start of the named.conf file. The basic elements of logging are "channel"s and "category"s, I will return to these shortly.

BINDs Start, Reload, and Reconfig Logging

The main, day-to-day use of the BIND logs is to find out if the changes you make to the configuration and zones are syntactically correct. For this reason you should always look at the BIND log when a zone or configuration file is updated and loaded. If you don't notice that a zone is rejected by BIND because of syntax errors your server will become *lame*, not able to answer queries about a zone it was supposed to be authoritative for. After the expiry interval set in the SOA record the slave servers will expire the zone and they too will become lame. At this point names in the rejected zone will become impossible to resolve, and all service, mail, Web or otherwise will fail. Similarly, a syntax error early in the named.conf file might stop all further processing of it, causing the zones appearing later in the file to not be loaded with the same disrupting results. A simple log inspection would have revealed all. Running "tail -f" on the log file when restarting or reloading bind is good practice.

The prudent DNS admin will either read, or set up a log analysis tool to read the DNS logs for her periodically to discover problems, no matter if a change was made to her own configuration or not. Network configuration, or other problems at remote sites might cause zone transfer of slave zones to your server. This might not be obvious to the master admin, but should be plain to the slave admin because BIND will complain.

There are ways to automate quality control of your DNS. Some of them are described in Chapter 7, "The DNS Tool Chest."

Logging Channels

A channel is a logging method, a way to funnel log messages somewhere, usually the syslog daemon or a file. A channel can have several other properties as well. The general syntax for a channel is quite complex:

```
channel channel_name {
  facility
  [ severity ( critical | error | warning | notice |
               info  | debug [ level ] | dynamic ); ]
  [ print-category yes_or_no; ]
  [ print-severity yes_or_no; ]
  [ print-time yes_or_no; ]
};
```

Severity is like syslogs priority concept. And indeed, when BIND logs to syslog it logs at the analogous syslog priority. The severity field gives the cutoff level of messages sent to the channel. The severities above are given in order of increasing verbosity. If you specify "critical" only critical messages will be sent there. If you specify "notice" all levels from "critical" down to "notice" will be sent there. If you desire debugging output specify "dynamic" and use "ndc trace" and "ndc notrace" to change the debugging level dynamically. There is an example of this earlier in this chapter, when I discussed zone transfer by NOTIFY.

If you want to find out what category a message is setting "print-category" to, "yes" will be helpful. Ditto for "print-severity." yes_or_no should be "yes" or "no," but "true" or "false" and "0" or "1" is also recognized. By default all the print settings are off. Setting these will help you customize BINDs logging exactly to your needs, because you can see at what levels and in which categories the interesting messages occur. It can also help automated reading of the logs because words such as "critical" are a lot easier to identify automatically than the wording of a message, which can change. The default severity is "info."

The facility is a logging facility, and is specified with this syntax:

```
( file path_name
   [ versions ( number | unlimited ) ]
   [ size size_spec ]
 | syslog ( kern | user | mail | daemon | auth | syslog | lpr |
           news | uucp | cron | authpriv | ftp |
           local0 | local1 | local2 | local3 |
           local4 | local5 | local6 | local7 )
 | null );
```

As you see there are three ways to log: to file, to syslog, and to null—the great bit bucket in the sky.

Time to concentrate. BIND has logging facilities. These are places to put log entries. Syslog is one of these facilities within BIND, a simple file is another. Syslog has facilities as well, but they are not the same. In syslog a facility is a message originator, or category. A syslog facility bears a name such as "kern," "user," "mail," or "local0," to "local7" as shown earlier. BIND facilities does not have names beyond "file," "syslog," and "null." Please don't confuse the two kinds of facilities.

If BIND is to log to the syslog facility you also need to specify with which of syslog's facilities you want the messages to be associated. Thus, the appearance of syslog facility names in the listing shown earlier. The syslog priority is given by BINDs own severity. If you check, you'll see that the syslog priorities match the severities well. If you want to run a chroot'ed BIND, you must log to file because the syslogd is not available from a chroot environment. See Chapters 8, "Security Concerns," and 15, "Compiling and Maintaining BIND," for more information about BIND in chroot'ed environments.

The file facility is quite advanced for a file logging facility. It can rotate its own logs. The log is rotated whenever it becomes bigger than the size and is kept for the number of generations given by the "size" and "versions" clauses. If your OS services include log rotation, be careful to not let syslogs own log rotation be interfered with by the OS log rotation. When logging to file it's usually a good idea to add "print-time yes." Syslog adds timestamps automatically, but output to file does not. The size_spec should be a number or "unlimited." The number can be followed by one of K, M or G, possibly in lowercase. The letters mean exactly what you think they mean.

Logging Categories

By this BIND refers to the category of messages. The syntax goes like this:

```
category category_name {
        channel_name; [ channel_name; ... ]
};
```

The channel names are the channels you have named with your channel clauses as described earlier, or one of the default channels, described later. The category name gives the category of messages that should go to that channel. It should be one of these:

- config—Configuration file processing
- parser—Low-level parsing of the configuration file
- queries—Log every query received (but briefly)
- lame-servers—The warnings about lame servers
- statistics—Various statistics
- panic—The last "eeeep!" from the server before exiting after a fatal a error is discovered
- update—Notices about dynamic updates
- ncache—About negative caching

- xfer-in—Zone-transfers to the server
- xfer-out—Zone-transfers to other servers
- db—Database operations
- eventlib—The latest from the event loop. Only one file channel can be specified.
- packet—The packets BIND sends and receives are decoded into the channel associated with this category. Only one file channel can be specified.
- notify—Everything about NOTIFY events
- cname—CNAME warnings
- security—Of approved and unapproved requests
- os—Problems with the OS
- insist—Failures of internal consistency checks
- maintenance—Internal maintenance events
- load—Zone loading events
- response-checks—Problems found in answers BIND receive

BINDs Default Logging Configuration

This is shamelessly stolen from the named.conf man page (see Appendix A):

```
logging {
        channel default_syslog {
                syslog daemon;      # send to syslog's daemon facility
                severity info;      # only send priority info and higher
        };

        channel default_debug {
            file "named.run";
            # write to named.run in the working directory
            # Note: stderr is used instead of "named.run" if the server
            # is started with the -f option.

            severity dynamic;
            # log at the server's current debug level
        };

        channel default_stderr { # writes to stderr
            file "<stderr>";
            # this is illustrative only; there's currently no way of
            # specifying an internal file descriptor in the
            # configuration language.

            severity info;         # only send priority info and higher
        };
        channel null {
```

```
        null;                   # toss anything sent to this channel
    };

    category default { default_syslog; default_debug; };
    category panic { default_syslog; default_stderr; };
    category packet { default_debug; };
    category eventlib { default_debug; };
};
```

This puts channels and categories in context. "Packet" and "eventlib" messages are sent to default_debug. "Panic" messages to default_syslog and default_stderr, while the "default" category is sent to default_syslog and default_debug. The "default" category is made up of all the categories that are not assigned to one or more channels explicitly. So, any category not listed in your logging directive will end up in "default."

The shown channels are defined no matter what, and cannot be redefined. The shown categories on the other hand will only be defined if you don't define anything for those categories, and they are meant to be overridden, if needed.

Controlling Debug Logging

The debug channel, shown earlier, and the my_log channel, which was declared like this earlier in this chapter both use "dynamic" severity setting.

```
channel my_log {
            file "/var/log/named.db";
            severity dynamic;
            print-category yes;
            print-severity yes;
    };
```

This allows you to control the level of output sent to the channel dynamically with the "ndc trace" and "ndc notrace" commands. This is very handy because there is no need to restart the server to adjust the log level. The downside is of course that all active channels are affected by the global debug level, which "ndc trace" adjusts. It might be a bit much to look through when looking for a problem. Too much information is overwhelming, and too little is of no use. The following declaration has the same effect as the combined "dynamic" severity and "ndc trace 3" command used earlier in this chapter, because it simply sets the debug level for the channel to 3, statically:

```
channel my_log {
            file "/var/log/named.db";
            severity debug 3;
            print-time yes;
    };
```

Of course, it will spew debug messages as long as BIND runs, too. And a lot at that, even a quite unloaded DNS server risks filling its disk quite quickly this way. But, by replacing and/or customizing BINDs default logging configuration you can get pretty much any result you want.

Adding More Domains

To add a new domain to your server you just add the needed forward and reverse zones in your named.conf file(s). There is no limit in BIND on how many zones it can serve, but in practice it is limited by how many requests your server can handle, and how fast it can be restarted and/or reloaded. There are BIND nameservers, in production use, that uses more than 30 minutes to start, just because of the number and size of the zones they serve. In BIND 9 we have been promised ways to solve this problem by using back-end databases, so that BIND can load records on demand, rather than a whole zone at a time.

It is reasonable to expect that any modern computer can handle the load of several hundreds of zones—depending on the size and popularity of course. One thing you should note is that BIND loads all the zones in entirely into memory. You will need enough RAM to store all of BIND, without swapping for preference. Additionally the cache will use up your RAM. In principle BIND will continue to use memory as long as it needs it and can. In practice few people have a problem with this. If this scares you, please have a look at the section on BIND resource limits in Chapter 8.

Contingency Planning

A question often asked is "Why do I need redundant DNS servers? When my services fail they don't work anyway so DNS is of no use." This is false. RFC 2182 (alias BCP 16) is about the placement, selection, and operation of redundant nameservers. You should read it. Section 3.3 in it deals with this myth:

"An argument is occasionally made that there is no need for the domain name servers for a domain to be accessible if the hosts in the domain are unreachable. This argument is fallacious.

■ "Clients react differently to inability to resolve than inability to connect, and reactions to the former are not always as desirable.

■ "If the zone is resolvable yet the particular name is not, then a client can discard the transaction rather than retrying and creating undesirable load on the network.

■ "While positive DNS results are usually cached, the lack of a result is not cached. Thus, unnecessary inability to resolve creates an undesirable load on the Net.

■ "All names in the zone might not resolve to addresses within the detached network. This becomes more likely over time. Thus a basic assumption of the myth often becomes untrue.

"It is important that there be nameservers able to be queried, available always, for all forward zones."

The most notable reaction of clients is that mail will bounce if there are no MX records available. Lost emails are lost opportunities, although some might find the effective way it stops spam a relief.

Regarding the second item: If a DNS query first fails the DNS server will try and try again. It will retry it every which way it can in a determined effort to succeed. This causes extra network traffic. If a lot of clients are retrying in this manner it can add up to a lot of extra load. And then perhaps the client decides to retry the query as well, and causes the DNS server to go through the whole retry dance again.

While new versions of BIND does cache the lack of results, avoiding storms of retries, this caching is in itself disruptive when your service comes up. It will be unavailable due to negative caching even if it is in fact available.

The last point goes to the fact that over time most companies will place one or more services outside their own network—for example, a secondary mail server, a Web server in Web hotel, or perhaps an application at an ASP. Thus the servers are in fact available even if your own network is cut off. In these cases your provider will likely be willing to be a DNS slave for your zones, so this is easily solved.

Internal Redundance

All in all, you should provide several nameservers. Internally in your company you might want to set up servers that are used as resolvers by the machines on the inside. Having at least two of them eliminates a single point of failure, which is simply good design. Internal name service is not a heavy task in most cases. You can give the job to almost any machine. Just list up to three of them in /etc/resolv.conf (or equivalents on other OSes) and your OS resolvers will try each one in turn until they find one that works.

If you have a large network inside one large building or across several buildings, you might want to section your network and set up each section to be as autonomous as possible, providing as many as possible of the network services each section needs inside the section. Setting up just one nameserver in each section, and using the servers outside the section as secondary servers would make sense in such a case. But if you have a large, or huge, organization please see the section on practical uses of forwarding later in this chapter.

Having at least DNS work will allow people to get a lot of things done that they might not have been able to do if DNS did not work. Even if other, independent things in your network are nonfunctional. As long as DNS and your external link are up they can at least keep themselves entertained while the file servers are down.

External Redundance

Externally you should also have redundant name service. Your ISP is a likely candidate for having secondaries, but an out-of-town, or even a foreign company you work or partner with is better. The less infrastructure, public or Internet, the servers share the better. They will be less likely to fail all at once. Another important factor is that the Internet does in fact suffer from failures quite often, even though most of us don't notice it. This can, for example, cut a nameserver connected to Qwest in Norway off from the rest of the Internet for hours, or in bad cases for days. You should plan for bad cases such as back-hoe operator error, or, say, irresponsible anchoring practices close to undersea cabling, or what insurance companies refer to as acts of God. These occurrences can keep things down for many days, or even weeks. Norway, and a large part of the world, is blessed with extremely stable power, few floods, and few quakes or volcano eruptions. But you might live in, or be affected by, parts of the world where normalcy is disrupted for days or weeks by floods or storms, which can bring down a lot of things that normally never have problems. You should plan for this; your DNS should be available all through these kinds of catastrophes.

For these reasons it should be easy to understand that having your "redundant" nameservers on one box with two IP addresses defeats the purpose of having redundant servers. Sure, you fulfill the requirement, but only to the letter. Placing your external nameservers on one and the same LAN segment is also unwise as is placing them in the same building where power can go out all at once.

In closing I'd like to recommend, once again, RFC 2182. Read it. Live it. It's not even expensive! An old 486 junker running Linux or a BSD can handle large amounts of DNS traffic.

Extended Outages

Extended outages cause problems normally not encountered or considered. Consider the SOA record, it has one extremely important field, the expires field. When the time set by the expiry field has passed without any contact with the master server a slave server will consider the zone expired, null and void. The zone will cease to exist. A good, high value for the expiry field is important. In Chapter 2 we saw this SOA record for the penguin.bv zone:

```
@      3600     SOA      ns.penguin.bv.  hostmaster.penguin.bv. (
                2000041300     ; serial
                86400          ; refresh, 24h
                7200           ; retry, 2h
                3600000        ; expire, 1000h
                172800         ; minimum, 2 days
       )
```

A value of 1,000 hours is about 42 days. It has been usual practice to have the expiry field set to one week. A week is next to no time in the face of major breakdowns of civilization. Of course a company can go broke after 30 days without being able to restore itself, but at least you will not have contributed to it by setting the expiry value too low.

Practical Uses of Forwarding

Forwarding can be quite handy. If your Internet access is slow, or metered, if you pay for each byte that goes over your connection, using forwarding is recommended. Forwarding is simply telling your DNS to forward queries to another DNS server, which will resolve the query on its behalf. Or perhaps, forward it further. This has a synergy effect with caching. If several servers forward queries to one server its cache will grow large and it will be quite likely to have the answer cached.

The Australian Academic and Research Network

A rather extreme example of this is the Australian Academic and Research Network, AARNet2. The network is shared among many institutions in Australia, and they all share one Internet link to the US. The link is of course overloaded in addition to being very expensive, and even more expensive to upgrade to a faster speed. To help discourage unneeded traffic to the US, and to help keep the link usable, its use is in fact metered and paid for, by megabyte. When a FTP archive inside AARNet2 fetches a CD-ROM image, about 700MB, it is expensive. Due to the cost the Australians have been very organized about how they give access to the goods of the Internet. All manner of traffic is concentrated in a hierarchy, and only very few DNS servers inside AARNet2 have access to the US link. The same goes for Usenet and other traffic that can be organized in this way. They also have large software mirrors on AARNet2 so people tend to get software from them instead of from other places in the world.

The congestion of the US link also adds two other factors: First UDP packets, which DNS uses, are often discarded by routers when networks are congested. So the DNS query might not get through to the outside. This causes retries, which adds to the traffic. If many servers are doing retries the traffic will raise proportionally. Second, the network delay, both due to the congestion, but also due to the sheer length of the network link combined with the limited speed of light causes a significant delay even when queries and answers do get through. When the delay is longer than the timeout in BIND this also causes retries. They clearly do not want every other server to have its own BIND querying DNS across the US link.

A typical setup in Australia is that an AARNet2 member concentrates all its DNS traffic to one DNS server. This server has access to a regional DNS server, which then forwards to the national DNS service, which in turn puts the query on the US link. Each level of forwarding concentrates the traffic and increases the likelihood that a cached answer is found. The structure of AARNet2 and DNS forwarding in it is shown in Figure 3.1.

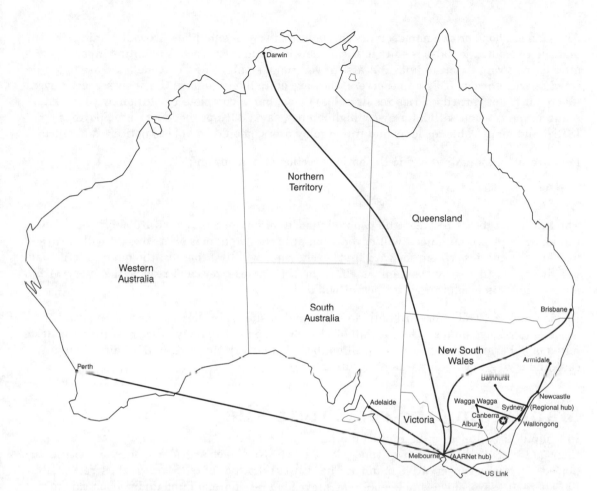

Figure 3.1   Within each region the members connect to the regional hub, which in turn con-
nects to the national hub. The DNS forwarding structure mirrors this, queries
being forwarded through each level until a cached answer is found or the
national hub resolves it.

Thanks to Glen Turner of the University of Adelaide for graciously providing information
about AARNet2.

Forwarding in Your Network

Although your network is probably smaller than AARNet2, using forwarding makes sense in
most corporate networks, or in any firewalled network with more than a few nameservers.

Allowing only one or two nameservers through the firewall simplifies firewall administration, and the concentration also results in the same wins from large caches resulting in fewer queries over your external link. But also, if you run a small company it makes sense to forward queries to your ISPs nameservers, they are quite likely to have the answer cached even if you don't. Forwarded queries result in less bytes than a complete resolution by your own nameserver. Anyone with a link with high latency, say a 33Kbps modem or even 64Kbps ISDN, and many cable modems and frame relay users, should be able to notice a difference.

Forwarding is configured inside the options section of named.conf:

```
[ forward ( only | first ); ]
[ forwarders { [ in_addr ; [ in_addr ; ... ] ] }; ]
```

The first line chooses between the two main modes of forwarding. "Forward only" does what the name implies, you named will never attempt to resolve names on its own, it will always forward the queries. When "forward first" is chosen it will first forward the query, and if that fails it will try to resolve the name itself. If the ISP nameserver can't resolve the query within a reasonable time your own nameserver will do it.

Inside many firewalls "forward only" to a designated site-wide DNS server will be needed to manage to resolve names. The firewall blocks DNS queries from any other host than the designated one. Peripheral nameservers will not be able to query the outside DNS directly in any case and trying to will only waste resources.

Maintaining the root.hints File

In Chapter 2 I alluded to the limited lifetime of a "root.hints" file. The set of rootservers and their addresses does change over time, albeit slowly. New ones are added, old ones retired, or moved—in a very conservative manner. The "powers that be" of DNS knows their responsibility. There are several ways to keep a root.hints file up-to-date, an updated version can be FTPed from a host, or DNS itself can be examined to determine if anything has changed—all automatically if you want. The quickest and easiest way is to use dig. First ask your own nameserver which root nameservers it thinks exist.

```
$ dig @127.0.0.1 . NS
...
;; ANSWER SECTION:
.                          5d23h56m30s IN NS  F.ROOT-SERVERS.NET.
...
.                          5d23h56m30s IN NS  H.ROOT-SERVERS.NET.

;; ADDITIONAL SECTION:
F.ROOT-SERVERS.NET.    6d23h56m30s IN A  192.5.5.241
...
H.ROOT-SERVERS.NET.    6d23h56m30s IN A  128.63.2.53
```

Then ask one of the root servers your nameserver lists the same:

```
$ dig @<root-server> . NS
; <<>> DiG 8.2 <<>> @<root-server> . NS
; (1 server found)
;; res options: init recurs defnam dnsrch
;; got answer:
;; ->>HEADER<<- opcode: QUERY, status: NOERROR, id: 6
;; flags: qr aa rd; QUERY: 1, ANSWER: 13, AUTHORITY: 0, ADDITIONAL: 13
;; QUERY SECTION:
;;      ., type = NS, class = IN

;; ANSWER SECTION:
.                       6D IN NS        L.ROOT-SERVERS.NET.
.                       6D IN NS        M.ROOT-SERVERS.NET.
.                       6D IN NS        I.ROOT-SERVERS.NET.
.                       6D IN NS        E.ROOT-SERVERS.NET.
.                       6D IN NS        D.ROOT-SERVERS.NET.
.                       6D IN NS        A.ROOT-SERVERS.NET.
.                       6D IN NS        H.ROOT-SERVERS.NET.
.                       6D IN NS        C.ROOT-SERVERS.NET.
.                       6D IN NS        G.ROOT-SERVERS.NET.
.                       6D IN NS        F.ROOT-SERVERS.NET.
.                       6D IN NS        B.ROOT-SERVERS.NET.
.                       6D IN NS        J.ROOT-SERVERS.NET.
.                       6D IN NS        K.ROOT-SERVERS.NET.

;; ADDITIONAL SECTION:
L.ROOT-SERVERS.NET.     5w6d16h IN A    198.32.64.12
M.ROOT-SERVERS.NET.     5w6d16h IN A    202.12.27.33
I.ROOT-SERVERS.NET.     5w6d16h IN A    192.36.148.17
E.ROOT-SERVERS.NET.     5w6d16h IN A    192.203.230.10
D.ROOT-SERVERS.NET.     5w6d16h IN A    128.8.10.90
A.ROOT-SERVERS.NET.     5w6d16h IN A    198.41.0.4
H.ROOT-SERVERS.NET.     5w6d16h IN A    128.63.2.53
C.ROOT-SERVERS.NET.     5w6d16h IN A    192.33.4.12
G.ROOT-SERVERS.NET.     5w6d16h IN A    192.112.36.4
F.ROOT-SERVERS.NET.     5w6d16h IN A    192.5.5.241
B.ROOT-SERVERS.NET.     5w6d16h IN A    128.9.0.107
J.ROOT-SERVERS.NET.     5w6d16h IN A    198.41.0.10
K.ROOT-SERVERS.NET.     5w6d16h IN A    193.0.14.129

;; Total query time: 794 msec
;; FROM: lookfar to SERVER: <root-server>  128.9.0.107
;; WHEN: Thu May  4 23:23:52 2000
;; MSG SIZE  sent: 17  rcvd: 436
```

If you examine this listing closely you will see that it has exactly the right syntax for a root.hints file. You can, in fact, capture the dig output directly into the root.hints file to update it. Updating it is not something you need to do often at all. Updating it whenever you upgrade your BIND would be a good habit.

If you set up automatic procedures to update the root.hints file be careful to handle errors, or you will be stranded with a nonfunctional BIND when a network error causes your root.hints file to be empty.

## 4

Getting a Domain

As discussed in Chapter 1, "DNS Concepts," it is not enough to simply set up a DNS server; to get your domain into DNS, you must get a TLD owner to delegate to you the domain you want to own. This involves a registration process and possibly money and finding someone to run slave DNS servers for redundancy. So, how do you go about accomplishing this?

Top-Level Domains and Their Owners

When you first get an Internet connection, your Internet service provider (ISP) will be able to help you establish your domain. In most cases, it can maintain your domain for you as well. In a startup phase, this might be the easiest way to go. Then, you can have the domain re-delegated to you and your own name server later. When that happens, you can probably get your ISP to provide your secondary, slave, name service so you can fulfill the requirement for two or more name servers you will find everywhere.

If you want to register your own domain(s) in foreign TLDs, you might have to do a bit more work.

Finding the TLD Owners

Each national TLD has a different national registrar, which has gotten the domain delegated by the Internet Assigned Numbers Authority (IANA). The appointed registrar has absolute power over the running of the TLD—as far as the law permits.

The requirements for registering under different TLDs vary. In some national TLDs, you must own a company registered in the country and will be allowed only one domain per company. In some, though, you will be able to register as many domains as you want; all you have to do is request multiple domains and pay the required fees.

IANA maintains Web pages enumerating every TLD and their registrars, including the three-letter TLDs such as `com`, `net`, and so on. These are available at `http://www.iana.org/top-level-domains.html`. If, or when, any new three-letter TLDs are established, you should be able to find the registrars for them there as well. The `.com`, `.net`, and `.org` domains can be registered through many accredited registrars. You can find more information about them at `http://www.internic.net/`.

After you have found the correct TLD registrar, you can proceed with the prescribed registration process. I'll discuss more about that later.

Finding the Reverse Zone Owners

Your ISP is the correct organization to contact to get your reverse lookups working. As you will recall from Chapter 1, an unbroken chain must exist from `in-addr.arpa` to your network block for reverse lookups to work. Your ISP will, usually, have all the IP network blocks it owns delegated to it, and can in turn assign authority over the block it assigned to you to your name servers. Unfortunately, not all ISPs take reverse lookup equally seriously and might not be very helpful. In that case, you might need to educate them or change ISPs.

You can use `dig` to follow the chain of delegations from `in-addr.arpa` to where it ends, or, as the case may be, dead-ends. The SOA records should tell you who to contact about delegating the reverse domain to you, or an intermediary if needed. In addition, whois knows about assigned IP blocks and who got it assigned in the first case.

The whois Database

whois is the name of a database the Internet registrars maintain. It's not actually one database anymore, though; it has been regionally segmented. It contains information about all domains and networks delegated and assigned on the Internet. If you want to find out about a domain and network or who owns what, whois is the answer. Table 4.1 contains the whois databases as of this writing.

Table 4.1   whois Databases

whois Server	Web Interface	Serves
whois.internic.net	whois.internic.net	.com, .net, .org, and the TLDs themselves
whois.ripe.net	www.ripe.net	Europe and surrounding areas
whois.arin.net	whois.arin.net	The Americas and sub-Saharan Africa
whois.apnic.net	whois.apnic.net	Asia and the Pacific

Each of the whois servers supports a `help` command. They might have slightly different options, so it's worth checking the possibilities in each.

A couple versions of the command-line tool `whois`, which is used to query the whois databases, are available.

whois

The classic `whois` tool essentially takes one option, `-h`. The `-h` option takes one argument, which is the name of the server to query. The other options are, as a rule, just passed on to the whois server.

The even older versions of `whois` query now-defunct whois servers. If you have one of these, you must use the `-h` option to specify a now-working server whenever you use `whois`.

Newer versions of `whois` use `whois.internic.net` as the default server.

fwhois

`fwhois` is more similar to the old UNIX command `finger` than to `whois`, thus the `f` in its name. The syntax is, as with `finger`

```
fwhois query@server
```

If you need to give it multi-word queries, or include `whois` options, you must pass it all as one single query (quoted if necessary), as in the following example:

```
$ fwhois help@whois.internic.net
[rs.internic.net]

Whois Server Version 1.1

Domain names in the .com, .net, and .org domains can now be registered
with many different competing registrars. Go to http://www.internic.net
for detailed information.
```

```
<WHOIS help>
Select a sub-topic for help; '?' (with no RETURN) for a list of options;
RETURN key to return to WHOIS.

<OVERVIEW>
WHOIS is used to look up records in the registry database.  Whois can provide
information about domains, nameservers, and registrars.

Enter a string to search the database.  By default, WHOIS performs a very
broad search, looking in all record types for matches to your query in
these fields: domain name, nameserver name, nameserver IP address, and
registrar names. Use keywords to narrow the search (for example, 'domain
root').
...
```

Similar to the normal whois, fwhois uses whois.internic.net as the default server.

Using whois

Because fwhois is what I have on the computers I use, I will use its syntax here. As mentioned earlier, when you use regular whois, use the -h option to specify the server.

Let's see what whois can tell us about LinPro. We can start by looking up the C net that has been assigned to LinPro:

```
$ host linpro.no
linpro.no has address 195.0.166.23
$ whois 195.0.166
[rs.internic.net]

Whois Server Version 1.1

Domain names in the .com, .net, and .org domains can now be registered
with many different competing registrars. Go to http://www.internic.net
for detailed information.

   Server Name: SMP.LINPRO.NO
   IP Address: 195.0.166.3
   Registrar: NETWORK SOLUTIONS, INC.
   Whois Server: whois.networksolutions.com
   Referral URL: www.networksolutions.com


>>> Last update of whois database: Tue, 14 Mar 00 03:31:24 EST <<<

The Registry database contains ONLY .COM, .NET, .ORG, .EDU domains and
Registrars.
```

As you saw in an earlier chapter, the block was actually assigned to eu.net and then reassigned by it to LinPro. Therefore, following the actual delegation chain with dig is a much safer way to locate who owns the network block if you have problems with your reverse lookups.

But, whois knows more about LinPro:

```
$ whois 'linpro.no'@whois.ripe.net
[joshua.ripe.net]

% Rights restricted by copyright. See http://www.ripe.net/ripencc/pub-services/db/copyright.html

domain:      linpro.no
descr:       LinPro AS, Oslo
admin-c:     DA16-RIPE
tech-c:      DA16-RIPE
zone-c:      DA16-RIPE
nserver:     smp.linpro.no
nserver:     ns1.xtn.net
nserver:     ifi.uio.no
notify:      ripe-notify@uninett.no
changed:     Steinar.Haug@runit.sintef.no 19951023
changed:     hostmaster@uninett.no 19960128
changed:     Jarle.Greipsland@runit.sintef.no 19960522
changed:     Jarle.Greipsland@runit.sintef.no 19960930
source:      RIPE

person:      Dag Asheim
address:     LinPro AS
address:     Waldemar Thranes gate 98B
address:     N-0175 Oslo
address:     Norway
phone:       +47 22 38 00 35
fax-no:      +47 22 80 63 80
e-mail:      postmaster@linpro.no
nic-hdl:     DA16-RIPE
notify:      ripe-notify@uninett.no
changed:     Steinar.Haug@runit.sintef.no 19951023
changed:     hostmaster@uninett.no 19960320
changed:     Bjorn.Myrstad@runit.sintef.no 19990202
source:      RIPE
```

The previous code shows that the domain linpro.no has been registered by LinPro AS in Oslo and that the administrative, technical, and zone contacts are all the same person, identified by the handle DA16-RIPE. This is a handle for a person, and the query helpfully reports to whom the handle corresponds, which in this example is Dag Asheim of LinPro AS. The address, phone numbers, email address, and handle (again) are all provided.

If you run, or have ever taken part in, the registration of a domain, look it up in whois. Is the information correct? If not, contact your TLD registrar and have the information corrected. You might also amuse yourself by finding my handle and checking whether anyone else you know is in there.

Getting the Domain

You should start by checking whether or not the domain name you want is already registered by someone else. Both `dig` and `whois` should be consulted. `dig` will tell you something only if the domain registration is complete. If it is in progress, or somehow incomplete, `whois` should, or could, have some information.

Because each TLD registrar has different requirements you must meet to get your domain registered, you need to pursue IANA's TLD listing and contact the registrar or find the needed information on its Web site to ensure you know what it requires.

If something legal such as forming and registering a legal company is required, it will probably be time consuming and a bit expensive. Therefore, you should start the required activities immediately.

Another common requirement is having working nameservers for the domain before the registration is finalized. You will need to set up all, or at least the required number, of your redundant nameservers. They will all need to be authoritative for your domain. To do this, simply follow the guidelines in Chapter 2, "DNS in Practice."

After you have met all these and any other requirements, you will get your new domain delegated. Not too long after that, it should be known all over the Net.

Slave Servers

You will be required to run at least two nameservers for your domain. This is for your own good because it ensures that your domain is robust and can handle failures. Strictly speaking, the requirement can be fulfilled by setting up two machines in the same room on the same Internet connection. It would be better, though, if you were able to get another company—or even your ISP—to run your secondary service. The more remote your domain's slave servers are, the more robust your domain will be in case of a failure somewhere.

When Your Domain Is Taken

You might find yourself in a situation in which the domain you want is unavailable to you because someone else has already registered it. This someone might be a domain pirate or an entirely benign person pursuing whatever it is people pursue.

This is a situation that requires diplomacy. `whois` will tell you who owns the domain, along with his address, phone number, fax number, and email address. You can approach him and possibly reach an agreement. Or, you might have to resort to the TLDs conflict resolution policy, which usually requires involving a lawyer.

Paying for Everything

If you look around on Web sites dealing with DNS, you will most likely find ads that offer to register the domains you want in the TLDs you want, or at least in the TLDs where it's easy to register domains. Some will even do all the legal paperwork needed to set up a pro-forma legal entity in the country in question if that is necessary to secure a domain. This is a perfectly good way to register domains and it can save you a lot of work and time, if not money.

You should make sure of a couple things, though. Most of these outfits provide excellent service, but some will provide rather dubious service. As usual, a cautious attitude should be applied to anything having to do with the Internet.

You should ensure that the domain registration will list you or your organization as the administrative contact. If that is the case, the TLD registrar will respect your requests for changes at a later date, and you will not be hindered by the whims of your service provider. If the service provider is listed in all the contact fields, you can run into trouble dislodging your domain from a bad service provider. It should be entirely safe to use the accredited registrars of the .com and other three-letter TLDs for such service.

5   Using Dig and nslookup

6   Troubleshooting DNS

7   The DNS Tool Chest

8   Security Concerns

9   Dynamic DNS

10   DNS and Dial-Up Connections

11   DNS on a Closed Network

12   Interfacing DNS in Programs

13   Resource Records

5

USING DIG AND

NSLOOKUP

Dig is the best tool you can use, but most people use nslookup because it's available almost everywhere. Both of these tools, as is true for most of the other tools in the BIND distribution, do not use the OS resolver library. They use DNS only. If you set up your resolver in that way, Telnet, ping, and the other non-DNS tools will first look in /etc/hosts and then query DNS. Your resolver setup configures the way the C library call family gethostby* works. Telnet, ping, and most other software use these calls, but Dig, host, and nslookup do not. So, Dig and Telnet might see things differently depending on your resolver setup and the contents of /etc/hosts. This does have an upside, though. nslookup and Dig present an unfiltered view of DNS; when you examine things with these tools, the OS C library won't get in your way or obscure things. However, all these tools have one thing in common—they all use /etc/resolv.conf.

Dig

Dig is a powerful tool, as you have already learned in Chapters 1, "DNS Concepts," and 2, "DNS in Practice." The following is the most general command-line syntax for Dig:

```
dig [@server] domain [<query-type>] [<query-class>] [+<query-option>]
        [-<dig-option>] [%comment]
```

Behind this inoffensive command line, Dig hides more options than you can shake a stick at.

Dig requires that you think about what kind of record you want retrieved and that you stop to think about the correct name to look up. A tool such as host will gladly look up 192.168.55.3 for you, understanding that you want the PTR record of 3.55.168.192.in-addr.arpa. Dig will not, and its default record type is A. In addition, dig -h will print usage information. Dig is documented extensively in its man page, but let's examine each command-line term here:

- @server—This is optional. If unspecified, the server in /etc/resolv.conf is used. This is either the server's address or name. If DNS is not working on your host, it might be because a name can't be resolved, so you might have to provide an address. The server also might be specified in the LOCALRES environment variable, which is Dig specific and will not be picked up by any other software.

- domain—This is the domain name you want to look up. Dig obeys the domain and search directives in /etc/resolv.conf. It also obeys the convention that names ending in a period (.) are FQDNs and won't be subject to the search and domain directives. See the -x option for a convenient way to specify reverse queries.

- query-type—The type of the record you want. See the following section, "Query Type," for a list of available types.

- query-class—The class of record you want. in, which stands for Internet, is the default and what you want in most cases. any is a special value and acts as a class wildcard. See RFC 1035 for a list of classes.

- +query-option—This affects the contents or processing of queries in Dig or in the nameserver. See the section "Query Options" for a list of available keywords.

- -dig-option—These options change Dig's behavior. See the section "Dig Options" for a list of options.

- %comment—All command-line words starting with the percent sign (%) are ignored. This is meant to be used as documentation. In the following example, @ provides the numerical address of the nameserver and the comment tells which nameserver it is:

```
dig @192.168.55.2 %ns.penguin.bv mail.herring.bv. A
```

Query Type

The *query type* is the type of record you want. If omitted, it is set to a, which causes you to get an A record back (if any of them match the domain name). The following are some of the record types:

- A—Network address.
- MX—Mail exchanger.
- NS—Nameserver.
- SOA—Start of Authority.
- HINFO—Host information.

- AXFR—Zone transfer. Zone transfers require that you query an authoritative server. You must locate this by looking up NS records for the zone. Some authoritative servers will deny zone transfer if you're requesting it from an unauthorized location. See Chapter 8, "Security Concerns," for more information.
- TXT—The TXT record.
- SRV—Service. This is a relatively new record type, but it's very useful. It is used heavily by Windows 2000 to locate services within domains. This record is also flexible enough to replace the MX and NS records. If you're designing a new protocol, consider using this record.

For a complete list of record types, see Chapter 13, "Resource Records."

Query Options

Query options affect the processing of queries in nameservers and in Dig. Their format is as follows:

```
+keyword[=value]
```

Table 5.1 shows the keywords available and their values.

Table 5.1   Keywords for Query Options

Keyword	Abbrev.	Value	Default	Description
[no]debug	[no]deb	nodeb		Enables and disables debugging output.
[no]d2	nod2			Enables and disables even more debugging output.
[no]recurse	[no]rec	rec		Enables and disables recursive lookup.
[no]defname	[no]def	def		[Don't] use the default domain name.
[no]search	[no]sea	sea		[Don't] use the default search list.
domain	do	<domain>		Sets default domain name.
retry	ret	#	4	Number of retries.[1]
time	ti	#	4	Timeout length in seconds.[1]
[no]ko			noko	[Don't] keep open. ko implies vc.
[no]vc			novc	[Don't] use virtual circuit. Uses a TCP connection for the query.
[no]primary	[no]pr		nopr	[Don't] use the primary server. Primary is not implemented.
[no]aaonly	[no]aa		noaa	Only authoritative answers wanted. aaonly is not implemented.

Table 5.1   Continued

Keyword	Abbrev.	Value	Default	Description
[no]cmd			cmd	Echo parsed arguments.
				This is the ; <<>> DiG... line.
[no]stats	[no]st		st	Prints query statistics.
				This is the tail containing the time of query, time used, and so on.
[no]Header	[no]H		H	Prints (basic) reply header information. This is the information starting with ->>HEADER<<-. Note the capital H in the option.
[no]header	[no]he		he	Prints reply flags. This is the line starting with ;;flags:.
[no]ttlid	[no]tt		tt	Prints TTL information.[2]
[no]cl			nocl	Prints class information.[2]
[no]qr			qr	Prints outgoing query.
[no]reply	[no]rep		rep	Prints reply.
[no]ques	[no]qu		qu	Prints the question section.
[no]answer	[no]an		an	Prints the answer section.
[no]author	[no]au		au	Prints the authoritative section.
[no]addit	[no]ad		at	Prints the additional section.
pfdef				Sets print flags to default output.
pfmin				Sets print flags to minimal output.
pfset		#		Sets print flags.
pfand		#		Performs bitwise and on printflags.[3]
pfor		#		Performs bitwise or on printflags.[3]

1. The retry and time options affect the resolver's retransmission strategy when sending queries by UDP. It uses an exponential backoff loop; time is the initial timeout; and time doubles for each of the retries.
2. As of this writing, the nott and nocl options are nonfunctional.
3. These options can only be used meaningfully if you've read the source of Dig. However, I don't recommend that; I would use the regular print options.

Dig Options

The query options are not the end of it; several more Dig options exist:

- -x <dotted.address>—This is the fast lane to dotted.address-reversed.in-addr.arpa. In other words, it's a convenience switch for reverse lookups. The default query type is changed from A to ANY.

- -f <file>—Batch file. Stuff a file with queries and Dig batch will execute it. See the following section, "Dig Batch Files," for more information.

■ -T <time>—Time in seconds between the starts of successive queries in a batch. This can be used to keep two batches roughly in synch.

■ -p <port>—Query a non-standard port. The default is 53.

■ -P [<ping-string>]—Executes ping for response time comparison. By default, ping -s server_name 56 3 is executed, and on the three last lines, the timing summary is executed.

■ -t <query-type>—Alternative way of specifying the query type. Here the numerical value is allowed as well as the symbolical ones discussed in the previous bullet and in Chapter 13.

■ -c <query-class>—Alternative way of specifying the query class. Numerical class as well as symbolic is allowed.

■ -k <keydir:keyname>—Sign the query with the named TSIG key.

■ -envsav—Save the parsed settings and options in the file named by the environment variable LOCALDEF; or, if it is undefined, a file called DiG.env in the current working directory. If you dislike Dig's defaults, this is a nearly permanent way of overriding them. Each time Dig is run, this file is loaded, if present. (See also -envset.)

■ -envset—Used for batches. After the Dig environment has been set up, it becomes the default for all subsequent queries, until -envset occurs again. The options on later lines then modify this default.

■ -[no]stick—Used for batch runs and makes the Dig environment sticky (or not).

Dig Batch Files

Dig can process queries in batches. After you realize this, some of the options in Dig's feature set make more sense. After a Dig or query option is set, it is persistent, or *sticky*, and you need a way to reset it. You can use the +ko option to keep a TCP connection open for several queries. The following is an example of a batch file:

```
www.penguin.bv. A +pfmin +ko +vc
ns.penguin.bv. A
```

The first line executes the given query. The options given on it are persistent, so +pfmin will be in force for the next query as well. If, sometime later in the batch file, you want to reset the print flags, just specify +pfdef.

The previous batch file results in this output:

```
$ dig -f dig-batch
;; res options: init usevc recurs defnam styopn dnsrch
;; got answer:
;; ->>HEADER<<- opcode: QUERY, status: NOERROR, id: 19036
;; QUERY: 1, ANSWER: 1, AUTHORITY: 2, ADDITIONAL: 1
```

The STATS SECTION is the last section. It contains information about when the query was sent, from where it was sent, to which server it was sent, and how much time it took to get the answer. This can be indicative of line load, latency, packet loss, and many other things.

Using Dig

But I was supposed to tell you how you use Dig. Of course, you have already seen Dig being wielded in Chapter 1. If you go back and look at the commands in that chapter, you should be able to understand them this time around. Here is a Dig command you would not have been able to come up with based on any documentation I know. I learned it by "word of Usenet":

```
$ dig CHAOS version.bind TXT

; <<>> DiG 8.2 <<>> CHAOS version.bind TXT
;; res options: init recurs defnam dnsrch
;; got answer:
;; ->>HEADER<<- opcode: QUERY, status: NOERROR, id: 4
;; flags: qr aa rd ra; QUERY: 1, ANSWER: 1, AUTHORITY: 0, ADDITIONAL: 0
;; QUERY SECTION:
;;      version.bind, type = TXT, class = CHAOS

;; ANSWER SECTION:
VERSION.BIND.           0S CHAOS TXT     "8.2.2-P5"

;; Total query time: 54 msec
;; FROM: lookfar to SERVER: default -- 127.0.0.1
;; WHEN: Fri Apr 21 00:30:45 2000
;; MSG SIZE  sent: 30  rcvd: 63
```

This code tells you what version of BIND I was running on April 21, 2000. Some DNS servers either do not implement this or have the version string set to wouldn't you like to know or something similar for reasons of security.

nslookup

nslookup is Dig's older cousin, and in fact, Dig shares a lot of source code with nslookup. The general command-line syntax is as follows:

```
nslookup [-option ...] [host-to-find | -[server]]
```

nslookup has two main modes of operation, interactive and command line:

```
$ nslookup -query=any www.penguin.bv
Server:  localhost
Address:  127.0.0.1

www.penguin.bv  CPU = PC        OS = Tunes
www.penguin.bv  preference = 10, mail exchanger = mail.penguin.bv
```

```
www.penguin.bv   preference = 20, mail exchanger = mail.herring.bv
www.penguin.bv   internet address = 192.168.55.3
penguin.bv       nameserver = ns.penguin.bv
penguin.bv       nameserver = ns.herring.bv
mail.penguin.bv  internet address = 192.168.55.2
ns.penguin.bv    internet address = 192.168.55.2
```

The interactive mode is perhaps a bit more interesting when you explore a DNS problem, because it lends itself to the exploration of DNS. Dig is better for this, but sometimes it's not available, so you must use nslookup. Whether or not you have Dig depends on whether you have a new or old BIND installed on your machine. Windows can also be a factor—nslookup is provided with it, but Dig is not. Here is how the interactive mode is used:

```
$ nslookup
Default Server:  [127.0.0.1]
Address:  127.0.0.1

> set norecurse
```

The things you can set in nslookup are identical to the query options in Dig because Dig borrowed this code from nslookup. The following repeats the process of finding the address www.amazon.com:

```
> www.amazon.com.
Server:  [127.0.0.1]
Address:  127.0.0.1

Name:    www.amazon.com
Served by:
- I.ROOT-SERVERS.NET
          192.36.148.17

- E.ROOT-SERVERS.NET
          192.203.230.10

- D.ROOT-SERVERS.NET
          128.8.10.90

- A.ROOT-SERVERS.NET
          198.41.0.4

- H.ROOT-SERVERS.NET
          128.63.2.53

- C.ROOT-SERVERS.NET
          192.33.4.12

- G.ROOT-SERVERS.NET
          192.112.36.4
```

```
- F.ROOT-SERVERS.NET
          192.5.5.241

- B.ROOT-SERVERS.NET
          128.9.0.107

- J.ROOT-SERVERS.NET
          198.41.0.10

> server i.root-servers.net.
Default Server:  i.root-servers.net
Address:  192.36.148.17
```

In the following, the server is changed to one of the ones listed in the answer instead. This server will be used until the next server command is issued:

```
> www.amazon.com.
Server:  i.root-servers.net
Address:  192.36.148.17

Name:    www.amazon.com
Served by:
- AUTH00.NS.UU.NET
          198.6.1.65
          AMAZON.com
- NS2.PNAP.NET
          206.253.194.97
          AMAZON.com
- NS1.PNAP.NET
          206.253.194.65
          AMAZON.com
- NS-1.AMAZON.com
          209.191.164.20
          AMAZON.com

> server NS2.PNAP.NET.
Default Server:  NS2.PNAP.NET
Address:  206.253.194.97

> www.amazon.com.
Server:  NS2.PNAP.NET
Address:  206.253.194.97

Non-authoritative answer:
Name:    www.amazon.com
Address:  208.216.181.15

> exit
```

Interestingly, ns.pnap.net returns a non-authoritative answer even though it was listed as an authoritative nameserver for the zone. This is not unheard of; in fact, it happens way too often. The technical term for ns.pnap.net is *lame server*; it should be authoritative for amazon.com but is not. In this case, at least you got an answer—sometimes the server will not be willing to provide an answer. If your resolver comes upon one of these, it will log it. In extreme cases, this will be logged:

```
query(********************.in-addr.arpa) All possible A RR's lame
```

This means that the domain is delegated but that no (authoritative) answers can be found. I've disguised the name to protect the guilty.

nslookup also has a useful `help` command. Additionally, other than the `server` command, the most interesting command is probably the following, which changes the query type:

```
set query=<query-type>
```

Another command available in nslookup is the `lserver` command. One problem with nslookup is that if you use the `server` command to set a server that is not responding to queries, you will be unable to use the `server` command again because it needs to resolve the name you give it. `lserver` is useful for getting out of that particular corner. It queries the initial, local name-server to resolve the server name you provide.

6

TROUBLESHOOTING DNS

Being a distributed database, there are quite a few things that can affect
how DNS operates. Perhaps the first place you should turn when you
encounter a problem you can't solve yourself is the `comp.protocols.`
`tcp-ip.domains` FAQ. Chris Peckham maintains it and posts it regularly on
the newsgroup. It is also archived and is available by anonymous FTP from
`ftp://rtfm.mit.edu/pub/usenet/news.answers/internet/tcp-ip/domains-faq` and
in hyperlinked HTML format at `http://www.intac.com/~cdp/cptd-faq/`.
Andràs Salamon maintains a DNS Tricks and Tips page at `http://`
`www.dns.net/dnsrd/trick.html`. Of course, the whole DNSRD at `http://`
`www.dns.net/dnsrd/` is a valuable source for information about DNS on the
whole. Another valuable resource is Ask Mr. DNS at `http://www.acmebw.com/`
`askmr.htm`.

Staying Out of Trouble

RFC 1912 is titled "Common DNS Operational and Configuration Errors"
and deals with common DNS configuration and data problems. It also
comes with software—dnswalk, which is described in Chapter 7, "The DNS
Tool Chest." dnswalk checks for a lot of these problems. Running some of
the DNS checking tools described in Chapter 7 or found on the Net will help
ensure that your setup stays healthy, so you can avoid troubleshooting
DNS. Reading RFC 1912 is also a good idea. Reading RFC 2181,

"Clarifications to the DNS Specification," will also help you gain insight into some of the things talked about in this chapter. For old-timers, it gives the reasons for some of the changes seen in DNS recently, which can cause problems in some older setups.

Another good idea is to read the logs whenever you restart or reload named after you've edited the configuration or zone files. This enables you to know what BIND thinks of your edits right away, and lets you fix them before your boss, or a customer, comes looking for you. The `logging` statement (discussed in Chapters 3, "Maintenance and Enhancements," and 15, "Compiling and Maintaining BIND") enables you to log things any way you want, anywhere you want. Of course, grep or a simple log analysis tool can be of considerable help if you have more than a few zones, because the log output when loading the zones can be a handful.

Taking a look through Chapter 8, "Security Concerns," will also help you avoid problems. Some of the things there, such as restricting recursive queries and zone transfers, turning off glue fetching, and blackholing bogus addresses are simple to implement and make it harder to sabotage you.

Finally, Chapter 2, "DNS in Practice," and Chapter 3 are simply filled to the brim with good advice about everything. Make sure you know everything in them.

Network Problems

DNS is wholly dependent on acceptable network conditions. If your network is congested, DNS will be one of the first services to suffer. Most network routers know that the UDP packets DNS uses are disposable, and they are the first to be thrown away, giving TCP traffic priority. Network congestion can be diagnosed by tools such as ping and traceroute, or by suitable network surveillance tools such as MRTG and HP OpenView. If you run a BSD, you can also look at how DNS traffic fares with the nsping tool mentioned in Chapter 7. Another way to see whether DNS traffic suffers is to look at the time information at the bottom of the output from dig:

```
;; Total query time: 136 msec
```

A couple of tenths of a second is good. If multiple dig queries result in high query times, your system might be suffering from network problems.

Most IP stacks are tuned for high performance with relatively few large packets. However, DNS uses many small packets. On your DNS server, you might see the data rate flatten out earlier than if it was transferring a file from memory to the network. This is not very likely to happen, though.

Another network problem can be firewalls and packet filters. A common misconception is that DNS uses only UDP port 53, and that TCP is used for only zone transfers. This is wrong. Whenever a DNS query or answer exceeds 512 bytes, TCP is needed. If the query is more than

512 bytes (very unlikely), the querier takes up a TCP connection to the server at once. If the answer is more than 512 bytes, a truncated answer is sent by UDP with the TC (Truncation) bit set. The querier is then meant to connect to the DNS server with TCP and ask the question again, to receive the complete answer. If it can't, the query fails. Although a UDP packet can carry more than 512 bytes over most transmission mediums, RFC 883 specified that a DNS UDP message is restricted to 512 bytes, and to remain compatible, it has stayed so.

You can test whether you can connect to the DNS server you want to test by using telnet. Simply initiate a telnet connection to port 53 on the server; if the connection is opened, you have a clear net all the way to the server. If the connection is refused or times out, the most likely cause is firewalling or packet filtering. Another way is to run dig with the +vc switch. The +vc switch instructs dig to use a virtual circuit, which means it uses TCP. With more sophisticated firewall setups, this might be the only sure way to verify correct operation because it snoops on the protocol to check which kind of protocol it is, and terminates the connection if it is illegal.

You can watch, analyze, and get statistical information about network traffic with programs such as netstat, snooper, tcpdump, trafshow, iptraf, and ethereal. Several of these will take your network traffic to pieces and show you what the bits mean, helping you in a troubleshooting effort.

Delegation Problems

As should be clear from Chapters 1, "DNS Concepts," and 2, it is vital that your authoritative servers have gotten your domains delegated to them. Lack of delegation can result in problems ranging from servers being incapable of looking up hostnames from the IP address to everyone outside your own network being unable to look up your hostnames. This is a problem mainly when the domains and networks are new and delegations are not propagated yet. Reverse delegations have proven to be especially difficult to get right. Unfortunately, it seems that some ISPs simply don't understand them or their uses. In that case, you will either need to educate your ISP or change ISPs.

Tools such as dnswalk and DOC (see Chapter 7) should be able to detect delegation problems. Run the tool on both your forward and reverse zones. Another way to check delegation problems is to use a Web-based DNS tool, such as DigIt, which will show you what DNS looks like from a vantage point other than your usual one (see Chapter 7).

Another thing that can cause problems is that you didn't pay your domain registration to your registrar's satisfaction. This has happened to several large corporations in the first half of 2000. If your domain suddenly disappears from the outside world, you had better check with your registrar. If it has expired, just pay the bill quickly, no matter who FUBARed. It takes as much as 24 hours to get things back in order, after you've paid, if the delegation from your TLD has been yanked.

There is also an inverse problem here. When a nameserver is listed in the zone or the parent zone, but is not authoritative for the zone—in other words, it is not a slave or master server for the zone even though DNS data says it is—a situation known as a *lame server* exists. (The NS records for the zone inside the zone itself and in the parent zone should match.) Lame servers are rife on the Internet. Usually, a lame server situation is temporary and is caused by the removal or moving of a nameserver before the updated NS records are available all around the network. In reverse zones, the problem is often more permanent. Older versions of BIND didn't make any noise about this, but newer versions do. They log messages similar to these:

```
Lame server on 'xx.xxx.xxx.xxx.in-addr.arpa' (in
      'xxx.xxx.xxx.in-addr.arpa'?): [xxx.xx.xxx.xxx].53 'NS.xxx.NET'
ns_forw: query(xx.xx.xxx.xxx.in-addr.arpa) All possible A RR's lame
```

The IP numbers and names have been changed to protect the innocent. The first message means that the server that should now have the PTR record (presumably) for xx.xxx.xxx.xxx.in-addr.arpa does not give authoritative answers for that zone. The second message means that no authoritative servers could be found, and that BIND has to give up resolving the name.

Reverse Lookup Problems

A lot of services, especially on UNIX, but also security-sensitive services on other platforms, try to perform reverse lookups of the origin hosts of all incoming connections. If the lookup fails, the service might deny the connection on the grounds that it wants to know to whom it talks, or because it simply is not allowed to talk to strangers.

But, even if the query works, the service might deny the connection. A common UNIX security mechanism, known as tcp wrappers or tcpd,performs a lot of checking. One of the checks it performs is whether the reverse lookup matches the forward lookup. If the IP address 10.35.129.219 has a PTR record saying its name is foo.penguin.bv, and foo.penguin.bv has an A record saying 10.35.129.218, which is a different address, the connection will be denied. It is usual practice that all services run out of inetd on UNIX runs under tcpd. This includes telnet, ftp, rsh, rlogin, pop-3, and imap. It is not usual to run Web servers under tcpd.

For these two first problems, the cure is to have correct reverse zone setups. Not only must you ensure that your setup is correct, but you must also ensure that the reverse zones are delegated correctly. Check the section before this one for more information about delegation problems.

A third scenario is that telnet, rsh, rlogin, and similar services will attempt to perform a reverse lookup as described previously, but that because of network problems, or simply because name service has been broken, the query is not answered and the connecting party will have to wait for DNS to complete the query or to time out. When the query is finally timed out, the connection might be denied, even if it would have been accepted if DNS was working, depending on the host configuration.

Masters, Slaves, and Serial Numbers

The serial number of the SOA record is very important to the correct operation of slave servers. Each time you edit your zone, the serial number must be increased so that the slave server can detect that the zone has been updated. Whenever the slave server notices that the serial number has changed, it performs a zone transfer and updates its cached zone file. In Chapter 3, you can find a discussion of how the SOA controls zone transfers and tips about how to plan changing zone data so server moves and similar changes can be done in a planned and orderly manner.

If some users are getting old data from DNS, the cause could be that one of your slave servers is still serving the old zone data because it has not seen that the master has been updated, or because it has failed to complete the zone transfer, for whatever reason. The problem that caused zone transfer failure might soon go away, but it might also be caused by misconfiguration of the slave or a firewall between the master and the slave preventing the zone transfer. You can easily check the SOA record on the slave servers with dig. If it keeps staying at an old serial number, you know you have a problem. If it takes too long to get updated zones, you might have a network problem.

If the slave-server is incapable of transferring the zone for the time set in the expire field of the SOA record, it expires the zone and stops serving data from it. Some sources recommend setting the expire value as high as four weeks. If the master server—or the network—stays down for a long time, the zone can be prevented from expiring by editing the file making the slave server think that the zone is fresher than it is. This is a rather desperate measure, but is sometimes required, especially when the expire time is only one week.

Manual editing of the serial number can result in mistakes, one of which is entering a serial number that's too small, causing the slave to think it is more up-to-date than the master. This is easily fixed by entering the correct, larger number. A mistake that takes a bit more work to correct is entering a serial number that is too large. When the slaves pick up the new zones, they will have this large serial number, and if you try to enter the correct, smaller serial number, the slaves won't want to update their zones. This is because, by serial number comparison, they know their zones to be newer than the one they see on the master server. This too can be solved.

This is the easy way: If you control all the slave servers, simply log into them, remove the slave zone files, and ndc restart the server—this forces a retransfer of the slave zones.

This is the hard way: The DNS serial number is a 32-bit unsigned quantity, and because the DNS designers wanted to plan for the future, they designed the serial number mechanism in a tricky way. It is a bit difficult to follow if you're not familiar with two's complement binary arithmetic. If the new serial number (minus the old one), performed in signed 32-bit arithmetic with no overflow correction, is a positive number, a zone transfer is needed. That is a bit complicated, but the practical upshot is this (follow these steps):

1. Take your erroneous serial number and add 2,147,483,647 (2^31) to it.
2. If the result is larger than 4,294,967,296 (2^32), subtract 4,294,967,296 from it.
3. You now have a new, temporary serial number. It will either be numerically less than the correct serial number or much bigger. It will cause the slave servers to trigger a zone reload. Enter it in the zone file, and wait until all your slave servers have picked it up.
4. When you have ensured that all the slave servers have the temporary serial number, enter the correct serial number and your slaves will pick up the zones with the new, now correct serial number.

Another upshot of this is that you can change your zones often. If you keep your serial number in numeric form rather than the traditional YYYYMMDDNN form, you can make up to 4,294,967,296 zone changes in each expire period—provided that the expire period is 4 weeks, the zone can be updated 887 times a second.

If you use DDNS, or something else that automatically manages your serial number, to maintain your zones, you won't ever run into this problem.

Caching and TTLs

The $TTL zone directive and the TTL of the SOA record are also important parameters. Besides old zone data on slave servers, a source of old data is caches. This can't be avoided. The caches are out of your reach; you can't troubleshoot them. All you can do is set the TTLs correctly. The $TTL directive sets the default TTL for the zone. If your BIND version does not support the $TTL directive, the default TTL is taken from the minimum TTL field of the SOA. In modern caches, the SOA minimum TTL is used as the TTL for negative caching. Negative caching is described in RFC 2308. If a name is looked up and not found, the fact that it does not exist is cached for the time set by the minimum TTL. Older versions of BIND and DNS software did not perform negative caching. *Negative caching* means that if you ask about a name before it is available in DNS and then ask again but before the negative-caching expires, the entry is masked. The name is not available to you, even though it is available in DNS, because the cache knows it's not available. Running ndc restart flushes your cache.

The one thing about caches that you can troubleshoot, though, is what is in your cache. Problems with the cache can stem from cache corruption or DNS poisoning. *DNS poisoning* occurs when your cache receives and stores bogus DNS data, whether due to misconfiguration or ill will. Poisoning is discussed further in Chapter 8. *Cache corruption* stems from a bug in BIND causing the cache data structure to decay. I can honestly say that I have never experienced cache corruption; I have only read descriptions of it.

The contents of your cache can help you track down these things, but only if you enable a handy little option:

```
options {
    ...
    host-statistics yes;
    ...
};
```

This enables accounting on the host level, including remembering where the cached records came from. It also keeps a lot of statistics about all the hosts BIND talks to. All in all, it uses a lot of memory. With `ndc dumpdb`, you can cause named to dump its cache into `/var/named/named_dump.db` (if `/var/named` is your named directory). The contents of the file changes a bit with the versions of BIND. With BIND 8.2, the start of the file lists the sources of its authoritative zone data. The file reads like a zone file (see Listing 6.1).

Listing 6.1   A Database/Cache Dump

```
$ORIGIN .
.         314073  IN      NS      E.ROOT-SERVERS.NET.     ;Cr=auth [128.9.0.107]
          314073  IN      NS      D.ROOT-SERVERS.NET.     ;Cr=auth [128.9.0.107]

...
ORG       314090  IN      NS      A.ROOT-SERVERS.NET.     ;Cr=addtnl [192.33.4.12]
          314090  IN      NS      E.GTLD-SERVERS.NET.     ;Cr=addtnl [192.33.4.12]
...
$ORIGIN uio.noi.
;www      765     IN      SOA     A.ROOT-SERVERS.NET. hostmaster.nsiregistry.NET. (
;                 2000081201 1800 900 604800 86400 );.;NXDOMAIN   ;-$    ;Cr=auth [192.36.148.17]
$ORIGIN ORG.
OPENNAP   164385  IN      NS      NS1.KINETIC.ORG.        ;Cr=addtnl [207.200.81.69]
          164385  IN      NS      NS1.WIREDGLOBAL.COM.    ;Cr=addtnl [207.200.81.69]
          164385  IN      NS      NS2.WIREDGLOBAL.COM.    ;Cr=addtnl [207.200.81.69]
...
$ORIGIN ROOT-SERVERS.NET.
K         400473  IN      A       193.0.14.129            ;NT=89 Cr=answer [128.9.0.107]
L         400473  IN      A       198.32.64.12            ;NT=147 Cr=answer [128.9.0.107]
...
$ORIGIN penguin.bv.
emperor   172800  IN      NS      ns.emperor.penguin.bv.  ;Cl=2
          172800  IN      NS      ns.herring.bv.          ;Cl=2
lbt       172800  IN      HINFO   "PC" "Linux"            ;Cl=2
          172800  IN      A       192.168.55.132          ;Cl=2
```

If the cache is corrupted, it should be easy to see either by corrupted names or corrupted data. Corrupted data should be especially easy to spot in an HINFO or a TXT record; you would expect them to contain sensible strings, not line noise or other garbage.

The commented entry is a negative cache entry, showing the SOA of the zone as well as the reason for the negativity: NXDOMAIN (nonexistent domain). As you see, someone typed www.uio.noi, a nonexistent name, instead of www.uio.no, which results in this negative entry.

The NT field in the comments indicates the RTT in milliseconds. In the case of nameservers, this is very significant. BIND prefers servers with lower RTTs. The Cl flag indicates that the data was loaded from a zone file, whereas the Cr flag says how credible BIND thinks the data is. auth is best and is set when an authoritative answer is received. answer is next best, and is set for non-authoritative answers, and addtnl is for data from the authority and additional sections of the answer. The credibility rating is used to decide whether cached data should be replaced when new data for the same name and record type arrives. Cached data is replaced when new data with a higher credibility rating arrives. As you see in Listing 6.1, the penguin.bv data was loaded from a zone file, and only one answer is in the data—the address of k.root-servers.net.

The format and contents of the database dump has changed over time. The previous dump is from 8.2.2. In 8.2.3, there will be an additional section in the dump about forwarding zones.

You can control the name of the dump file with the dump-file option:

```
options {
    dump-file "/var/named/better_name_here.db";
};
```

Zone Data Mistakes

I mentioned RFC 1912 earlier. Much of the RFC deals with mistakes in zone data files. Running nslint or dnswalk (for both, see Chapter 7) helps you find such mistakes. Some of the most common are as follows:

- The HINFO record takes two items of data: the CPU and the OS fields. If one of the fields contains whitespace, it must be quoted as follows:

  ```
  tdr    HINFO   "IBM PC"  OpenBSD
  ```

  Always quoting the values is a good idea.

- Matching A and PTR records. The named A record pointed to by a PTR record should point back to the address of the PTR record. Even if a host has several A records pointing to it, only one PTR record is expected. Using a tool such as mkrdns (see Chapter 7) to generate reverse zones is a good idea, but nslint and dnswalk will also discover this.

- The SOA record has two fields before all the numerical fields:

  The first field is the domain name of the primary master server. This must not be a CNAME. The second field is the email address of the hostmaster, the person to contact about DNS matters. This field can't contain a @; instead of the @, use . (period). If the email address of the hostmaster contains periods then they can be escaped like this: \.. So, if the email address of the hostmaster is `nicolai.langfeldt@penguin.bv`, the SOA record should start this way:

```
@        SOA     ns.penguin.bv nicolai\.langfeldt.penguin.bv (
    ...
```

Otherwise, the SOA record must contain sensible values for the rest of the fields. See Chapter 2 for a discussion of this. Additionally, the mailbox referred to by the SOA record should be read frequently. Important mail, such as a message telling you your domain is broken and how to fix it, could arrive there at any time.

■ Zones should not contain glue A records for any zone that is not directly delegated from the same zone. BIND 8 rejects such inappropriate glue records, logging them each time. A glue A record is the A record belonging with an NS record. For example, penguin.bv contains this NS record:

```
@        NS      ns.herring.bv.
```

But it does not contain any A record for ns.herring.bv because the A record can be found other ways, and including it in your zone requires that you update it whenever ns.herring.bv's address is changed. In the old days, we did include such glue records, but in practice they were not kept up-to-date and were found to be a liability. On the other hand, for zones delegated from the penguin.bv zone, a glue record is required:

```
emperor          NS      ns.emperor
ns.emperor       A       192.168.56.3
```

Otherwise, because emperor is a subdomain of penguin.bv, no way to find the address of ns.emperor.penguin.bv exists.

■ MX, SOA, and NS records referring to a CNAME are not legal. These records can refer only to names that have A records.

■ Wildcards don't always work as you hoped. For more about them, and CNAME records, please refer to Chapter 3.

■ Forgetting the ending . in fully qualified names. If you write

```
esr    MX mail.penguin.bv
       MX mail.walruss.bv
```

in the penguin.bv zone file, you will see MX records pointing to mail.penguin.bv.penguin.bv and mail.walruss.bv.penguin.bv in DNS.

In general, after editing and reloading a zone, it's a good idea to try to resolve the names you added or made changes to, to verify that BIND thinks your edits mean the same as you think they do. As mentioned before, you should look at the logs when (re)loading zone data—BIND might reject the whole zone due to some silly mistake and stop serving the zone.

The Log File(s)

BIND writes things to log file(s). You can direct what gets written where with the logging statement, which is discussed in Chapters 3 and 15. By default, named logs to syslog, and usually you will find the named log messages in /var/adm/messages or /var/log/messages, but not always. It depends on your syslog configuration. The format and wording of the messages, and what messages you will find, varies a bit over time, but the complaints mostly stay the same. This list is based on BIND 8.2.2P5. Kevin O'Neil maintains a list of log messages at http://www.acmebw.com/askmrdns/bind-messages.htm. It can provide more varied comments on these messages as well, having the DNS newsgroups to draw on. The following list is not by any means complete. It does not contain any debug-level messages because too many exist to list, nor does it contain most of the panic messages because few exist and they are very easily understood. Also available are a host of memory and filesystem management–related errors. These are not listed because they never occur as long as your server has enough memory and the disk has room enough, and there are simply too many of them.

Zone File and Configuration Errors

Several zone file and configuration errors exist because we humans are such lousy typists and have memories like sieves. Most of the errors in the named.conf file stem from one simple error: lacking semicolons (;) at the end of option statements and sections. Another cause is using the wrong comment characters. C-style (/* ... */), C++ style (// ...), and shell style (# ...) is allowed. Zone file style (; ...), however, is not allowed.

pz/penguin.bv:55: xxx error near (foobar)

Severity: Notice

This is a range of messages originating in the zone file loader. The message means that you need to check your syntax for errors—for example, for missing fields, typos, and quoting. A complete list of these errors alone would fill several pages, and while I could list them all, it would be very boring. Most of them are self-explanatory, but a few are worth commenting on.

IP Address

IPv6 Address

The syntax of the IP or IPv6 address is incorrect. One likely cause of this is using a comma (,) instead of a period (.). Another is putting leading 0s in the IP numbers, such as 096 instead of 96. Leading 0s cause named to interpret the number as octal; 9 is not a valid octal digit, thus the error message appears. And, of course, all your IP numbers with leading digits will probably be something different from what you intended.

Priority

PX Priority

The priority of an MX, an AFSDB, an RT, an SRV or a PX record is illegal. It should be a number 0–65,535. You might have forgotten to give the priority?

NAPTR Flags too big

NAPTR Service Classes too big

NAPTR Pattern too big

The string representing these can be only up to 255 characters long.

$TTL bad TTL value

TTLs must be in the range 0–2,147,483,647.

pz/penguin.bv: Line 47: $GENERATE unknown type: FOO

pz/penguin.bv: Line 54: Unknown type: FOO

Severity: Info

Named expected something such as A or PTR but got FOO. The most likely cause of this is forgetting to enter the type field.

pz/penguin.bv:54: Database error near (foo)

Severity: Notice

The zone file loader did not understand something on line 54. There might or might not be a more specific error message about it just before this message.

db_load could not open: pz/penguin.bv: Permission denied

Severity: Warning

The file named could not be read due to the reason given. "Permission denied" or "No such file or directory" are the most likely reasons. In the latter case, someone forgot to create the file, or a typo occurred somewhere so it does not exist, and is not supposed to.

Zone "penguin.bv" (file pz/penguin.bv): No default TTL set using SOA minimum instead

Severity: Warning

A $TTL directive is missing in the named zone file, and the old policy of using the SOA minimum TTL as the default TTL is used instead. In a future version of BIND, a missing $TTL can become a fatal error causing the zone to be rejected. So, insert $TTLs in all zones that are missing them.

pz/penguin.bv: Line 1: TTL > 2147483647; converted to 0

pz/penguin.bv: Line 10: SOA minimum TTL > 2147483647; converted to 0

Severity: Info

You have tried to set a TTL that is too big. The maximum is 2,147,483,647 seconds, which is 24,855 days, or approximately 68 years. It might be due to a typing error. A TTL of 0 is unfortunate because things will expire from caches at once, so this should be fixed.

pz/penguin.bv:22: SOA for "penguin.bv" not at zone top

Zone "penguin.bv" (file pz/penguin.bv): no SOA RR found

Zone "penguin.bv" (file pz/penguin.bv): multiple SOA RRs found

Severity (respectively): Error, warning, warning

All zone files must have exactly one SOA record, at the top of the zone file. If it is on the top, try adding some ;s (comment chars) to any empty lines coming before it.

pz/penguin.bv:5: WARNING: new serial number < old (200008080 < 2000080801)

Severity: Notice

This is probably a typing error. If you're in the process of fixing a serial number as described earlier in this chapter, you probably made a mistake.

pz/penguin.bv:45: data "ns.herring.bv" outside zone "penguin.bv" (ignored)

Severity: Info

Records for ns.herring.bv do not belong in the penguin.bv zone. You're not supposed to put data that does not belong in the zones domain in the zone file. This is typically an old zone file with glue (A) records in it meeting BIND 8 for the first time.

Zone "penguin.bv" (file pz/penguin.bv): no NS RRs found at zone top

Severity: Warning

All zones must also contain the NS records for the zone itself.

master zone "penguin.bv" (IN) rejected due to errors (serial 2000080803)

Severity: Warning

The named zone was rejected due to errors and was not incorporated into the database. named does load the remaining zones normally after this, but does not answer authoritatively for the zone.

master/slave/stub zone "penguin.bv" (IN) loaded (serial 2000080804)

hint zone "." (IN) loaded (serial 0)

Severity: Info

The named zone was loaded, and the server will answer authoritatively for the master and slave zones. Stub zones are used for the glue. This does not mean that the zone file was without errors, though, just that it was acceptable.

pz/penguin.bv:52:penguin.bv: CNAME and OTHER data error

Severity: Notice

The zone contains a CNAME with other data as well. Please see Chapter 3 about CNAMEs and its associated issues.

pz/penguin.bv:2: Unknown $ option: $tlt

Severity: Notice

You've entered an unknown $ option; in the previous example, a simple typing error caused this.

pz/penguin.bv:2: expected a TTL, got "foo"

Severity: Notice

named did not recognize the data found as a ttl, which was what it expected.

pz/penguin.bv:5: decimal serial number interpreted as 1000

Severity: Info

You've used a decimal serial number, and it was interpreted as the number shown. Don't use decimal serial numbers because they are unpredictable.

pz/penguin.bv:67: unexpected EOF

Severity: Info

named was in the midst of reading something, perhaps a record, and instead of finding more record contents, it found the end of the file. The record, or whatever, proceeding it might be correct. The message might be due to a missing newline after the last line in the file. UNIX conventions call for an empty line to end all text files.

pz/penguin.bv: WARNING SOA expire value is less than SOA refresh+retry (21600 < 21600+1800)

pz/penguin.bv: WARNING SOA expire value is less than refresh + 10 * retry (21600 < (21600 + 10 * 1800))

pz/penguin.bv: WARNING SOA expire value is less than 7 days (21600)

pz/penguin.bv: WARNING SOA expire value is greater than 6 months (18748800)

Severity (respectively): Notice, warning, warning, warning

These are sanity checks on your SOA field values. Abide by the rules they set, except in special circumstances. In any case, the expire field should be at least 7 days, and perhaps even something like 28 days. But 6 months is probably too long.

zone 'penguin.bv' did not validate, skipping

Severity: Error

A check on the zone declaration in named.conf failed; the error message will be shown prior to this. Because of this, the zone could not be loaded.

NSMAX reached for zone 'penguin.bv'

Severity: Error

You are trying to add too many masters to the zone. In BIND 8.2.2P5, the limit is 16.

duplicate also-notify address ignored [10.5.66.126] for zone 'penguin.bv'

duplicate global also-notify address ignored [10.5.66.126]

Severity: Warning

You've listed the same address more than once in an also-notify list.

limit "datasize/stacksize/..." not supported on this system - ignored

Severity: Warning

The named resource limit is not supported by BIND on this system. If your system does support this limit and BIND does not, a little source code patching is in order. Send the patch to the ISC afterward.

setrlimit(datasize): Operation not permitted

Severity: Warning

You're probably trying to raise the resource limit beyond what the OS allows.

couldn't create pid file '/var/run/named.pid'

Severity: Error

You probably do not have write permission in the directory. This is probably because you've run named with the -u option, so it won't run as root. Also, only root has write access to the /var/run directory. This is as it should be; opening /var/run to be written in by anyone is a security risk that approaches, if not exceeds, the risk of running named as root. Create another directory, such as /var/named/run, with the proper write permissions to have the pid file in.

pz/penguin.bv: WARNING SOA refresh value is less than 2 * retry (3000 < 1800 * 2)

Severity: Warning

Another sanity check of your SOA values. Let the refresh value be at least two times the retry value, or this message will appear.

host name "rms.penguin.bv.25/0.56.168.192.in-addr.arpa" (owner "25/0.56.168.192.in-addr.arpa") IN (primary) is invalid - rejecting/proceeding anyway

Severity: Warning

In this case, someone forgot an ending period in the right side of a PTR record in a reverse zone. The name should have been typed rms.penguin.bv., with the ending period, but was not. In general, this error means that an illegal character is in the name. In this example, it was a slash (/); another favorite is the underscore (_). By default, in master zones, this error results in the zone being rejected, and in slave zones, it results in a warning. This behavior can be adjusted with the check-names option; see Appendix A, "named.conf Man Page."

owner name "sub_domain.penguin.bv" IN (primary) is invalid - rejecting/proceeding anyway

Severity: Warning

The zone name is invalid because it contains an underscore. The TLD registrars will not accept such registrations. See the previous error for more information.

invalid class IM for zone 'penguin.bv'

Severity: Error

The zone directive specifies an illegal zone class for the given zone. Did you mean IN?

no type specified for zone 'penguin.bv'

Severity: Error

You forgot to specify a type clause in the zone specification.

only the root zone may be a cache zone (zone 'penguin.bv')

only the root zone may be a hint zone (zone 'penguin.bv')

Severity: Error

You tried to specify that a zone other than . is a cache or hint zone. This is illegal.

'file' statement missing for master zone penguin.bv

Severity: Error

You can't have a master zone without a zone file to load it from and store it in. You can, however, have a slave zone without a file to store it in, but I don't recommend it.

'master's statement present for master/hint/cache zone 'penguin.bv'

no 'masters' statement for non-master zone 'penguin.bv'

'allow-{update,transfer}' option for non-{master,slave} zone 'penguin.bv'

'allow-query' option for non-{master,slave,stub} zone 'penguin.bv'

'notify' given for non-master, non-slave zone 'penguin.bv'

'also-notify' given for non-master, non-slave zone 'penguin.bv'

'forward' given for hint zone '.'

'forwarders' given for hint zone '%s'

Severity: Error

All these result from using zone options in the wrong kinds of zones. Please see Appendix A for the allowed combinations.

Zone "penguin.bv" declared more than once

Severity: Error

Do not define the same zone more than once, and if you copied a zone statement, remember to edit the name.

directory /var/named is world-writable

Severity: Warning

It is considered insecure to have the named directory world-writable. You should chmod it. Think long and hard before ignoring this message.

can't change directory to /var/named: No such file or directory

unix control /var/runn/ndc failed: No such file or directory

Severity (respectively): Panic, warning

The error message on the end of the message can be something else entirely—Permission denied, for example. Check whether the directory is there, that you typed its name correctly in the configuration file, and that it has proper permissions and so forth.

the maximum number of concurrent inbound transfers is 20

Severity: Error

You are trying to raise the transfers-in limit beyond the hard-coded maximum, and the value has been truncated to the maximum. The maximum is 20 in BIND 8.2.2P5.

cannot set resource limits on this system

Severity: Info

Your system does not support setting system limits, such as datasize, because it does not have the getrusage, getrlimit, and setrlimit system calls. If this is not correct, the port of BIND to your platform must be fixed.

forwarder '192.168.0.2' ignored, my address

Severity: Error

Don't use yourself as a forwarder.

Unsupported TSIG algorithm foo

Severity: Error

Only HMAC-MD5 is supported as of BIND 8.2.2P5. Refer to Chapter 5, "Using Dig and nslookup," for more information about dynamic DNS and TSIGs.

Invalid TSIG secret "CuTaNDPaSTEErrOR"

Severity: Warning

The secret string was not a valid BASE64 encoded string, probably because of a cut and paste error.

must specify a file or null channel for the eventlib category

only one channel allowed for the eventlib category

must specify a file or null channel for the packet category

only one channel allowed for the packet category

Severity: Error

The eventlib and packet logging categories funnel so much data that you are allowed to channel them only to a file, and only one file.

re-establishing default options

Severity: Warning

You have previously specified logging options, which no longer appear in named.conf; therefore, the default logging options have been re-established.

chrooted to /var/BIND-chroot

Severity: Info

Your chroot setup is working, at least so far.

Ready to answer queries

Severity: Notice

Your name daemon is ready to answer queries. This is good.

named shutting down

Severity: Info

For some reason or other, named is shutting down—probably because ndc stop was run.

reloading nameserver

Severity: Notice

Someone issued a ndc reload command.

/etc/named.conf:33: cannot redefine...

While parsing the named.conf file, the parser found another definition of something that can be defined only once. Only one options section is possible; only one listen-on is possible; only one server section for each server is possible; and only one definition of each zone name is possible. Except for views of course, each view can have only one, but each view can have one each (zone definition, that is).

Zone Transfers, Slave Zones

Err/TO getting serial# for "penguin.bv"

Severity: Info

Your named tries to determine whether a zone transfer of penguin.bv is necessary, but fails to communicate and get the serial number from the master server.

Zone "penguin.bv" (IN) SOA serial# (200008080) rcvd from [192.168.0.2] is < ours (2000080803): skipping

Severity: Notice

Count the digits carefully. The master has a serial number less than the one we have. If only one host is used as master, someone made a typing error that stops the updated zone from being transferred. Please see the previous section dealing with masters, slaves, and serial numbers for how to deal with this.

If you're using slaves as additional masters to help zone propagation, you will see this from time to time when you have succeeded in getting an updated zone transferred, but your other master (a slave of the origin master) has not gotten it updated yet.

attempted to fetch zone penguin.bv from self (192.168.0.2)

Severity: Notice

This is probably due to some misconfiguration. I have seen this on multi-homed nameservers that did not have a listen-on option set (see Chapter 2) and thus did not detect that the master for the zone was itself.

startxfer: too many xfers running

Severity: Warning

A zone is due for a serial number query (because the refresh interval for the zone has passed), but the maximum number of zone transfers is already running. The serial number query will be tried again later. The number of concurrent inbound zone transfers is limited by a compiled constant called MAX_XFERS_RUNNING. In BIND 8.2.2P5, its value is 20. A related message appears when you try to set transfers-in higher than this limit.

zone transfer timeout for "penguin.bv"; pid 4711 killed

Severity: Notice

The zone transfer timed out. This is normally due to temporary network problem and will pass. If it is not temporary, you might need to increase max-transfer-time-in to fix the problem. Or you might have to get a better connection to your master. It's 120 minutes by default. See Chapter 17, "Miscellany," for more information.

zone transfer timeout for "penguin.bv"; pid 4711 missing

zone transfer timeout for "penguin.bv"; kill pid 4711: Not owner

zone transfer timeout for "penguin.bv"; pid 4711 kill failed Not owner

zone transfer timeout for "penguin.bv"; second kill pid 4711 - forgetting, processes may accumulate

Severity: Warning

This should never happen under normal circumstances. All these errors happen when named notices that a zone transfer has been running too long, and then when it tries to abort, it fails to do so.

named-xfer "penguin.bv" exited with signal 7

Severity: Notice

The named-xfer that was transferring the given zone exited because it was sent the given signal. This could indicate a number of things, but don't worry if it happens only occasionally.

xfer vfork: Resource temporarily unavailable

can't exec named-xfer: Resource temporarily unavailable

Severity: Error

The reason given can vary, but Resource temporarily unavailable indicates that a memory, process table, or other OS or machine resource shortage has occurred. Do you need to buy more RAM or enlarge some key kernel tables?

Sent NOTIFY for "penguin.bv IN SOA" (penguin.bv); 1 NS, 1 A

Severity: Info

named has sent out the NOTIFY messages for an update in the penguin.bv zone. This occurs at random intervals after a zone reload to avoid everyone trying to zone transfer everything at once.

suppressing duplicate notify ("penguin.bv" IN SOA)

Severity: Info

named has already sent NOTIFYs for this zone and doesn't want to be redundant. This can be due to listing a slave server in both the NS records for the zone and in the also-notify list.

rcvd NOTIFY(penguin.bv, IN, SOA) from 192.168.0.1

Severity: Info

A NOTIFY was received, meaning that the indicated zone might have been updated. The server compares the serial number on the master with its own and then, if necessary, starts a zone transfer.

rcvd NOTIFY for "penguin.bv", name not one of our zones

NOTIFY(SOA) for non-secondary name (penguin.bv), from [192.168.0.2].2375

Severity: Info

Someone is telling us that a zone we know nothing of has been updated.

NOTIFY(SOA) from non-master server (zone penguin.bv), from [192.168.0.2].3256

Severity: Info

A server we don't recognize as master for the given zone tried to tell us that the zone was updated. This is probably caused by a multi-homed master not sending NOTIFYs from the right address. See Chapter 2 and the section "Forwarding source address is [0.0.0.0].1033" later in this chapter.

Received NOTIFY answer from 192.168.0.1 for "penguin.bv IN SOA"

Severity: Info

This should arrive shortly after the NOTIFYs are sent out. If it does not, the NOTIFYs might have been lost or rejected.

unapproved AXFR from [192.168.0.1].3782 for "penguin.bv" (acl)

unapproved AXFR from [192.168.0.1].3782 for "penguin.bv" (not master/slave)

unapproved AXFR from [192.168.0.1].3782 for "penguin.bv" (not authoritative)

Severity: Notice

The given server was denied its request for AXFR (or IXFR). In the first case, this is because it was forbidden by an allow-transfer option. In the second case, this is because the zone was not a master or slave zone, but rather a hint or stub that does not make sense to the zone transfer. In the third case, this is because if we don't have that zone, we're not authoritative for it.

approved AXFR from [192.168.0.1].3959 for "penguin.bv"

Severity: Info

The server approved a zone transfer request from 192.168.0.1 for the penguin.bv zone.

NOTIFY(SOA) for zone already xferring (penguin.bv)

Severity: Info

We're being told that the zone penguin.bv has been updated, while we're still transferring the last update. The NOTIFY is ignored.

zoneref: Masters for secondary zone "penguin.bv" unreachable

Severity: Notice

Your nameserver is incapable of reaching any of the masters for the given zone. This is probably temporary, but if the condition persists, it should be investigated. If it persists too long, the zone will expire as set in the SOA record.

secondary zone "penguin.bv" expired

Severity: Notice

The expire interval for the zone has passed without any contact with any master server. If you need to reinstate the zone, touch the file and reload the nameserver. The cached zone file's last modification date is used to calculate its age.

secondary zone "penguin.bv" time warp

Severity: Notice

The named slave zones file has a modification time in the future. This makes no sense. But, it can happen if the nameserver is restarted or reloaded right after the servers clock has been adjusted, or if the clock adjustment was big.

zone transfer (AXFR) of "penguin.bv" (IN) to [192.168.0.1].3112

Severity: Info

The outgoing zone transfer is initiated.

Dynamic DNS

Some of the errors possible with dynamic DNS are the same as with static DNS. See the previous zone file messages if you can't find something.

unapproved update from [10.212.103.201].61762 for dyn.penguin.bv

Severity: Notice

Someone at the given address is trying to send you a dynamic DNS update, but your nameserver denies the request. Dynamic DNS is discussed in Chapter 9, "Dynamic DNS."

cannot delete last remaining NS record for zone dyn.penguin.bv

Severity: Debug

You're trying to remove the last NS record of the zone. A zone must have at least one NS record, so this is forbidden. As you see, this error is at debug level, so you might never see it. You will notice only the NS record not being deleted in spite of your best efforts.

invalid log file pz/dyn.penguin.bv.log

Severity: Error

While maintaining the dynamic zone, the change log was found to be invalid. Either look at the log and fix the error or rename it, restart the nameserver, and then send the updates you find in the log file to the server with nsupdate.

fopen() of pz/dyn.penguin.bv.xyz failed: Permission denied

error dumping zone file pz/dyn.penguin.bv

Severity: Error

Is your disk full? Do you run named as nonroot? If so, does named have write permissions in that directory?

Resolving

Among the chief problems when resolving are lame delegations.

Lame server on 'news.penguin.bv' (in 'penguin.bv'?): [10.55.0.181].53 'ns0.nic.bv'

Severity: Info

You nameserver queried ns0.nic.bv for news.penguin.bv because it thought it was authoritative for the zone penguin.bv, but ns0.nic.bv did not answer authoritatively. The reason it asked ns0.nic.bv in the first place was that someone said it was an authoritative server for the zone.

Because several lame delegations are out there, your named logs might be dominated by messages about lameness. You can disable lamer logging:

```
logging {
    ...
    category lame-servers { null; };
    ...
};
```

Another option that affects lameness is `lame-ttl`. Lameness is cached to reduce the number of queries that can result only in rediscovering the same lame condition. By default, the TTL for this is 10 minutes, but it can be raised up to 30 minutes:

```
options {
    ...
    lame-ttl 1800;
    ...
};
```

A lame server is not a fatal condition; the nameserver will continue to query the other nameservers for the zone until an answer is found, until the following messages are logged.

ns_forw: query(news.penguin.bv) All possible A RR's lame

ns_forw: query(news.penguin.bv) No possible A RRs

Severity: Info

While trying to resolve news.penguin.bv, only lame servers were encountered and the name could not be resolved. This mainly occurs for reverse zones because they and their delegation and maintenance are blind spots for administrators. This is also why it can take some time before you receive your reverse zones delegates properly.

tcp_send([192.168.0.2].53) failed: Network is unreachable

sendto([192.168.0.2].53): Connection refused

Severity: Info

The trailing error message need not be the same as shown. `Network is unreachable` means that the network is incapable of relaying the request packet for some reason. It could be because the IP address is bogus, or because your routing tables are incomplete. `Connection refused` means that no one was listening on the port the server tried to talk to.

domain name too long: <long name>

Severity: Info

This is an internal buffer overflow, which should never happen. If you ever find `Name_Too_Long` in your cache, you'll now know why.

unapproved query from 192.168.0.3 for "news.penguin.bv"

Severity: Notice

The given host is not allowed to ask for that. See `allow-query` in the index.

"baddomain.bv IN NS" points to a CNAME (ns0.baddomain.bv)

Severity: Info

The admin of baddomian.bv is not following the rules about not using CNAMES for NS records (or MX or SOA). Send a friendly email pointing out the error, if you want. It can only make things better.

Response from unexpected source ([192.168.0.1].53)

Severity: Info

A response packet came from an unexpected place and got dropped in the bit bucket. Again, this is something that a multi-homed server can cause. It also can indicate a very old spoofing attack being executed.

wrong ans. name (news.penguin.bv != mail.penguin.bv)

Malformed response from [192.168.0.1].8762 (answer to wrong question)

Severity: Info

An answer was received for the wrong question. In the first case, the query was for mail.penguin.bv and news.penguin.bv was received.

`Malformed response` appears in several other contexts and indicates an error discovered while decoding an answer. It can mean that an implementation error occurred in your server or in the remote server.

bad referral (penguin.bv !< walruss.penguin.bv)

Severity: Info

While querying the walruss.penguin.bv nameservers for a walruss.penguin.bv name, the nameserver received a referral to a nameserver closer to the root. A properly authoritative nameserver would return the answer or a referral one more step away from the root. This probably means that the server queried about walruss.penguin.bv is not authoritative, in spite of what earlier referrals indicated. Some server is holding bad NS records for walruss.penguin.bv.

MAXQUERIES exceeded, possible data loop in resolving news.penguin.bv

Severity: Info

The error message says it all. More than 20 (MAXQUERIES in BIND 8.2.2P5) queries are needed to resolve the name. Something is afoul.

sysquery: findns error (NXDOMAIN/SERVFAIL) on ns.penguin.bv?

Severity: Info

Your nameserver was trying to find the A record of a nameserver named in an NS record but failed. NXDOMAIN means that the name ns.penguin.bv does not exist, which is very bad in the case of a nameserver. SERVFAIL means that the servers that should know the answer are tripping.

ns_forw: query(foo.penguin.bv) xxx (langnese.nvg.ntnu.no:127.0.0.1)

Severity: Info

The xxx complaint can be due to several different things, but they all boil down to a clearly bogus answer, such as referrals to nameservers with 127.0.0.1, 0.0.0.0, or a multicast address. Contains our address means that the referral was to the server itself, clearly a lame delegation because the server would have known that itself. Forwarding loop means that the server was referred to the host that issued the query in the first place, which is also a lame delegation— the querier would have known that it is authoritative. NS points to CNAME means just that: Someone was not thinking when he set up the NS records in question.

unrelated additional info 'www.walruss.bv' type A from [192.168.0.2].52

Severity: Info

The answer contained information unrelated to the query and the rest of the answer. The information is ignored. It can indicate a server bug, or less likely, a spoofing attempt.

Miscellaneous

rcvd IP_OPTIONS from 192.168.6.66 (ignored)

Severity: Info

Use IP option is normally associated with attacks on your computer. If a connection is made with options set, named disables the options and logs this message.

dropping source port zero packet from [192.168.6.66].0

Severity: Notice

UDP packets from port 0 are not allowed and are invariably associated with attacks or badly configured or unstable machines.

refused query on non-query socket from 192.168.6.66

Severity: Notice

A query arrived at the socket that named itself is using to send queries. This should not happen; queries should arrive on the socket at port 53.

Socket(SOCK_RAW): Too many open files

Severity: Panic or error.

When named is starting up, this is a panic condition. After startup, during the periodic interface scanning (see Chapter 17), it is an error. The condition is detected during the interface scanning when named finds and binds each interface's TCP and UDP port 53 to listen for queries. Each port it binds requires one file handle, and during startup it uses file handles for each zone file it reads. If you get this message, raise the files limit.

listening on [127.0.0.1].53 (lo)

listening on [192.168.0.2].53 (eth0)

Severity: Info

Several of these should exist—one for each network interface on your system. Or, if you use the listen-on option, one should exist for each of the interfaces you listed.

There may be a name server already running on 192.168.0.2

bind: Address already in use

Severity: Error

A nameserver is probably already running on the host. If you've set up for two or more servers with listen-on options, you might have two nameservers with the same configuration running or a conflict in your configurations.

deleting interface [127.0.0.1].53

deleting interface [192.168.0.2].53

Severity: notice

The interface could not be bound; named gave up on it and removed it from the listen-on list. See the description of the bind: Address already in use message.

ctl_server: bind: Address already in use

Severity: Error

The control socket could not be established. The Address already in use message indicates that someone else is already using the socket. ctl_server means that it has to do with the socket ndc talks to named over; the usual path for this is /var/run/ndc. The path can be overridden with the controls option in named.conf. If you need to run multiple instances of BIND, they will need one control connection each—each with a distinct name.

not listening on any interfaces

Severity: Warning

Your named could not find any interfaces on which to listen, and so does not listen on any. This is probably caused by another nameserver running on the machine.

Forwarding source address is [0.0.0.0].1033

Severity: Info

This is the source address that will be used when issuing queries, NOTIFYs, and other traffic from this host. If the address is 0.0.0.0 then the OS will tack on the address of the network interface the packet leaves by when it leaves. On multi-homed servers that are masters or slaves, this can cause problems because the master might be expecting zone transfer queries from a specific address, and the slaves are expecting NOTIFYs from one of the hosts listed as master in the slave zone configuration. You should specify the query-source option, as described in Chapter 2.

forwarding interface [192.168.0.2].53 gone

Severity: Panic

The interface configured to be used as forwarding origin has disappeared. It should be gotten back up; then restart your named.

named restarting

Severity: Info

Named is restarting because someone told it to, probably with `ndc restart`.

query log on/off

Severity: Notice

You should take notice when this is turned on. It uses a lot of disk space, and do I mean *a lot*.

Suppressed qserial_query(penguin.bv)

Severity: Info

You have configured named as being on a dial-up connection and a serial number query has been suppressed; it will be executed later.

Heartbeat: qserial penguin.bv

Severity: info

The dial-up heartbeat is causing serial number queries to be sent out now, all in a lump. Instead of when the whim of TTLs and refresh intervals dictates.

Cleaned cache of 42 RRsets

Severity: Info

The cache was cleaned and 42 resource record sets were removed because their TTLs had expired.

unapproved recursive query from [192.168.0.1].53 for news.walruss.bv

Severity: Notice

You've restricted recursive queries (with the `allow-recursion` option) and received one from an unapproved source. If the host is supposed to be allowed to make recursive queries, adjust the `allow-recursion` option.

ns_req: no address for root server

Severity: Notice

You didn't put any A records for the root servers in the `root.hints` file.

findns: No root nameservers for class HESIOD?

Severity: Info

If you have a server without any hints zones, or are playing with some non-IN zones (such as a Hesiod zone) for which you don't have any hint files, you'll see this message. Don't worry unless you're supposed to know the root servers for that class. This could also happen if your hint file is empty.

check_hints: no NS records for class IN in hints

check_hints: no A records for E.ROOT-SERVERS.NET class IN in hints

Severity: Error

Your hint file is without NS, or A, records. You need a new hint file.

dumping nameserver stats

done dumping nameserver stats

Severity: Notice

Someone wanted statistics, and now they're getting them or have gotten them. They were probably requested by `ndc stats`. The default filename for this is `named.stats`.

dumping nameserver data

finished dumping nameserver data

Severity: Notice

A database and cache dump is, or was, written to `named_dump.db` in the directory named in the directory option. Earlier in this chapter I gave a description of this dump file.

foo.penguin.bv CNAME and other data (invalid)

Severity: Info

A name cannot have both a CNAME record and other records. See Chapter 3 for a discussion of this.

Too many open files

This message can appear at the end of several other messages in your logs. If can indicate that you must raise the files resource limit using the `files` option in `named.conf`. named keeps two open files/handles/sockets per network interface on your host; moreover, it uses one handle for the control socket and one handle for the query socket. Some sockets are also used when files (zone and configuration) are read from disk at startup, at reload, and after zone transfers and dynamic updates. Software such as lsof can be very helpful in finding out why you've run into this. This is the normal output of lsof on a Linux system running BIND:

```
# lsof -c named
COMMAND PID USER   FD   TYPE     DEVICE     SIZE   NODE NAME
named 11536 root   cwd   DIR       3,8      4096 227650 /var/named
named 11536 root   rtd   DIR       3,1      1024      2 /
named 11536 root   txt   REG       3,5    511440 170342 /usr/sbin/named
named 11536 root   mem   REG       3,1    340663  12140 /lib/ld-2.1.3.so
named 11536 root   mem   REG       3,1   4101324  12143 /lib/libc-2.1.3.so
named 11536 root    0u   CHR       1,3             22092 /dev/null
named 11536 root    1u   CHR       1,3             22092 /dev/null
named 11536 root    2u   CHR       1,3             22092 /dev/null
named 11536 root    3u  unix 0xc2ef4340         3316436 socket
named 11536 root    4u  IPv4      3316446          UDP *:1035
named 11536 root    5u  unix 0xc1285480         3316438 /var/run/ndc
named 11536 root   20u  IPv4      3316442          UDP localhost:domain
named 11536 root   21u  IPv4      3316443          TCP localhost:domain
          (LISTEN)
named 11536 root   22u  IPv4      3316444          UDP 192.168.0.2:domain
named 11536 root   23u  IPv4      3316445          TCP 192.168.0.2:domain
          (LISTEN)
```

NSTATS...

USAGE...

XSTATS...

Statistics information. Please see Chapter 17 for more information about this.

ns_udp checksums NOT turned on: exiting

Severity: Panic

UDP checksums are not enabled on this host. Because DNS relies on UDP, we want UDP checksums. Some old versions of SunOS had UDP checksums disabled. UDP checksums have been recommended to be enabled for…oh, 10 years?

ns_udp: check sums turned on

Severity: Warning

UDP checksums were not enabled, but now they are. See the previous message.

7

THE DNS TOOL CHEST

The Internet

I'm risking sounding trite, but the Web—and Internet in general—is an important tool. It's especially important for DNS. The newsgroups and mailing lists mentioned in Chapter 15, "Compiling and Maintaining BIND," are excellent places to learn of, and about, DNS and the tools people use. If you don't have time to read them everyday, they are still an excellent resource if accessed through a service such as the Usenet archive at deja.com, which has a searchable archive of news. If in doubt, search there first. The URL is `http://www.deja.com/usenet`.

Web sites do, of course, exist that are dedicated to DNS. One of the best known is the DNS Resources Directory at `http://www.dns.net/dnsrd/`. It is really the only URL you'll ever need when it comes to DNS. A separate, very extensive, Tools to Manage DNS page is also available there.

Internet-Based Tools

Getting someone else's view of your domain can be useful, especially if you are experiencing complaints from outside your organization about things not working, and you can't figure out why from the inside.

ZoneCheck

ZoneCheck is a Web-based tool used by the French NIC to enable their clients to check whether the zones they want to register are available. You can use this prior to registration, and periodically thereafter. It is at `http://www.nic.fr/zonecheck/english.html`. You also will find the source code there.

DigIt

DigIt is a Web interface to dig provided by Men&Mice. It enables you to see how your domain resolves from the outside, using the nameserver at Men&Mice if you want. Its URL is `http://us.mirror.menandmice.com/cgi-bin/DoDig`.

Internet Query Tools

This very diverse service is provided by Demon Internet. It lets you check almost anything you can think of, including whois lookups. You can find it at `http://www.demon.net/external/ntools.shtml`.

Maintenance Tools

A large class of the tools called maintenance tools helps you maintain zone files in various ways. The following are some of them.

h2n

h2n is a popular tool; it's a Perl script written by Cricket Liu, one of the authors of the O'Reilly book *DNS and BIND*. h2n formats a /etc/hosts style file into DNS zone files and a BIND 4 or 8 configuration file. The software is available from the O'Reilly FTP site, but the most updated version is included in the BIND 8 contrib bundle in the directory nutshell. It's a simple, yet effective tool. Consider this /etc/hosts file:

```
195.0.166.251    lookfar.linpro.no
195.0.166.130    rcp.linpro.no      rcp
195.0.166.200    nfsd.linpro.no     nfsd
195.0.166.201    false.linpro.no    false
195.0.166.2      mail.linpro.no     mail
195.0.166.140    lpd.linpro.no      lpd
```

In addition, consider this simple command: `h2n -v 8 -d linpro.no -n 195.0.166`. From it, you get several files:

`named.boot`	Named in the style of BIND 4, but containing BIND 8 `named.conf` syntax
`db.127.0.0`	The reverse lookup file for the 127.0.0 network
`db.linpro`	The forward file for the linpro.no domain
`db.195.0.166`	The reverse lookup file for the 195.0.166 network

The following is the `db.linpro` file it produced:

```
@ IN  SOA lookfar.linpro.no. root.lookfar.linpro.no. (
         2 10800 3600 604800 86400 )
   IN  NS  lookfar.linpro.no.

localhost          IN  A    127.0.0.1
lpd                IN  A    195.0.166.140
lpd                IN  MX   10 lpd.linpro.no.
mail               IN  A    195.0.166.2
mail               IN  MX   10 mail.linpro.no.
false              IN  A    195.0.166.201
false              IN  MX   10 false.linpro.no.
nfsd               IN  A    195.0.166.200
nfsd               IN  MX   10 nfsd.linpro.no.
rcp                IN  A    195.0.166.130
rcp                IN  MX   10 rcp.linpro.no.
lookfar            IN  A    195.0.166.251
lookfar            IN  MX   10 lookfar.linpro.no.
```

Either these files can be used as starting points for maintaining your DNS or the entire maintenance of your DNS can be based on h2n. Each time h2n is run, it rewrites the files, all the while maintaining the SOA record sequence number in the correct manner. That, however, is the only thing saved from the zone files; any changes you might have made to them are lost. If you maintain a hosts file in NIS (the name service formerly known as YP), h2n can be used to trivially generate zone files from it. h2n has a rich set of options, making it powerful enough to be used for almost anything.

As you might have noticed, each host in the previous zone file is its own mail server. You can suppress all MX records with the `-M` option, and you can add MX records with the `-m` option.

If you feel more comfortable with the hosts format, or simply like the idea of maintaining just one file instead of all the files BIND needs to work—and h2n is powerful enough for you—this is a good tool. In addition, it is written in Perl and therefore is easy to hack if you know how to program.

Webmin

Webmin is a GUI UNIX administration tool. It can do a lot of things, among which is DNS management. Plus, it can work with both BIND 4 and 8. Webmin has not even reached version 1 as I write this; it's at 0.80 and is already spoken well of on the Net. Its home page is at `http://www.webmin.com/webmin/`. Figures 7.1 and 7.2 show a browser-based interface, to `named.conf`, and all the zone files you manage, letting you add, delete, and alter zones and records. It supports setting all types of parameters, globally and per zone as BIND allows. Additionally, it can use https, as well as http, as a transport.

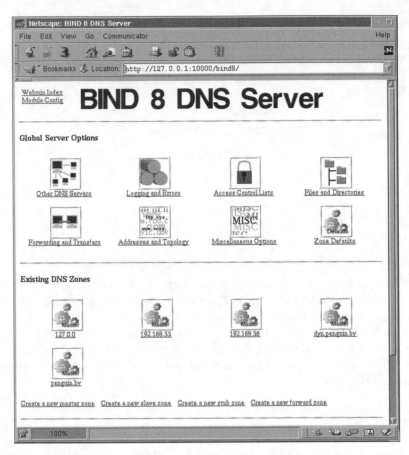

Figure 7.1 Webmins BIND 8 interface.

mkrdns

mkrdns takes care of writing reverse zone files for you. Given a `named.conf` file and a set of forward zones, written by you, it will write the appropriate reverse zone files. You must have the files for all the forward zones that use the given reverse zones to be able to do this, but the advantage is that one source of errors is eliminated—your reverse zones *will* match your forward ones. One reverse zone can correspond to several forward zones, and mkrdns needs all of them to be available locally. If you're not the master for the zones, you should make reverse maps to enable you to at least be a slave. However, you can very easily just enter slave zone entries in `named.conf` to gather the necessary data.

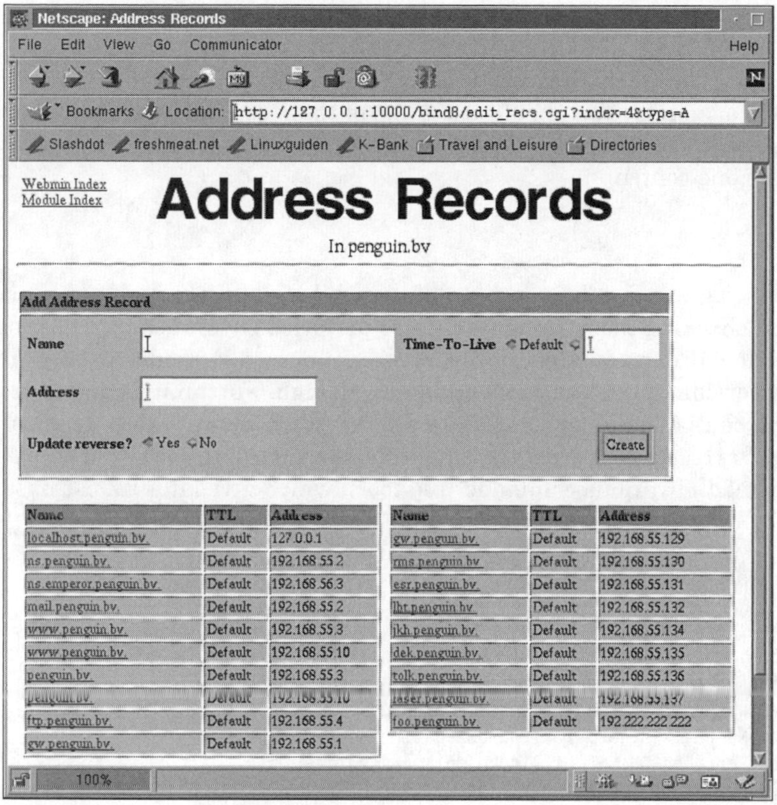

Figure 7.2 Editing penguin.bv A records and the reverse zone.

You can leave mkrdns directives embedded in your named.conf file, hiding them from BIND as comments. The map directive enables mkrdns to support classless reverse zones. The serialt directive, on the other hand, controls which kind of serial numbers you use. In other words, it controls whether you use a serial number in the YYYYMMDDNN date format, which is traditional, or whether you simply use a number. Handling it as a number enables you to make more than 100 changes in a day, and this is, perhaps, why BIND's dynamic zones are maintained with a numerical serial number as well. The serial number format can be global or zone by zone.

The skip directive instructs mkrdns to ignore certain records when generating the reverse zone. This enables you to create multiple A records for one address, but to have only one PTR record for the same address, as expected. It also enables you to ignore addresses whose reverse zone you're not responsible for. mkrdns also entirely skips zones named with the skipzone directive, because you do not maintain the reverse zones for the addresses used in that forward zone.

Quality Control

Quality control tools are tools that will help you ensure that your zone data and DNS service are healthy and consistent. You should use some of them regularly to check certain things. For example, you should use dnswalk—alone or DOC combined with nslint—to check both your delegations and zone contents.

dnswalk

dnswalk, a Perl program that has been around a while, walks through your zone(s), looking at its contents and checking those contents. It also performs several sanity and consistency checks on your domain and subdomains. A version of dnswalk resides in the BIND contrib directory. That version does have some problems, though. Fortunately, another version is available, which can be found at http://sourceforge.net/project/?group_id=1103. Its homepage is at http://www.visi.com/~barr/dnswalk/. dnswalk is a complete rewrite using the Net::DNS Perl module instead of various command-line tools, which gives it a robust base for future development.

The following is an example:

```
$ ./dnswalk -rFl linpro.no.
Checking linpro.no.
Getting zone transfer of linpro.no. from smp.linpro.no...done.
SOA=smp.linpro.no       contact=hostmaster.linpro.no
BAD: linpro.no NS ns1.xtn.net: lame NS delegation
WARN: loghost.linpro.no CNAME pot.linpro.no: unknown host
WARN: covehold.frs.linpro.no A 193.212.244.37: no PTR record
Checking ddns.linpro.no
BAD: ddns.linpro.no has only one authoritative nameserver
Getting zone transfer of ddns.linpro.no from smp.linpro.no...done.
SOA=smp.linpro.no       contact=hostmaster.linpro.no
WARN: mangellan.ddns.linpro.no A 192.168.55.200: no PTR record
0 failures, 3 warnings, 2 errors.
```

In the first warning, pot refers to the Norwegian civil surveillance organization, Politiets ÅkningsTjeneste. Linpro obviously hasn't bothered to do more than enter a joke CNAME record for loghost. Someone also forgot to enter a reverse record for covehold.frs.linpro.no. But, worst of all, only one nameserver is available for our ddns experiment—ddns.linpro.no— and no reverse exists for mangellan, either.

The -F (fascist checking) switch is particularly useful, because it checks whether your A and PTR records match up. If you maintain your zones by hand, as many people do, having a software tool check for you is very beneficial. Another switch, the -l switch, enables lame delegation checking, which detects servers that are listed as authoritative but are not answering as if they are. In the Linpro example, ns1.xtn.net is such a server. The -r switch simply turns on recursion, causing subdomains of Linpro to be checked, in this case, it's ddns.linpro.no.

The original dnswalk was written alongside RFC 1912, "Common DNS Operational and Configuration Errors," and checks for the errors mentioned there.

DOC

DOC (Domain Obscenity Control) is another tool that interrogates the DNS, looking for problems. It is a collection of csh and awk scripts distributed in the BIND contrib bundle—in contrib/doc to be exact. A more current version might be available at the FTP site (`ftp://ftp.his.com/pub/brad/dns/`), but you should also check the DNS Resource Directory Web site mentioned earlier in this chapter.

The following is an example:

```
$ doc -v linpro.no
Doc-2.1.4: doc -v linpro.no
Doc-2.1.4: Starting test of linpro.no.   parent is no.
Doc-2.1.4: Test date - Sat Aug  5 11:08:18 CEST 2000
soa @ifi.uio.no. for no. has serial: 2000080461
soa @nac.no. for no. has serial: 2000080461
soa @nn.uninett.no. for no. has serial: 2000080461
soa @ns.eu.net. for no. has serial: 2000080461
soa @ns.uu.net. for no. has serial: 2000080360
WARNING: Found 2 unique SOA serial #'s for no.
Found 3 NS and 3 glue records for linpro.no. @ifi.uio.no. (AUTH)
Found 3 NS and 3 glue records for linpro.no. @nac.no. (non-AUTH)
Found 3 NS and 3 glue records for linpro.no. @nn.uninett.no. (non-AUTH)
Found 3 NS and 3 glue records for linpro.no. @ns.eu.net. (non-AUTH)
Found 3 NS and 3 glue records for linpro.no. @ns.uu.net. (non-AUTH)
DNServers for no.
    === 1 were also authoritatve for linpro.no.
    === 4 were non-authoritative for linpro.no.
Servers for no. (not also authoritative for linpro.no.)
    === agree on NS records for linpro.no.
NS lists for linpro.no. from all no. servers are identical
    === (both authoritative and non-authoritative for linpro.no.)
NS list summary for linpro.no. from parent (no.) servers
    == ifi.uio.no. ns1.xtn.net. smp.linpro.no.
soa @ifi.uio.no. for linpro.no. serial: 2000080401
soa @ns1.xtn.net. for linpro.no. serial: 2000080401
ERROR: non-authoritative SOA for linpro.no. from ns1.xtn.net.
soa @smp.linpro.no. for linpro.no. serial: 2000080401
SOA serial #'s agree for linpro.no.
WARN: SOA records differ for linpro.no. from authoritative servers
Authoritative domain (linpro.no.) servers agree on NS for linpro.no.
NS list from linpro.no. authoritative servers matches list from
    === all parent (no.) servers
Checking 1 potential addresses for hosts at linpro.no.
    == 195.0.166.3
```

```
in-addr PTR record found for 195.0.166.3
Summary:
   ERRORS found for linpro.no. (count: 1)
   WARNINGS issued for linpro.no. (count: 2)
Done testing linpro.no.  Sat Aug  5 11:08:26 CEST 2000
```

As the previous example shows, DOC does not perform the same checks as dnswalk. DOC also does not come with a published RFC like dnswalk does; however, DOC does come with a draft RFC, as well as a man page that describes the tests DOC implements. DOC checks the structure of your domains, the delegations, the SOA records, and the NS and A records. It does not verify the zone contents beyond that. If you plan to use it, it should be combined with a tool that checks zone contents, such as nslint.

nslint

The traditional C programmer's tool lint is described thus in the Solaris man page: "lint detects features of C program files which are likely to be bugs, nonportable, or wasteful." nslint, on the other hand, checks your zone files. You can find a copy in the BIND contrib directory, but the home site (ftp://ftp.ee.lbl.gov/) is likely to contain a newer version. nslint is written in C and comes with a GNU automatic configure script, so it is very easy to compile. In addition, nslint reads your /etc/named.conf file and finds all the domains it defines and then checks your zone files. Similar to its C equivalent it is very picky. See the following example:

```
$ nslint
nslint: /var/named/pz/penguin.bv:22 "ns" target missing trailing dot:
        ns.emperor
nslint: /var/named/pz/penguin.bv:24 "a" name missing trailing dot:
        ns.emperor
nslint: /var/named/pz/192.168.56:20 bad ttl
nslint: /var/named/pz/192.168.56:22 bad ttl
nslint: missing "ptr": ns.penguin.bv. -> 192.168.55.2
nslint: missing "ptr": ns.emperor.penguin.bv. -> 192.168.56.3
nslint: missing "ptr": penguin.bv. -> 192.168.55.3
nslint: name referenced without other records: mail.herring.bv.
nslint: missing "a": localhost. -> 127.0.0.1
nslint: missing "ptr": localhost.penguin.bv. -> 127.0.0.1
nslint: 127.0.0.1 in use by localhost.penguin.bv. and localhost.
nslint: 192.168.55.2 in use by mail.penguin.bv. and ns.penguin.bv.
nslint: 192.168.55.3 in use by www.penguin.bv. and penguin.bv.
```

In this example, nslint complains about valid constructs, but not without reason: Some of the valid constructs I've used in the Penguin zone files are, in some ways, risky and should perhaps be avoided. nslint is a very useful tool, but it is also a strict master. The upside is that tools such as dnswalk probably will not find anything to complain about if you verify your zones with nslint. But, if you use it, you should change your zone style to suit it, not you—especially if several people are maintaining the zone files using nslint, or dnswalk.

All the bad ttl messages stem from the fact that the nslint version I tested does not understand the new 1D, 1H, and so on, on syntax that BIND supports.

nsping

nsping is a more system- and network-oriented tool. It sends DNS query packets to a server, measures how long it takes to get an answer, and determines whether the answer arrives at all. In this way, it is very much like the ordinary network ping tool. If you run FreeBSD, you will find nsping in the ports collection, but it is also available as source code from http://www.enteract.com/~tqbf/nsping.tar.gz. However, running FreeBSD and getting it from the ports collection is your best bet for getting it running. The following is an example:

```
$ nsping -h www.world-online.no ns000.world-online.no
NSPING ns000.world-online.no (213.142.64.170): Hostname
        "www.world-online.no", Type = "IN A"
+ [  0 ]    204 bytes from 213.142.64.170:    9.304 ms [   0.000 san-avg ]
+ [  1 ]    204 bytes from 213.142.64.170:   11.241 ms [  10.273 san-avg ]
+ [  2 ]    204 bytes from 213.142.64.170:    0.880 ms [  10.142 san-avg ]
+ [  3 ]    204 bytes from 213.142.64.170:    9.922 ms [  10.087 san-avg ]
+ [  4 ]    204 bytes from 213.142.64.170:    9.924 ms [  10.054 san-avg ]
+ [  5 ]    204 bytes from 213.142.64.170:    9.916 ms [  10.031 san-avg ]
+ [  6 ]    204 bytes from 213.142.64.170:   10.286 ms [  10.068 san-avg ]
+ [  7 ]    204 bytes from 213.142.64.170:    9.924 ms [  10.050 san-avg ]
^C
Total Sent: [  8 ] Total Received: [  8 ] Missed: [  0 ] Lagged [  0 ]
Ave/Max/Min:   10.050 /   11.241 /    9.304
```

If packet loss occurs, you might be experiencing a network or server (or BIND) problem. This is useful to know because such things are usually hidden by retransmission strategies in the resolver library and recursive servers.

Software such as top, trafshow, and netstat show you your resource usage and pinpoint resource hogs. If no problems occur on the server or with its network interfaces, you can check the network with the usual ping tool. However, if that shows problems, you should alert the network administrator(s). But, if no problems show up, you can lean back and feel happy and confident about your DNS installation and how it works for your clients.

My thanks to Anders Nordby of WorldOnline for help with nsping.

## 8

Security Concerns

About Security

Network and computer security used to be an obscure subject. These days, though, anyone administering computers and network services should have some knowledge of it to do their job properly. This is especially true for DNS administrators because of the key role DNS plays on the network.

Some years ago, it was not uncommon to run BIND unprotected on firewalls and other critical machines because BIND was thought to be a safe program. But that was before stack overruns and other powerful exploit methods became commonplace. Security mailing lists, such as Bugtraq, now announce such attacks weekly if not several times daily (but to be fair, not very often against BIND), often with code to demonstrate the weakness. These days, no software should be considered safe. If you just got worried about your firewall security, read this chapter and then go fix it.

To keep up with DNS security developments, you should, at the very least, read the bind-announce mailing list. However, you really should also read the bind-users list (both these lists are described in Chapter 15, "Compiling and Maintaining BIND"). Another excellent source of security information not only about BIND is the Bugtraq mailing list. Bugtraq is hosted by Security Focus, which has a Web site at http://www.securityfocus.com/. Check the Forums section on the Web site or mail your subscribe bugtraq lastname, firstname message to listserv@securityfocus.com, filling in your name, of course. Another good source of computer security information is the SANS Institute at www.sans.org; they have some mailing lists and digests that are worth subscribing to.

How Secure Is DNS and BIND?

The way DNS was (and is) run was not very secure. Running the latest recommended version of BIND is the very least you should do. If you're running any version of BIND 4 or a version of BIND 8 that's not current, you're open to numerous weaknesses in the code. The most threatening thing in old versions of BIND is how easy it is to feed it bogus information, known as *spoofing* or *poisoning*. It would then spread this bad information on to its clients. If you consider how important DNS information is for many (most?) of the security mechanisms used in UNIX, this is quite chilling. Spoofing or poisoning is still possible, but it's much harder now, and by configuring DNS restrictively, it can be made even more difficult. As BIND 9 is completed and DNS-SEC is deployed across the Internet, things will get even better. However, add to this that BIND has had (and we might still find new) remote root exploits, and the scenario is pretty grim for security.

> **Spoofing and Poisoning**
>
> Spoofing and poisoning are two terms often used in connection with attacks on, through, or using DNS in some way.
>
> *Poisoning* places bogus information in a DNS cache. The cache then spreads the poison on to its clients, spreading it throughout the network like poison spreads throughout the body. A possible object of poisoning can cause a software client to connect to the wrong server. This, in turn, can enable a fraudulent person to set up a Web site that looks identical or a lot like some other site, and then collect something useful from the users misdirected there—credit card numbers, for example. A sidebar later in this chapter discusses a famous poisoning episode—the AlterNIC attack. Forwarding chains, as discussed in Chapter 3, "Maintenance and Enhancements," are especially vulnerable to this kind of attack. If someone manages to poison a cache fairly close to the root of the chain, the effect will be widespread.
>
> The term spoofing is used in many contexts of network security, not only DNS. *Spoofing* involves forging a network packet in some way that causes software to accept it as legitimate. BIND can be vulnerable to spoofing (see the section about the use-id-pool option later in this chapter). Successful spoofing of a DNS query answer is one of the ways DNS can be poisoned.

Spoofing DNS

Spoofing BIND used to be as easy as sending it a properly formed answer package—it would store the information, regardless of whether it had asked for the information. If you run an old BIND 4, you are likely still vulnerable to this attack, which has been widely known for years. It is still possible to spoof BIND 8, but it's much more difficult.

The basic method is to set up a nameserver to issue query replies with an extra, poison, record in them (this can involve creative zone files or source code hacking). The trick then is to get other nameservers to query it, and when the poisoned answer arrives with the extra record, the record is stored in the nameserver's cache. Thereafter, until the cached answer expires, any queries to that server are resolved based on the bogus information in the cache, quite possibly spreading the poison further in the process.

The AlterNIC Attack

In the summer of 1997, the AlterNIC (a company running an alternative DNS structure), from alternative root servers and up, pulled off a cache poisoning attack against most of the Internet. They caused DNS servers all over the Net to query one of their DNS servers. This server provided the requested information, as well as some additional information (the poison) that the querier cached. The attack is described at `http://www.wired.com/news/technology/0,1282,4715,00.html`. After this attack, up to 90% of the Internet recognized some of AlterNIC's extra TLDs. The attack was quickly followed by a fix to BIND and a lot of BIND updating activities all over the Net.

Most BIND installations will act as recursive resolvers for anyone asking. This makes getting a given installation to retrieve bogus information from other nameservers quite easy. Another scenario in which a DNS server will retrieve information that might be poisoned is when it attempts to retrieve glue information for NS records it is about to put in a query answer. Both, however, can be turned off in named.conf:

```
options {
    ...
    recursion no;
    fetch-clue no;
    ...
}
```

This is fine if your nameserver does not act as a recursive resolver for anyone, but it probably needs to perform recursion for your own machines—the ones using it as their local name-server. So, instead of disabling recursion altogether, you might want to restrict it to your own networks instead. The penguin.bv nameserver needs to act as a recursive resolver for the Penguin network, which is 192.168.55.0/255.255.255.0 (also written as 192.168.55.0/24 because the network address is 24 bits). Penguin AS has one other network— 192.168.56.0/255.255.255.128, alias 192.168.56.0/25. And the nameserver should also act as a nameserver to itself, 127.0.0.1. Here is the example:

```
options {
    ...
    allow-recursion {
        192.168.55.0/24;
        192.168.56.0/25;
        127.0.0.1;
    };
    ...
};
```

You can be still more restrictive, though. If your nameserver is not acting as an authoritative server for zones, you don't want it to answer queries from strange computers at all. You, again, want only the internal networks inside Penguin AS to be capable of querying the server:

```
options {
    ...
    allow-query {
        192.168.55.0/24;
```

```
        192.168.56.0/25;
        127.0.0.1;
    };
    ...
};
```

ACLs

Enumerating all those networks multiple times throughout the config file is tedious and error prone. Therefore, BIND offers named Access Control Lists (ACLs), which you can define and then use in permissions and denials. An ACL statement can include any number of network addresses and single addresses you want. Rewriting the previous allow-recursion and allow-query statements, this is the new configuration:

```
acl penguinets {
    192.168.55.0/24;
    192.168.56.0/25;
    127.0.0.1;              // Use "localhost" instead
};

options {
    ...
    allow-recursion { penguinets; };
    allow-query { penguinets; };
    ...
};
```

Four predefined ACLs exist: any, which matches anything; none, which matches nothing; localhost, which matches all the addresses of all the interfaces on your BIND server; and localnets, which is the networks directly attached to those interfaces. You should probably use localhost instead of 127.0.0.1, so I loose one point for the previous ACL I wrote. As is usual for these things, the ACL is processed one element at a time until a match is made. ACLs or ACL components can be negated by prefixing an exclamation mark (!).

These restrictions stop whomever the nameserver wants to answer queries from. But, the Penguin nameserver is authoritative for a number of zones, and its job is to answer queries about all those zones. So, it must answer queries about the penguin.bv zone as well as all the other zones it holds. That is configured like this:

```
zone "penguin.bv" {
    type master;
    file "pz/penguin.bv";
    allow-query { any; };
};
```

The allow-query option must be repeated for every zone for which the server is authoritative, if you restrict allow-query in the way shown in the previous code. This, and continued enhancements to the logic of BIND, is the best we can do for now. Your BIND should really be configured like this in any case.

Restricting access to DNS servers is one of the subjects of AUS-CERT advisory AL-1999.004; it deals with DoS attacks leveraging DNS servers. The advisory is available at `ftp://ftp.auscert.org.au/pub/auscert/advisory/AL-1999.004.dns_dos`. The advisory makes for good reading, and describes ACLs very well; I highly recommend it.

The AUS-CERT Advisory

The *AUS-CERT* advisory deals with network traffic amplification using DNS servers. The amplification mechanism is such that a DNS query originating with the attacker is small, whereas the server's query answer is large. If the attacker forges the source address, indicating that the system being attacked is the originator of the query, the answer is sent to the attacked system. This causes it to be bogged down in network traffic.

The advisory presents a work-around that widens the scope of the things to deny and control, somewhat. The advice is sound in any case, and you should seriously think about implementing this restrictive configuration no matter how secure your site needs to be. It recommends blackholing a large number of bogus addresses and otherwise restricting access to an absolute minimum. For example, the 0.0.127.in-addr.arpa zone should be able to be queried by only your own hosts, and be forbidden to zone transfer. All other zones should have carefully configured `allow-transfer` options. This is the blackhole they suggest:

```
acl "bogon" {
    0.0.0.0/8;      // Null address
    1.0.0.0/8;      // IANA reserved, popular fakes
    2.0.0.0/8;
    192.0.2.0/24;   // Test address
    224.0.0.0/3;    // Multicast addresses
    // These might be used internally in your organization,
    // remove them if so.
    10.0.0.0/8;
    172.16.0.0/12;
    192.168.0.0/16;
};

options {
    ...
    blackhole { bogon; };
    ...
};
```

Blackholing

Now you have secured your nameserver the best you and I know how, but as long as your server is acting as an authoritative DNS server, it still must answer queries from anyone. This cannot be avoided; it is the function of DNS. But, sometimes, when someone (due to misconfiguration, ill will, or intent, abuses your nameserver), you might want to bar them form contacting it entirely. It probably would be better to bar them by installing appropriate rules on a firewall, but you can do almost the same with the `blackhole` option. Incorporating the blackhole suggestion from the AUS-CERT advisory discussed earlier, the code becomes the following:

```
acl "bogon" {
    ...             // From the AUS-CERT advisory
};

acl rougenets {
    10.0.128.0/255.255.255.0;
};

options {
    ...
    blackhole {
        rougenets;
        bogon;
    };
    ...
};
```

But, of course, many attack techniques do not require the attacker to use his or her own return address on the query packets. Any source address can be used, forcing you to blackhole networks that are not attacking you, or even networks you can't blackhole because they are dependent on you, or you on them, for DNS service. When this is the situation, the only solution is to track down the real attacker and stop the attack. Or wait it out.

Bad Servers

As the AlterNIC episode clearly shows, DNS depends on DNS servers to be good and serve good data. In the case of the AlterNIC episode, a fixed version of BIND that would not accept that kind of bad data was out in short order. However, the possibility of someone setting up a bad server and succeeding in a poisoning scheme still exists. Another possibility is an ineptly setup nameserver that is spreading bad information. If you use the following syntax, your BIND will simply stop talking to the server:

```
server 10.156.82.33 {
    bogus yes;
};
```

Listing a server as bogus is not quite the same as blackholing it. If you blackhole it, your nameserver will not answer queries from the server. If you bogus list it, as in the previous code, your server will stop asking it, but it will not deny it answers.

Resource Use

In secure, reliability-focused environments you usually want to be able to predict the resource usage of the software used. Controlling, or at least knowing things about, typical resource usage helps keep the service stable because it has enough resources to run. It also keeps other services stable because there are still resources for them to run, and it can help prevent denial of service attacks based on exhausting limited resources. In addition, limiting how many resources one specific service can use helps prevent the other services from being taken out as a result of the attempts to take out BIND.

BIND manages a cache that, potentially, can use up all the memory on the machine on which it runs. Given a high enough query rate, BIND gladly uses all available CPU and much of the network capacity, as well. BIND manages its cache based on TTL, and nothing else. A future version of BIND 9 might implement its max-cache-size option.

Although you can restrict who you allow to send recursive queries to your nameservers, other ways are available to make something query them—sending mail to your site, for example. Your mail server queries for information about the sender's hostname, then your FTP server queries about the client hostname, your Web log analyzer queries about the Web client hostnames, and so on.

However, BIND enables you to set the OS resource usage limits. If they're not set in named.conf, BIND inherits them from the invoking shell. If you use a C shell–type limit to see to what the resource limits are set, or if you use a Bourne- or Korn-related shell type, such as ulimit -a, to view the resource limits, the code is as follows:

```
$ ulimit -a
core file size (blocks)      1000000
data seg size (kbytes)       unlimited
file size (blocks)           unlimited
max locked memory (kbytes)   unlimited
max memory size (kbytes)     unlimited
open files                   1024
pipe size (512 bytes)        8
stack size (kbytes)          8192
cpu time (seconds)           unlimited
max user processes           256
virtual memory (kbytes)      unlimited
```

Typically, the memory usage and CPU usage limits are unlimited. Several options for the options named.conf statement lets BIND adjust these values for its own private use:

coresize	Limits the size of core dumps. A size of 0 prevents core dumps from filling your filesystem. It also prevents you from analyzing the core dumps to figure out what has happened when a problem occurs.
datasize	The maximum size of the data segment.
files	The maximum number of open files the server can have at any one time.
stacksize	The size of the stack.

The downside of these limits is that you might find the limits set too low to enable BIND to operate. In that case, you can use the options to raise the limits. If your OS does not support manipulation of these limits, BIND will log warnings about it if you try to change them.

The problem with these options is that the OS might kill the named or start returning errors that are irreconcilable with continuing to run, if the limits are violated. So, if you set datasize to something reasonable for your environment and BIND later exceeds it, it might die. That might be preferable to eating your whole memory, but it requires you to run named inside a shell script loop or keep restarting BIND each time it dies:

```
while :; do
        named -f
done
```

The -f causes named to run in the foreground, so the shell will wait until named terminates before running it anew. named can also be run from init; most UNIX /etc/inittab files enable you to start, and keep restarting, system processes from it. Note, however, that most of them also keep resource usage in check by restricting how often a process is restarted. For example, if a process is restarted too often during one minute, init might stop restarting the process for five minutes, hoping whatever made it restart so often goes away. You might not want to be without your named for five minutes.

However, the cache isn't the only thing that uses memory; the zones your server is authoritative for also use memory. If you set the datasize and the zones grow, as time passes, your BIND might start using more memory than it is allowed, even when running normally. If this goes unchecked, it can in the end be killed by the OS before it completes startup. If you use datasize, or any other resource limits, you absolutely should monitor how your BIND is doing in the resource usage department and adjust the limits so that BIND stays within the limits when it runs normally.

Cache Cleaning

BIND 8 introduced a subroutine that walks the cache data structure looking for stale data. By default, it does this every 60 minutes. While this cleaning is being performed, BIND will not answer queries. If your cache server is buzzy and the cache is large (or the server slow), the interval when BIND does not answer might become larger than you want to tolerate. Then, you might want to disable cache cleaning entirely, or set it to perform less often, or even more often. You can double the interval as follows:

```
options {
    ...
    cleaning-interval 120;
    ...
};
```

Of course, enlarging the interval or disabling cleaning entirely causes your named to use more memory. If that is a cost you can tolerate, fine. By running normal cache cleaning, the cache size should stabilize within one or two days—most TTLs are one or two days, perhaps a week at the most.

If you enlarge the interval, your nameserver will still be unresponsive for a short while every interval, but it will be less often, which could well make it more tolerable. If you set the cleaning interval to 0, cleaning is disabled and stale data will be found and replaced only if the data is queried for.

One situation exists in which shortening the interval might be beneficial. If your server does not handle a lot of traffic, a relatively large percentage of the cached data might be stale at any one time. If your server is a vintage, very, very slow machine that has little memory, it will benefit it to run the cleaning subroutine more often to keep the expired items out, memory usage low, and the cache small so that the time used to do the cleaning stays low and the machine avoids swapping.

On the other hand, if you restart your named on a regular basis (twice per week or more often), all this is moot. When BIND is killed, the cache dies with it and it will not grow large between each invocation.

Zone Transfers

Two issues exist in relation to zone transfers. First of all, they are resource demanding, and second of all, some consider them to be problematic in the context of security because they help anyone locate the hosts and services in your network trivially. Knowing the names of all your hosts can help anyone with unfriendly intent guess which services your hosts run and perhaps even information about the structure of your network. This last is important, but I will not dwell on that here (see the section "Split DNS, NAT, and Network Hiding" later in this chapter). One situation in which better control of zone transfer is undeniable is in a split DNS scenario, which is also discussed later in this chapter. If you want, you can restrict zone transfers in the same way you can restrict recursive queries and queries in general. You know which servers are secondary for you, and you also know from which hosts you might want to run zone transfers by hand to perform checks or debugging. This is what the allow-transfer option is for. allow-transfer can be used in both the options statement and individual zone statements. You can also use ACLs here. A configuration might go like this:

```
acl slaves {
    198.162.80.1;    // Real slave
    localhost;       // My self for debugging
};

options {
    ...
    allow-transfer { slaves; };
    ...
};
```

To further control how demanding of resources zone transfers are—both for you and your peers—you can use three options: `transfers-in`, `transfers-out`, and `transfers-per-ns`. `transfers-in` limits how many named-xfer processes are forked concurrently to perform zone transfers. Raising this number increases memory and CPU usage. `transfers-out` is not implemented, but if it were, it would limit how many outgoing zone transfers BIND would allow at any one time. `transfers-per-ns` is a bit overlapping with `transfers-in`—it limits how many concurrent transfers will be started with any one nameserver. These are the default values:

```
options {
    ...
    transfers-in 10;
    transfers-per-ns 2;
    ...
};
```

`transfers-out` does not have a default.

chroot and Least Privilege

Software is vulnerable to various attacks that can cause different problems. One of the most insidious is attacks resulting in the attacker gaining root access to your mission-critical servers. BIND has been vulnerable to such attacks, but even so, the impact of such a compromise can be minimized. Not that gaining control of a nameserver isn't useful if you want to break into some network.

The principle of least privilege dictates that you run a service with exactly those access rights it needs, and you restrict its capability of accessing anything else. Although BIND does need to run as root to start, to be capable of listening on port 53, which is privileged, it does need to run as root after the port has been opened. To achieve this, BIND has the `-u` and `-g` command-line options, which instruct it to switch to the given user and group identity. The user called nobody and the corresponding group (sometimes called nobody, other times nogroup, and sometimes something else entirely) can be used. If you use these, the risk of root compromise is replaced with a nobody compromise, and no one worries about a nobody. A typical command line for running BIND this way follows:

```
named -u nobody -g nogroup
```

If you run several services on a machine, all as nobody, you run the risk of having insecurities in one allowing access to another. You might want to create separate accounts for each service that runs on the machine.

UNIX has another mechanism, called chroot, which enables software to be insulated into a chroot jail in the filesystem. After it's inside the jail, with the proper precautions taken, even if the software is compromised, the compromise cannot take over the whole machine because it is restricted to a few directories containing only a few files of limited value. (It has been repeatedly shown that chrooted programs can break out of chroot jails if the program does not take other precautions, which I will not go into here. Using a chroot call in your software and thinking you're safe is a fallacy. For these examples, we will, however, assume that BIND takes those precautions.) Figure 8.1 illustrates how chroot works, and Chapter 15 contains a section on setting up BIND in such a chroot environment. As noted there, the chroot option in BIND 8.2.2 is experimental, and changes might occur in how it works by the time you read this. Please check the release documentation. If you add the -u and -g options to drop root access to the -c option to chroot, you end up with a pretty secure setup. You should, however, police your BIND chroot jail to find out whether any files are changed unexpectedly. That will be a good compromise indicator.

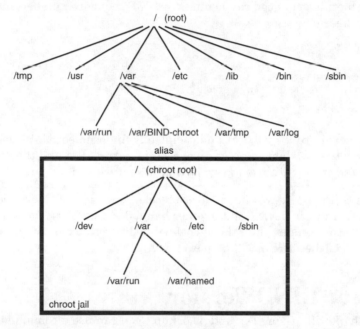

Figure 8.1   The chroot call moves the / of BIND to the machine's /var/BIND-chroot directory, and BIND is incapable of accessing the filesystem outside the jail.

Query ID Pool

BIND uses random query ID numbers to match queries and answers and to make spoofing answers more difficult. This is somewhat similar to the sequence numbers used in TCP, if you're familiar with that. In any case, the more random this number is, and the less the numbers are reused due to poor randomness, the better. BIND can, at the cost of 128KB, increase the randomness of the query IDs by keeping track of which numbers have been used and to which the answer is still outstanding. The use-id-pool option, set to off by default, enables this:

```
options {
    ...
    use-id-pool yes;
    ...
};
```

BIND 9 enhances its random number generator, and is capable of retrieving randomness from the OS. The BSDs and Linux, for example, have a special random device—/dev/random and /dev/urandom—which gathers randomness from the whole OS and which is used by the TCP/IP stack to generate very good randomness for TCP sequence numbers. BIND can gather randomness from these devices:

```
options {
    ...
    random-device "/dev/urandom";
    random-seed-file "/var/named/random-seed";
    ...
};
```

These options are new to BIND 9.0.0rc1 and completely undocumented. Please check the documentation available to you when you read this, especially the ARM and the named.conf man page. It might have revealing things to say about this feature and its use.

On Linux and the BSDs, the /dev/random device blocks the reader if the randomness is running thin. The /dev/urandom device, on the other hand, does not block the reader even if that is the case. Even if it is running thin, the kernel will deliver good randomness through these devices, and the use of the id-pool will help even more.

Hiding Your BIND Version

As described in Chapter 5, "Using Dig and nslookup," you can use a command such as

```
$ dig CHAOS version.bind TXT
```

to determine the version of your BIND. This can be considered a security risk. And indeed, it makes determining your BIND version easier, which might be a risk when a new security problem in BIND gets published. In named.conf enter the following:

```
options {
    ...
    version "Wouldn't you like to know?";
    ...
};
```

Of course, such an answer might inflame the temper of any attacker rather than stop the attack, so you might want to choose other language, or set it to blank. It has been argued that if the version string returned shows that you're using the latest, no-known-weaknesses BIND, the attacker will go on to the next target. On the other hand, if you conceal your version, the attacker will direct the whole arsenal of BIND compromise tools toward your server. But now we're into the realm of second-guessing the attacker. Do what you feel most comfortable with.

Earlier versions of BIND required you to set up a zone of class Chaos instead of the default IN, called bind. They also required you to define a CHAOS TXT record for the name version.bind, replacing the default one. That no longer works, which is just as well because the new way is less work.

BIND 9 and DNSSEC

The DNS of RFCs 1034 and 1035 is secure in the same way IPv4 is—not very. You must be able to trust people, which you could on the Internet of 10 years ago, but now this has turned out to be a bit of a liability. On the other hand, if the root servers sign their query answers with known keys so you could check that the answers were unaltered and from a legitimate root server, it's a different situation. Additionally, if they also provide the public key of the nameserver to which they refer you, so that when, in turn, the answer comes back from that server you can verify that the answer is legitimate and unaltered, you have a new situation. You can trust DNS in a new way. Of course, this will still not stop people from entering bogus data into the DNS either by accident or ill will, so it will not really guard against all poisoning attacks. Spoofing, though, will become much more difficult (if not impossible), at least as long as the private key remains private and secret.

RFC 2535 specifies DNSSEC. BIND 8 starts to implement it and BIND 9 will complete it. DNSSEC is not in wide deployment on the Internet today, and it is not easy to find documentation of it beyond the RFCs. DNSSEC also faces some difficult issues of key management and contingency mechanisms when secret keys are compromised. The ARM documents how to perform some specific operations relating to DNSSEC, but assumes you are familiar with the concepts already. Expect more documentation in the future.

One thing that is readily understandable is TSIGs for zone transfers. Chapter 9, "Dynamic DNS," discusses TSIGs for dynamic DNS updates, and BIND 9 easily can be configured to use TSIGs for zone transfers, as well. In the case of zone transfers, TSIGs ensure that the slave accepts only zone transfers signed by the master. This is a great step forward in DNS security. If you run BIND 9, you absolutely should configure the keys necessary to enable this. See Chapter 16, "BIND 9," for how to set it up.

DNS on Firewalls

A firewall is very security sensitive. If you're going to run BIND on your firewall, and some firewall solutions recommend this, you should secure your BIND in every way. In addition, you especially should run it in a chroot environment and with changed user and group IDs, as discussed earlier in this chapter.

If you run DNS on your firewall, it is usually used as a proxy for the internal DNS servers. This way, your internal DNS servers never talk to outside servers, and any DNS attacks can be directed at only the firewall, which is the point of a firewall, of course. The downside is that, unless your firewall is redundant, this is a single point of failure in your DNS. However, if your firewall fails, you won't have Internet connectivity either, so it's not a new single point of failure.

If your firewall is acting as a proxy and its internal address is 192.168.55.1, you should have the following configuration on your internal DNS servers:

```
options {
    ...
    forward only;
    forwarders { 192.168.55.1; };
    ...
};
```

This directs all queries to the firewall DNS and enables you to install quite restrictive DNS firewall rules.

Firewall Rules and DNS

At least two kinds of firewalls are available. The simplest is *packet filtering* firewalls, and at the more advanced end of the spectrum is firewalls such as FireWall-1, which maintains complete connection state engines capable of filtering traffic in a much more intelligent manner. A commercial, GUI-equipped firewall should be quite easy to set to allow DNS traffic to pass correctly. However, please check the documentation because it might have specific, not-so-obvious recommendations about DNS configuration that you should adhere to.

In the old days, when BIND 4 ruled the networks, setting up firewall rules for DNS was quite simple. Everything—TCP and UDP, information coming from port 53, information addressed to port 53—was DNS server-to-DNS server traffic and should be let through. As long as the clients on the inside used only the inside DNS server, the queries would get through. BIND 8 changed this: It sends queries from a random port to port 53 on the server it's querying. Then, the reply comes back from port 53 to the same random port. So, now the correct rule is that any TCP or UDP packet destined to port 53, no matter what the origin is, is a DNS packet. To spell it out, you must open for inbound UDP destined for any UDP port, as long as it originates from port 53 on some machine; the query originates on a random UDP port on the inside. This is a good reason for having a DNS proxy on the firewall because allowing UDP packets into your internal network is very dangerous business, at least if UNIX computers are on your network. Most UNIX computers run quite insecure services over UDP. If you don't control the firewall or don't want a DNS proxy on the firewall, you can instruct BIND to use port 53 to query from. This re-establishes the behavior of BIND 4 and makes things a bit easier again:

```
optons {
    ...
    query-source port 53;
    ...
};
```

If you don't have any recursive, resolving DNS servers on the inside, you will have a flock of machines on the inside trying to talk to a resolver on the outside. The inside machines will not be querying from port 53; the queries are generated by unprivileged processes and are forbidden to use port 53. The inside machines behave exactly like BIND 8, in other words (actually it's the other way around, BIND 8 is the late entrant; stub resolvers have always used high ports). So, again you must open up several ports, and again, this is insecure. It would be much more secure to just set up BIND on one of the internal hosts and have all the inside hosts use it, and indeed this is what most people with a firewall do, as should you.

It is important to note that while DNS usually uses UDP, it sometimes needs to use TCP. This happens whenever the amount of data to be transferred exceeds 512 bytes. 512 bytes was the maximum amount of payload in UDP packets dictated by the first RFCs, and it's still the limit. Zone transfers are always larger than 512 bytes, so make sure the firewall is open for the same TCP ports as UDP. It is, however, true that the internal DNS server always initiates queries itself, and that the query is answered on the same TCP connection. Therefore, no need exists to open for incoming TCP SYN packets, unless someone on the outside needs to perform zone transfers through the firewall, of course.

Split DNS, NAT, and Network Hiding

Many companies don't want to share the complete DNS information for their internal network with the world for security reasons. Another reason is that they might be using a NATing Internet gateway and that the complete DNS information contains hosts with IP numbers that are not routable over the Internet. So, they make this DNS information unavailable from the outside. But, they still want some hosts to be seen and used by the outside. They therefore provide that DNS information to the world.

The network management principle is known as *network hiding*, and the accompanying DNS configuration is known as *split DNS*. Many will argue that network hiding is an exercise in futility, that scores of things cross over from the internal network to the Internet that will give away names and internal addresses of hosts on the inside. Something as simple as a mail

> **Why Forward-Only?**
>
> If the cache servers are set up to forward first or without forwarding, they either partially or completely fail to work. When set to forward first, your BIND evaluates what it thinks of the answers from the forwarded-to host, and discounts them entirely if they seem unreliable. So, suddenly internal resolving could fail for no obvious reason. If you use forward-only, BIND slaves itself to your authoritative servers and never doesn't ask them.
>
> If the cache does not ask the internal authoritative servers for names in the penguin.bv zone, it has no other way to resolve the name than to consult its cache and `root.hints` and resolve the name from the root up. The query then ends up at the external DNS servers because these are the only servers that can be found from the outside. The external DNS servers have no knowledge of the internal names and the query then fails, which is not what we wanted. So, forward-only is obligatory on the nonauthoritative servers.

The external DNS servers are the ones penguin.bv registers with its TLD registrar; therefore, only the external servers are listed in the TLD and only they can be found by anyone outside penguin.bv asking for them. Because the external DNS servers contain zones that are a subset of the real zones, listing only those hosts that need to be known by the outside, they cannot give any secrets away. The external DNS servers are also configured in a completely normal manner. All in all, split DNS is quite simple: The only differences between the internal and external servers are the contents of their zone files and whether they are registered with the TLD registrar. The only magic involved is that the internal hosts and caches must query only the internal servers—something which is easily arranged.

Split DNS on a Firewall

Firewalls, NAT, and split DNS are different sides of the same story. Quite often, when you first get a firewall, you start performing network hiding and need a split DNS setup. It is tempting to not only use the firewall as a DNS proxy, but also to serve both internal and external zones from it. Doing so makes things simpler and reduces the number of machines required. Fortunately, this is possible using two instances of BIND and the `listen-on` option. However, it is much simpler to do this with BIND 9.0.0's views feature, which I mentioned earlier in the chapter, and you will soon see why.

Of the two instances of BIND, one is for the inside listening on the inside network interface, and one is for the outside listening on the outside interface. If the penguin.bv firewall has 192.168.55.1 as its inside address and 10.0.0.2 as its outside address, you configure the internal instance like this:

```
acl internalifs { // Internal interfaces
    192.168.55.1;
};

options {
    ...
    listen-on port 53 { internalifs; };
    ...
}
```

The external configuration simply replaces the address (and name) in the interface ACL. Otherwise, each BIND is configured as described previously: the external with the reduced zones and the internal with the complete zones. This enables you to get two nameservers for the price of one.

Several interfaces might be counted as internal or external, depending on your network. They should all be listed, but then again, it might not matter whether the clients consistently use only one address for each purpose.

That is not the end of it, however. As I said previously, this should all be performed inside a chroot jail, and to add a twist, preferably one chroot jail for each instance of BIND. Each jail will contain a separate `named.conf` and the appropriate zone files to accompany it. The chroot setup and scripts must be modified accordingly. This is a difficult bit to get right because a simple substitution of the ndc and named executables such as I describe in Chapter 15 will not work. Dave Lugo has made some notes at `http://www.etherboy.com/dns/chrootdns.html` about how to do this. They are a bit Linux specific, but replacing the `init` script and only using the `init-script` to manipulate named (and not ndc) is not a bad idea at all. All manual, simple invocations of named and ndc would fail in any case, and having two sets of ndc and named wrappers is a bit messy.

With BIND 9, you simply run one BIND and configure two different views that clients see based on their IP addresses. The 192.168.55 network is internal, and everything else is external:

```
acl internal {
    192.168.55/24;
    localhost;
};

view internal_penguin {
    match { internal; };

    zone "penguin.bv" {
        type master;
        file "pz-internal/penguin.bv";
        // Other zone statements here
    };

    // Other internal zones here
};

view external_penguin {
    match any;

    zone "penguin.bv" {
        type master;
        file "pz/penguin.bv";
```

```
        // Other zone statements here
    ];

    // Other external zones here
};
```

When a query arrives, the zones are checked in order for a match against the origin address of the query. In the previous configuration, any host not matching the first internal view falls through to the second view, which matches any origin address. This is quite a bit neater than the options required to give the two different BIND 8s as outlined earlier.

Large Networks and Split DNS

In Chapter 3, I describe forwarding, and inside a large network, using forward-only to a few resolving, recursive servers is an obvious solution. As the network grows, you can add levels of forwarding (but not many), such as used in Australia, also described in Chapter 3. This obviously has some scaling advantages because the chance of finding a cached reply increases as the query proceeds along the forwarding chain. The disadvantage though, is that all queries that cannot be satisfied from a cache end up at one of the resolving servers at the end of the forwarding chain. This is contrary to how DNS usually works—forwarding centralizes resolving, rather than distributing it as is intended. With a large enough network, the load on the central forwarding servers can become considerable. It can be eased by having several resolving servers and listing them in the forwarders statement in random order in the satellite servers. Adding resolving servers with full resolving powers and access to the Internet will scale linearly, if you manage to distribute the load evenly.

With this setup, you can still delegate subdomains to other servers and perform the usual tasks for large networks. But performance can become less than optimal. If you do it incorrectly, queries from a subdomain about a name in that subdomain proceed all the way to the central forwarding servers before being resolved by the normal method with the subdomain's own authoritative nameserver. To perform it correctly, the hosts within a delegated subdomain should have their own nameservers and be authoritative for the zone so that they are capable of resolving the names in the subdomain right away instead of forwarding the query.

At some point, the pressure of the query concentration that forwarding results in can become unmanageable. At that point, it's time to implement internal root servers. In Chapter 11, "DNS on a Closed Network," I describe such private, internal root servers. An internal root setup has the same scaling properties as DNS as used on the Internet, which is pretty good. The disadvantage, or what used to be the disadvantage, of an internal root setup is that it cannot resolve names outside your private network—the Internet DNS effectively becomes unreachable. Two ways exist to work around this, though, and the second is my favorite.

Using Application Proxies

One way, which fits in well with strict security policies, is using application proxies that have access to the Internet DNS namespace for all traffic to the outside. For example, the organization is likely to have one, or several, Web proxy machines that all Web content is fetched via. These Web proxies can be configured to use an Internet DNS rather than the internal DNS. Web proxies, such as Squid, even have configuration file options to override /etc/resolv.conf so that they can resolve things independently of the rest of the applications on the machine. Similarly, this can be done with mail and other application proxies set up around the perimeter of the internal network. Careful tricks with wildcard MX records and other records as needed can be used with this setup to achieve pretty much anything.

Using BIND

This method works only with BIND 8.2 and later versions. A new zone type was introduced that enables you to override the global forwarding policy for specific subdomains. This is exactly what we want.

First, you install an internal root setup exactly as described in Chapter 11, with internal hint files and everything. Then, by default, you forward all queries to an Internet-aware resolving server. As before, the code is

```
options {
    // Forward to servers with Internet root.hints files
    forward only;
    forwarders {
        10.0.0.2;
        10.1.0.2;
    };
};
```

Next, you override the forwarding for resolution for the local domains, penguin.bv, and the reverse zones:

```
zone "penguin.bv" {
    type forward;
};

zone "10.in-addr.arpa" {
    type forward;
};
```

This cancels the global forwarding policy forcing normal, non-forwarded, hint-using resolution of these domains and their subdomains. The scalability problem of a forwarding hierarchy is solved. Of course, you can add as many forward zones as you need, as the corporation grows into a multinational conglomerate acquiring companies that are folded into the network. However, this is not a perfect solution because maintaining and distributing the forwarding exception list can grow into a tedious task.

BIND 9.0.0 does not support forward zones, but a future version will.

Now that forward zones are available, the disadvantages that formerly dissuaded people from using internal roots are now either vanished or so small that I would now prefer to set up internal roots rather than organize a forwarding hierarchy when the need for scaling arises. It is less work and will not need to be heavily reorganized in any foreseeable future.

TSIG

Using TSIG updates is just a little bit harder than IP authentication and it is a lot more secure. *TSIG* is short for *transaction signature* and is a cryptographical signature that the server can check. If the signature is correct, the server knows that the update either came from the authorized client or from someone who has stolen the secret signing key. TSIG uses a mechanism called HMAC-MD5 to authenticate the sender and message content of the updates. HMAC is a mechanism for message authentication to be used in combination with a cryptographic hash routine, MD5 in this case. HMAC is described in RFC 2104; MD5 is described in RFC 1321. HMAC-MD5 is also specified for use in IP-SEC, and in RFC 2403 (a IP-SEC RFC) we find this nice summation:

> "HMAC is a secret key authentication algorithm. Data integrity and data origin authentication as provided by HMAC are dependent upon the scope of the distribution of the secret key. If only the source and destination know the HMAC key, this provides both data origin authentication and data integrity for packets sent between the two parties; if the HMAC is correct, this proves that it must have been added by the source."

HMAC-MD5, then, is a secret key, shared secret, or symmetric cryptography. This is different from public key cryptography, which is the kind of cryptography used for email. It is vital that the shared secret remains secret. If anyone manages to steal the key, they can trivially masquerade as you; then they don't even have to spoof their IP address. I'm not a cryptography expert and will not go farther into how this works, but see *Handbook of Applied Cryptography* or *Applied Cryptography* for more information on the subject of cryptography. TSIG is currently described in an Internet draft only; it is available at `http://www.ietf.org/internet-drafts/draft-ietf-dnsext-tsig-00.txt`. TSIG is based on HMAC-MD5.

These are also the properties we want for use with dynamic DNS.

The Dynamic Zone

An important thing to note is that a zone maintained dynamically cannot be maintained any other way. The primary master will maintain the zonefile automatically and BIND expects to be the sole updater of the file. Any effort to edit it manually will result in mayhem and confusion. Although, this does not stop you from maintaining the zone wholly with the dynamic DNS tools, and indeed you can do that.

But, due to this restriction and because they want to keep using the tools they know to maintain their normal zones, many sites set up separate zones for dynamic DNS.

The Penguin company has hired 16 new employees and wants to maintain their workstations in a dynamic zone. The company adds dyn.penguin.bv. This must be a separate zone, delegated in the normal way with NS records in the parent zone. In the penguin.bv zone, this is added to delegate the zone to the named servers:

```
dyn            NS ns
dyn            NS ns.herring.bv.
```

9

DYNAMIC DNS

With the appearance of dynamically allocated addresses in DHCP and dial-up protocols such as PPP, DNS has had some catching up to do. In April 1997 RFC 2136 was published, specifying a mechanism for dynamic updates of DNS, known as DNS-UPDATE. However, before getting into that I need to introduce some new terms.

Of RRsets

An RRset is the set of RRs associated with a name. In any zone there is at least one name which has several records associated with it. This is an extract from the penguin.bv zone as shown in Chapter 2, "DNS in Practice":

```
@       3600    SOA    ns.penguin.bv.  hostmaster.penguin.bv. (
                2000042924       ; serial
                86400            ; refresh, 24h
                7200             ; retry, 2h
                3600000          ; expire, 1000h
                172800           ; minimum, 2 days
                )
                NS       ns
                NS       ns.herring.bv.
                MX       10 mail
                MX       20 mail.herring.bv.
...
@               A        192.168.55.3
@               A        192.168.55.10
...
```

Associated with the name penguin.bv are one SOA record, two NS records, two MX records, and two A records. This makes one RRset. In RFC 2181, which updates RFC 1035, it is specified that all records in an RRset must have the same TTL. This RFC is listed as elective and this restriction is, in fact, not currently implemented in BIND 8. But acting like it is implemented in the case of dynamic zones might be a good idea, because in a dynamic zone the TTL of the records becomes very important. There is no mechanism to update cached RRs. They must be expired from the cache before any new value is requested from the zone servers.

Of Masters and Slaves

In the context of updates, what server to update becomes important, because there will be a need to know what server is the primary master. The primary master is named in the SOA record's first field. This field must not be used for the zone name. It must name the zone master server. Even if the server is otherwise unlisted, it must be named in the SOA record.

A slave server is a server that has a master. A master server is a server that acts as a master for a slave. The primary master is the zone origin server—it has no masters.

RFC 2136 specifies that, if a slave server receives an update request, the request shall be accepted and forwarded toward the primary master server. A slave server will not know who is authorized to update zones and so cannot check the authorization. It must store the update request and forward it. If the primary master is unavailable, it should forward it to any other master it knows. This allows the request to percolate through layers of protection that might be present between the zone updater and the primary master. That's the theory anyway. As of this writing (May 2000), BIND 8 does not implement this and the primary master must be present for an update to take hold. Even if you configure a slave to accept update requests and update the zone, the update will not find its way back to the primary master. Then, the next time a zone transfer from the primary master takes place, the update will be overwritten. So, the primary master must be available to the zone updater. This will be fixed in a future version of BIND.

Accepting and Doing Updates

The DNS Server

By default BIND DNS servers do not accept update requests. You must configure each zone on the server to accept updates from the appropriate clients. Those who are allowed to update zones can be defined in two ways. The easiest is to accept all update requests from a given host. This is not very secure and should only be contemplated within a firewall-protected network. Consider that it is relatively easy to spoof IP source addresses, and that anyone able to present the correct source address will be able to demolish the whole dynamic zone. Do not underestimate how simple this is; variations of spoofing have been used in a variety of attacks all over the Internet. So beware.

In named.conf dyn.penguin.bv is added in the normal way, less one detail—the allow-update ACL:

```
zone "dyn.penguin.bv" {
        type master;
        file "pz/dyn.penguin.bv";
        allow-update {
                192.168.55.2;
        };
};
```

This zone specifies which hosts are allowed to update the zone. In this case it is the nameserver's own IP address. It will also act as a DHCP server so all updates will come from itself. To use TSIG authentication of updates, a key pair must first be generated:

```
# dnskeygen -H 512 -h -n ns.penguin.bv.
Generating 512 bit HMAC-MD5 Key for ns.penguin.bv.

Generated 512 bit Key for ns.penguin.bv. id=0 alg=157 flags=513
```

Two files were created: `Kns.penguin.bv.+157+00000.key` and `Kns.penguin.bv.+157+00000.private`. They both contain the same secret key, but in different formats. The `.key` file is in DNS zone file format. The key must be stolen for the thief to be able to sign as you would and thus be indistinguishable from you for the DNS server. Keep your key on a secure machine, and as with sensitive passwords, change it now and then—especially when key staff leaves you or whenever you have security incidents. Keeping your keys secure is not a matter to be taken lightly.

The public key must be entered in the named.conf file, or in a file it includes, and the file containing it must of course be read restricted. The audience able to read it should be miniscule.

```
key ns.penguin.bv. {
        algorithm hmac-md5;
        secret "XBzxlscP7rw3vfqF/yONoGNDQKMKgAcndBhKednuwlgqMc2rTVO
                jdGv4VqGyhj5uqW/uJlciyn/MO45VFonxtQ==";
}
```

The key has been broken to fit in the book. In the file there should be no line break. The zone must be configured to allow for the holder of the key to change it:

```
zone "dyn.penguin.bv" {
        type master;
        file "pz/dyn.penguin.bv";
        allow-update {
                key ns.penguin.bv.;
        };
};
```

You can, of course, list several authorized keys and IP-numbers. I will get back to how the client uses the key in a second.

The next task is to seed the dynamic zone—to provide an initial zone file. It should include all the usual records for a zone, perhaps excepting any actual host records. You can add those later. Here then, is a seed file:

```
$TTL 1m
;
@       1m      SOA ns.penguin.bv. hostmaster.penguin.bv. (
                1               ; serial
                5m              ; refresh
                2m              ; retry
                6h              ; expire
                1m              ; minimum
                )
        1m      NS      ns.penguin.bv.
        1m      NS      ns.herring.bv.
```

Which values to use in the SOA record is an interesting question. The answer depends on how often your zone will actually change and how important it is for the change to be known immediately. In some settings the zone might be managed as a dynamic zone, but, in fact, the contents will be highly static. Hosts will keep their IP addresses for a long time, and if it does change it is no catastrophe if the change is not known at once. This is true for many office settings. In other settings hosts will change IP numbers fairly often, perhaps disappear, and when they reappear the new IP number should be known ASAP. This could be the case for a dial-up setting. Of course, whether a host changes an IP number often in a dial-up setting might be an administrative decision as well, and it might prove better not to change IP numbers often.

The SOA shown previously is suited for a highly dynamic zone, where hosts change IP numbers often—potentially several times a day. In the opposite case, the SOA values used for the main penguin zone in Chapter 2 are more appropriate. The thinking behind these values is that the serial number will be automatically maintained by the nameserver. It does not keep it in the yyyymmddnn format and giving the impression that it does by seeding the zone with a serial number in that format is liable to cause confusion.

The refresh interval is short. Normally the NOTIFY protocol discussed in Chapter 2 ensures that the update propagates promptly to all slave servers, but the UDP packed bearing the NOTIFY can get lost occasionally. In that case a five-minute refresh interval might not be too onerous to wait out. If the refresh fails, the transfer will be repeated every retry interval— every 2 minutes here. A shorter interval might be used if failures need to be corrected more quickly. This depends on your environment and requirements.

An interesting problem arises if the zone transfer fails repeatedly. How long is it before the zone expires? In a highly dynamic zone, the data will quickly become stale. Having the slave servers fail rather than serve stale data might be preferable, and possibly set off more alarms as well, which could help the situation to be resolved more quickly. Do not keep a zone

keys in /etc. The part after the colon (:) specifies the name of the key, not the name of the key file:

```
# nsupdate -k /etc:ns.penguin.bv.
> update add magellan.dyn.penguin.bv 1h A 192.168.55.200
> (blank line)
```

Upon getting the empty line, nsupdate sends an update request to the primary master server. The primary master server will check whether the client is allowed to perform the specified edits and, if so, check the prerequisites. Then, if they are met, it performs the updates all at once. You can now exit nsupdate, press Ctrl+D. Note that pressing Ctrl+D without entering the empty line first will abort the operation. It will not be submitted to the server. You can now test whether the update had any effect:

```
# dig @ns.penguin.bv. magellan.dyn.penguin.bv. ANY +pfmin
; (1 server found)
;; res options: init recurs defnam dnsrch
;; got answer:
;; ->>HEADER<<- opcode: QUERY, status: NOERROR, id: 62041
;; QUERY: 1, ANSWER: 1, AUTHORITY: 1, ADDITIONAL: 1
;; QUERY SECTION:
;;      magellan.dyn.penguin.bv, type = ANY, class = IN

;; ANSWER SECTION:
magellan.dyn.penguin.bv.   1H IN A   192.168.55.200
```

The A record I submitted with nsupdate is in place, so it worked. If you're not using TSIG, but rather IP number authentication, the -k option should not be used. Now the next job is getting the change to the slave servers.

nsupdate is not very good about displaying errors unless you specify the -d (debug) switch. But keeping an eye on the standard messages log file on the server will let you know whether the update was rejected due to authentication problems:

```
unapproved update from [192.168.55.2].2391 for dyn.penguin.bv
```

The contents in the zone log and ixfr files will tell you what updates arrive and are approved. This is the content of the dyn.penguin.bv.ixfr file after adding the record shown previously:

```
;BIND LOG V8
[DYNAMIC_UPDATE] id 27514 from [192.168.55.2].2390 at 958316354
        (named pid 3814):
zone:   origin dyn.penguin.bv class IN serial 9
update: {add} magellan.dyn.penguin.bv. 60 IN A 192.168.55.200
```

Similar information can be found in the zone log file. If you look at the zone file right after the update, it will (probably) not have been updated with the new information. Rewriting large zone files whenever they are updated is resource consuming. Instead the ixfr and log files are appended with the changes done, and upon occasion BIND will roll all the changes into the zone file and rewrite it. The log and ixfr files are transaction logs as used in databases and modern file systems. When an update is applied to the zone, BIND writes the updates to the logs at once. That way, if the server or BIND crashes, BIND can do a roll forward of the transaction log when BIND restarts and no changes will be lost.

The SOA serial number is updated automatically when an update is received. You do not need to update the SOA record.

Slave Server Issues

In the setting where the dynamic zone does not really change that often and immediate propagation of changes is not critical, there is nothing to add to what has already been said about slave servers in Chapter 2.

In the case where the dynamic zone changes often and immediate updates of slave servers is important, I would like to remind you of, and reinforce, some things said in Chapter 2. When an update is received, the server will follow the usual procedure when a zone is updated: After a random waiting period (in the order of tens of seconds), a NOTIFY request is sent out to all the listed nameservers and any additional servers listed in named.conf. In this setting keeping the list of nameservers up to date and ensuring that they really receive NOTIFY requests becomes important. Combining NOTIFY requests with appropriate intervals in the SOA record will ensure that your slave servers are current and up-to-date;.

There is one more thing. As long as your dynamic zone is not right under a TLD (as is the case for dyn.penguin.bv) and is almost exclusively used internally, which will also often be the case, the need for a slave server might not be that great—especially in small places. One server can handle large amounts of requests for the zone, so load will not be an issue. It is more an issue of reliability and redundancy, which might be less important in the dynamic zone, but more important in larger organizations.

Reverse Zones

I have not mentioned reverse zones at all thus far into the chapter. Of course you will need reverse zones as well as forward zones, and they are maintained exactly the same way. In the case of classlessly delegated reverse zones, you should send update requests for the real record name, not the correct name. In the case of the classless emperor.penguin.bv network in Chapter 2, the update request would be for names such as 129.128-255.56.168.192.in-addr.arpa, not 129.56.168.192.in-addr.arpa.

A One Host Zone

In some settings not having to set up a separate dynamic zone for dynamic updates would be the best scenario; or to enable a specific host, or key, to modify only the records of one specific domain name, a more fine-grained access control of who may change what. In the setting shown previously, anyone with the correct key or access to the right host is able to perform any updates on the whole zone. This might not be desirable, and if you find yourself in such a situation, you should consider not implementing dynamic DNS at all. If you can't trust your users at this level, they should perhaps not be able to alter DNS at all.

But there is a "hackish" way to work around it: It is possible to make a "one host" zone. The zone can have its own update ACL and thus the holder of the associated key or IP number can only update the zone, not anything outside it, and no one else can alter the zone either. The way to do this is to delegate the zone bearing the hostname to the nameservers you want, as shown previously, and then seed the zone. If the zone is for magellan.penguin.bv,

```
$TTL 1m
;
@       1m      SOA ns.penguin.bv. hostmaster.penguin.bv. (
                1               ; serial
                5m              ; refresh
                2m              ; retry
                6h              ; expire
                1m              ; minimum
                )
        1m      NS      ns.penguin.bv.
        1m      NS      ns.herring.bv.
        1m      A       10.10.10.10
```

it gives magellan.penguin.bv an A record with the value 10.10.10.10. This can be deleted and re-added just as described previously for magellan.dyn.penguin.bv. This gives finer update access control and the capability to have dynamic hosts directly under the main domain, but at the cost of configuration overhead and increased key/ACL maintenance. Of course, anyone able to update this zone can add subdomains of magellan.penguin.bv if he wants to, so it can't really be called secure or considered very restricted.

DHCP

DDNS and DHCP are complementary services. DHCP doles out the addresses and DNS helps you find the address.

The ISC is also implementing a DHCP server for UNIX systems. As I write this, DHCP 2.0 is the production version and in common use. DHCP 3.0 is in beta. The 2.0 distribution does not support dynamic DNS updates. The 3.0 beta does support dynamic updates but the documentation carries big warnings about not being final, so use it at your own peril and only if you need the features. But a production release might be available by the time you read this. As with BIND, you can get DHCP from the ISC ftp site: ftp://ftp.isc.org/isc/dhcp/. See its Web site at http://www.isc.org/products/DHCP/ for more information about the available releases, their status, and features. I will not even try to describe the design, implementation, and usage issues connected with DHCP; I will simply discuss some DHCP/DNS integration issues.

Please see *The DHCP Handbook* for more complete information about DHCP, both the standard and the implementation.

Mixing DNS and DHCP Implementations

Some people want to use Windows DHCP with BIND DNS, or vice versa. I have not had the opportunity to try either combination, but the general advice available on the Net about this is "don't." It apparently works better if you keep Windows DHCP paired with Windows DNS and ISC DHCP paired with ISC DNS.

DHCP and Static DNS Entries

Due to the lack of support for dynamic DNS support in DHCP 2 and, more significantly perhaps, the potential management overhead if everyone could grab any name and get an IP address to go, a lot of sites use fixed names for their DHCP range. In BIND 8 it's quite easy to enter such ranges in zone files too, using $GENERATE which was introduced in Chapter 2. In such a case, the 16 new penguin employee computers would be assigned an IP range, such as 192.168.55.220 to 229, and the names would be entered thus:

```
$GENERATE 220-229 dhcp$ A 192.168.55.$
```

The names would be dhcp220.penguin.bv and so forth. This is a good way to do it; it is simple and low maintenance. For hosts that you want to have fixed IP numbers or fixed hostname, ISC DHCP 2 provides a way for you to assign them. In the dhcpd.conf file, insert something like this:

```
host gentoo {
        hardware ethernet 00:60:1d:1f:1e:f7;
        fixed-address 192.168.55.55;
}
```

This assigns the given IP address to the host bearing the given Ethernet address. Just enter the name in DNS in the usual manner. The "gentoo" part of the host statement is arbitrary, but it would be good policy to assign 192.168.55.55 the name gentoo.penguin.bv.

DHCP and Dynamic DNS Entries

As I mentioned earlier, version 3 of the ISC DHCP distribution can do dynamic updates of DNS based on the hostname the client wants. However, the how of this integration has not been entirely worked out at this time so I'll refrain from teasing you with what you can't do. *The DHCP Handbook* has more information about how it is supposed to work.

The DNS update conditionals allow the DHCP server to specify update conditions to the DNS server such as "if the name already is in use" to forbid users from using new names or "if the name is not present" to forbid users from using names already in use. Whichever way you want it is a pure administrative decision and what you can allow depends on how much you trust your users. If you don't trust your users, I recommend that you give them static names.

Dynamic Updates by the Client

I have assumed that the DHCP server would do the DNS updates. Of course it does not have to, and indeed, on a limited scale it might be easier to do on the client's server. Doing it from the DHCP server gives low ACL/key maintenance overhead and, if need be, full control of what gets added. But there is nothing stopping you from giving the DHCP (or PPP) client access to update DNS. By running a simple script after the interface has been assigned, an address DNS can be updated:

```
#!/bin/sh

PATH=/sbin:/usr/sbin:/bin:/usr/bin
export PATH

IF=hme0
NAME=gentoo.dyn.penguin.bv
TTL=60

IP=`ifconfig $IF | awk '/inet/ { print $2; }'`

nsupdate <<EOC
update delete $NAME
update add $NAME $TTL A $IP

EOC
```

The script shown here works on Solaris. It needs to be adapted to other OSes; the interface names and the output of ifconfig vary wildly between OSes. Also add the -k option if you want to use TSIG signing.

10

DNS AND DIAL-UP
CONNECTIONS

BIND has a tendency to want to talk to nameservers every now and then. Quite often in fact. If you use a dial-up connection to the Internet and pay by the minute for your connection time, you're wasting money. Many companies connect to the Internet by auto-dialing ISDN or analog modems. These ISDN and analog modems can be connected to ISDN network routers, Linux machines, or other inexpensive UNIX machines used as firewalls or ISDN routers. The goal, then, is to minimize the connection time (at least before and after working hours) but still allow BIND, and people, to work.

Keeping your dial-up connection time as low as possible is important, but it also is important to note that if your server is master for any zones, the slaves *must* be capable of connecting to the master. To ensure this, your server should be online for at least two times the retry interval in the SOA record daily. Recall the pattern in which a slave tries to transfer zones from masters. This ensures that the slaves can check for new versions of the zone(s) and retrieve it if necessary, and that the zone docs not expire and become unavailable.

In addition, if your server is a master, it should be an unlisted server, as explained in Chapter 2, "DNS in Practice." If your master is unavailable most of the time, DNS resolvers on the outside just waste time and network resources when they try to get answers from it.

In any native auto-dial setup, the default behavior will take up the Internet connection and then keep it up until the disconnect timeout occurs. Because getting ISDN connections up is a quick process, a simple fix is to set a short timeout, such as 120 seconds without traffic, before disconnecting. Working with analog connections is a bit harder because they can take as long as 30 seconds to establish, and therefore are difficult to take up and down. As a result, most people want a long timeout. If the timeout is long enough, BIND can manage to keep the connection up all the time, all by itself. However, this can become quite expensive.

Moderating BIND

To alleviate high costs, BIND offers the following option in the `options` section of `named.conf`:

```
options {
    ...
    dialup yes;
    heartbeat-interval 360;
    ...
};
```

When this option executes, BIND concentrates maintenance activities (which normally are spread out over time) to a short time interval, so it occurs all at once. This activity occurs once every *heartbeat interval* minute. The heartbeat interval number should be many times higher than your dial-up connection timeout. If your timeout is 15 minutes and you set your heartbeat interval to 4 hours, BIND causes as many as 6 connections in 24 hours—in other words, roughly 90 minutes of connection time per day for nothing. Shortening the timeout and increasing the heartbeat interval will help decrease this.

When set up this way, BIND still originates traffic when the following occurs:

- A user, or software, causes a lookup to be performed. This usually occurs when the user, or software, wants to speak to a machine on the outside, so the line would get connected anyway.

- When the server is master for a zone, NOTIFY requests are sent to the slaves immediately. The disconnect timeout should be long enough that the slave has time to get back to the master and transfer the zone. The necessary timeout is several minutes—for example, 3–5. In most cases, this also takes care of all necessary contact between master and slave servers with regard to refresh and retry activities. But not in all cases. Therefore, the server should be kept online for longer than the longest retry interval of your zones so no chance exists for your slave servers to expire the zone(s).

Cutting Off BIND

If BIND does not reduce its activity enough, you have other options for keeping the network connection from going up. You can cut off BIND from the Internet. However, you must still ensure that master servers are online long enough and often enough that the slave servers don't expire the zones.

Doing this is quite technical and can require passwords and triggering commands by command line, GUI, Web, or some other interface. If a user does not have the necessary expertise and access rights to perform this, the user will be unable to both cut off BIND and cut BIND back in. Working without a functioning name service can be quite frustrating, as can being called to help the person trying to get connected to the Net.

All the software solutions can be regulated in two ways. One way is to regulate them by timer. For example, you can cut off BIND at 6 p.m. and restore connectivity at 7 a.m. The second way to regulate it is by command. You could have whoever is the first to arrive at the office in the morning execute a set of commands to bring up BIND, and then have whoever is last to leave at night execute a set of commands to cut it off. You could even combine these methods so that anyone coming in early or staying late could override the timed commands and get DNS and the Internet connection up. Of all the ways to cut off BIND, I like the software solutions least. They're complex, and if they fail, you're the one who gets called to come in and fix them—usually while you're home on a Sunday afternoon watching football.

Pulling the Plug

The simplest way to cut off BIND is by simply pulling the plug—of the phone, the Ethernet connection, or the router's power supply. Disabling the connection or any other necessary equipment is similarly effective. I recommend all these methods to clients.

These methods have several advantages:

- Documenting how they work is simple.
- Everyone will understand how they work.
- Anyone can cut off BIND when they come in or leave because it's simple to understand, implement, and debug, even for non-technical staff.

Killing BIND

Killing BIND has the advantage of being quite simple, but it causes the cache to die with `named` and all the cached RRs to be lost. However, this is not a big disadvantage. To implement it, simply run, as root, `ndc stop` and `ndc start` on your nameserver.

Packet Filter Rules

Packet filtering is mainly associated with firewalls, but it can be performed by some dedicated routers, too. If your dial-up router is capable of performing packet filtering, it can stop DNS packets and thereby stop BIND from tying up your line. Filtering packets destined to the outside world on TCP or UDP port 53 makes DNS traffic incapable of reaching the dial-up interface. Some routers can perform packet filtering, as can all the free UNIX versions (the BSDs and Linux). However, I would not recommend purchasing a firewall just to stop BIND from taking your dial-up connection up. After all, you want to save money, not spend money. A commercial firewall easily can cost much more than many years of phone bills.

You must be careful when blocking traffic. If your nameserver and router are the same box, when you filter incoming traffic, any traffic originating in named itself will not be stopped. The following is an example that works with Linux 2.2:

```
# ipchains -A output -p TCP -d 0.0.0.0/0.0.0.0 53 -j REJECT
# ipchains -A output -p UDP -d 0.0.0.0/0.0.0.0 53 -j REJECT
```

This stops traffic on port 53, TCP, and UDP with any destination address. For DNS to work again, the rules must be deleted. (Instead of showing an example of this, I'll leave it as an exercise for the reader.)

Auto-Dialing

The problem, if we are to see things in this perspective, is auto-dialing. DNS causes traffic, and the auto-dial mechanism takes the line up when you want it to be down. Disabling the auto-dial function and then hanging up the line is a good solution. The way to do this is OS/appliance dependent, but I won't get into that here.

On the other hand, when in a manual dial setting, the line easily can be taken up by a forced dial command or by simply setting the interface back to auto-dialing.

IP Routing and Interfaces

Another way, which is available on all UNIX versions and routers, is to modify the routing table or disable the external interface.

The following is a simple command to disable the external interface, Ethernet, and PPP, and disable all traffic over it:

```
# ifconfig ippp0 down
```

However, this won't work if your auto-dialer takes the interface up on demand.

In addition, your ISDN line is probably the default router of your network. So, if you remove the default router, no network traffic will find its way to the ISDN line. The exact command to accomplish this will vary, but the following will usually do the trick:

```
# route del default
```

Keep in mind, though, that this won't be very effective unless you also delete all the other routes leading to the ISDN line. A routing entry for the network usually is attached directly to the ISDN line, as well. This must be removed, too.

11

DNS ON A CLOSED
NETWORK

If you are on a network that is not connected to the Internet, DNS can still be used. Depending on how complex you want your domain setup, and how autonomous any other departments that influence your network are, you might need to set up root nameservers.

In a Simple Network

The basic principle you'll rely on is that a DNS server that receives a query will answer the query if it knows the answer. Thus, by merely setting up BIND with your zone and no root.hints, you have a working DNS service your DNS clients can use. The normal root.hints file is, of course, useless inside your closed network. For redundancy, you then can set up secondary servers for your zone in the normal manner, but also without a root.hints file. In a simple scenario in a simple company, this is all you must do.

> **Harmless Error Messages**
> When you drop the root.hints file, you get errors about it being missing and messages such as sysquery: nlookup error on ?. These are all harmless and can be safely ignored.

If you're not alone on your network and other people control other parts of the network, you should probably have several zones so that each network administrator can take care of her own zone, which will help expedite things. In that case, you still might not need any rootservers as long as all your DNS servers are authoritative for all the zones in your network, they are masters or slaves for all the zones, or they have NS records for any subzones in your domains.

So, using our previous Bouvet scenario, a simple network of slaves and masters would be set up, they would all be authoritative for each other's zones, and all names would be available from all nameservers at all times.

Internal Rootservers

Internal Rootservers and the Internet

A thing you must consider is reserving the domain name you want to use with the appropriate Internet name authority. If you connect to the Internet or use it to exchange email or other documents, you—and those with whom you communicate—can use your reserved name in all contexts, eliminating any need to duct-tape together things with mismatched naming schemes. Reserving a domain is discussed in Chapter 4, "Getting a Domain."

Implementing internal rootservers is a good option if one of the following is true: Your organization is somewhat complex; you want to use several TLDs internally because your organization is international; you want to use several TLDs internally because your organization is made up of several divisions within a corporation that has separate domains; or replicating the zones around to all the DNS servers is impractical.

A Traditional Rootserver

While root nameservers are special, they are not that special. The root zone is just another zone; however, the rootservers you set up obviously do not need a `root.hints` file. Instead, they are masters and slaves for the root zone, so no hints are needed to find a rootserver.

The following is a (very basic) rootserver configuration:

```
options {
        directory "/var/named";
        allow-recursion { none; };
        notify yes;
};

zone "." {
        type master;
        file "root.zone";
};
```

Note that if the rootservers are rootservers *only*, you probably should limit recursive queries to them so they aren't used as regular nameservers. Incorrectly configuring DNS clients to use your rootservers because it seems to work can cause you headaches later.

The following is the `root.zone` file:

```
; Internal root zone for Bouvet
;
$TTL    1D
;

@                       IN SOA  @ root.penguin.bv. (
                                2000022043      ; serial
                                24H             ; refresh
                                1H              ; retry
                                4W              ; expiry
                                1H )            ; min ttl

                        NS      ns.penguin.bv.
                        NS      nic.walruss.bv.

penguin.bv.             NS      ns.penguin.bv.
                        NS      ns2.penguin.bv.

walruss.bv.             NS      nic.walruss.bv.
                        NS      ns.penguin.bv.

0.1.10.in-addr.arpa.    NS      nic.walruss.bv.
                        NS      ns.penguin.bv.

0.10.in-addr.arpa.      NS      ns.penguin.bv.
                        NS      ns2.penguin.bv.

; Glue records

ns.penguin.bv.          A       10.0.0.2
ns2.penguin.bv.         A       10.0.10.2
nic.walruss.bv.         A       10.1.0.2
```

Notice that no separate bv zone file exists, because it's unnecessary. Instead, you immediately can begin listing the nameservers you want to define. The root zone is just like any other zone in that respect, too. The maintenance overhead is low as long as the nameservers don't change addresses or names. This last point is very important. An internal DNS with delegated subdomains will break if someone running the delegated domains changes a nameserver's address without telling the rootserver administrator. I can't emphasize enough that you always should be conservative when making a decision about DNS servers. Otherwise, things won't work properly.

Stub Zones Only

One other, untraditional, way exists to accomplish this. Depending on how many zones, changes, and rootservers you have, using a *pseudo* rootserver that only holds stub zones might be beneficial. This will add administration overhead in some circumstances, though, because using a root zone enters all the pertinent data in a zone that BIND can transfer. In addition, using stub zones moves the maintenance into the configuration file. Therefore, because BIND doesn't have a configuration distribution or update mechanism, you must roll your own transfer mechanism.

The following demonstrates how you can set this up:

```
options {
        directory "/var/named";
        notify yes;
        allow-recursion { none; };
};

zone "penguin.bv" {
        type stub;
        masters { 10.0.0.2; 10.1.0.2; } ;
        file "stub/penguin.bv.zone";
};

zone "0.10.in-addr.arpa" {
        type stub;
        masters { 10.0.0.2; 10.1.0.2; };
        file "stub/10.0.zone";
};

zone "walruss.bv" {
        type stub;
        masters { 10.1.0.2; 10.0.0.2; };
        file "stub/walruss.bv.zone";
};

zone "0.1.10.in-addr.arpa" {
        type stub;
        masters { 10.1.0.2; 10.0.0.2; };
        file "stub/10.0.1.zone";
};
```

The advantage of this approach is that you will have a working root nameserver as long as the masters are capable of answering the stub queries—SOA and NS.

A Rootserver with Stub Zones

You can even accomplish this using a third method. And in some situations, this next method is the best method. If you combine a root zone with stub zones, you will not need any glue records. That's because in this method, when a zone transfer is performed, the server supplies the necessary glue records from the stub zones. In other words, the stub zone listing must occur only on the master rootserver. On the slave servers, they are unnecessary because when the root zone is transferred, it contains all the necessary data. An example follows:

```
options {
        directory "/var/named";
        notify yes;
        allow-recursion { any; };
};

zone "." {
        type master;
        file "root.zone";
};

zone "penguin.bv" {
        type stub;
        masters { 10.0.0.2; 10.1.0.2; } ;
        file "stub/penguin.bv.zone";
};

zone "0.10.in-addr.arpa" {
        type stub;
        masters { 10.0.0.2; 10.1.0.2; };
        file "stub/10.0.zone";
};

zone "walruss.bv" {
        type stub;
        masters { 10.1.0.2; 10.0.0.2; };
        file "stub/walruss.bv.zone";
};

zone "0.1.10.in-addr.arpa" {
        type stub;
        masters { 10.1.0.2; 10.0.0.2; };
        file "stub/10.0.1.zone";
};
```

The previous code ensures that the nameservers in the root zone always have updated A records. In addition, it doesn't require you to roll your own transfer mechanism for the config file.

It can still be argued, though, that the first version—a root zone file only—is simpler because any changes have to be made to only one file. On the other hand, the mixed approach requires only two files to be changed: the zone file and the configuration file. Either option will work; you just have to decide which one will work best for you.

Slave and Cache Servers

Just as with normal zones, you can (and should) set up slave servers for your root zone, as in the following:

```
zone "." {
        type slave;
        masters { 10.0.255.2; };
        file "slave/root.zone";
}
```

Please note that with the previous stub zones–only configuration, this will *not* work because the server doesn't have a root zone—it just has the information that would be in a root zone if it had one.

As with DNS on the Internet, you also can set up caching nameservers. The only difference is the root.hints file, which obviously will need to contain information relevant to your network rather than the Internet. An appropriate root.hints file can be constructed with the dig(1) command, as shown earlier in this chapter, with appropriate adjustments for your setup, of course.

The following is the code for our Bouvet scenario:

```
$ dig @10.0.255.2 ns .

; <<>> DiG 8.2 <<>> @10.0.255.2 ns .
; (1 server found)
;; res options: init recurs defnam dnsrch
;; got answer:
;; ->>HEADER<<- opcode: QUERY, status: NOERROR, id: 6
;; flags: qr aa rd ra; QUERY: 1, ANSWER: 2, AUTHORITY: 0, ADDITIONAL: 2
;; QUERY SECTION:
;;      ., type = NS, class = IN

;; ANSWER SECTION:
.                       1D IN NS        rootns.penguin.bv.
.                       1D IN NS        nic.walruss.bv.

;; ADDITIONAL SECTION:
rootns.penguin.bv.      23h59s IN A     10.0.255.2
nic.walruss.bv.         1D IN A         10.1.0.2

;; Total query time: 0 msec
;; FROM: barbar to SERVER: 10.0.255.2
;; WHEN: Sun Feb 20 14:54:35 2000
;; MSG SIZE  sent: 17  rcvd: 104
```

It is, of course, much shorter than the Internet equivalent because Bouvet has only two root-servers. As before, the output of dig can be placed directly into the root.hints file. With the stub zone–only configuration, getting a root.hints file like this automatically isn't possible.

You must write one yourself, listing your root-capable server NS and A records exactly as you would in a normal root zone.

Structuring Your DNS

The structure of your rootserver network should be planned just as if you were setting up a corporate DNS without rootservers. You should disperse your servers over your network, taking into account such things as network connectivity, latency, how links are likely to fail, and so on. This is discussed in more detail in Chapter 6, "Troubleshooting DNS."

12

INTERFACING DNS IN
PROGRAMS

Using DNS and Name lookups is really a network programming topic.
However, even though this is not a network programming book, I will
scratch the surface in this chapter to provide a starting point from which
you can further pursue this.

Different programming languages have different interfaces for resolving
hostnames. On UNIX, most have at least a binding to the standard UNIX
resolver, which is usually contained in libc. As described in Chapter 2, "DNS
in Practice," the UNIX resolver can use multiple services to attempt hostname resolution. Therefore, because it's not strictly using DNS, it is not
DNS resolving. In most cases, though, this is still what you want, and the
API will work even without the presence of DNS.

Of course, you can write software that uses the DNS protocol described in
RFC 1035 directly. The protocol, however, can take up a good amount of
time, and for most applications this would be a waste of the programmer's
time. In most cases, using the standard resolver API, or some other API provided by your OS or language, is a better solution.

The UNIX Resolver
The UNIX resolver implements a number of API calls, the most frequently
used of which are gethostbyname and gethostbyaddr. These calls are available
in most programming languages on the UNIX platform in some form.

`gethostbyname` and `gethostbyaddr`

gethostbyname and gethostbyaddr are probably the most frequently used calls in the UNIX resolver library. They work the same for both IPv4 and IPv6 and provide the basic functions of looking up the A or AAAA record of a host (gethostbyname) and looking up the PTR record of an IP address (gethostbyaddr). Complete descriptions of these calls are found in your OS man pages, as well as in network programming texts such as *UNIX Network Programming*.

The data types involved in these calls are opaque, which enables them to carry information about different addressing families—for example, IPv6 as well as IPv4 (for which they were designed) and also OSI addressing, in theory. The opaqueness of the data types makes the calls a bit difficult to use and remember, but don't let that bother you. I don't know any programmers who don't have to look up these calls in manual pages, other documentation, or previously written code. In fact, a lot of the code out there looks very similar to the code samples found in *UNIX Network Programming*.

If you want to look up the address of a host in C, the code is as follows:

```
void do_lookup(char *name)

{
  /* Look up the IP address of the host named by the variable "name" */
  struct hostent *rhost;      /* Host lookup address */
  struct in_addr addr;        /* TMP: Address for inet_ntoa */
  unsigned long inaddr;       /* IP address (IPv4 only) */

  char *ipstr;                /* IP address as a string */
  int tcp_port;               /* Port number */
  int cd;                     /* Connection descriptor */

  /* First try to convert IP number to address */
  if ((inaddr = inet_addr(name)) != INADDR_NONE) {
    ipstr=name;
  } else {
    /* Look up A (or AAAA) record of the host.  This code should work
       for any address protocol. */
    rhost = gethostbyname(name);

    /* Check return value */
    if (rhost==NULL) {
      printf("%s could not be resolved\n",name);
      return;
    }

    memcpy(&addr,rhost->h_addr,rhost->h_length);

    ipstr = inet_ntoa(addr);
  }

  printf("The address of %s is %s\n",name,ipstr);
}
```

Other Functions in the Resolver

What you find available in a random OS resolver will vary, but if you installed BIND as described in Chapter 15, "Compiling and Maintaining BIND," you will have a libresolv in /usr/local/lib, which has quite a lot of functionality. This is described in resolver (3) of your man pages. It's probably not in the OS man pages, though, so look in /usr/local/man or in the BIND distribution. I will not describe it here, but if you are interested in functions beyond gethostby*, you should look for them there.

DNS from Perl

Perl has gethostby* functions available in libc, and these are the ones most people use. The use of the gethostby* functions is documented in the perlipc man page. Because DNS lookups are (or can be) slow, the results are prime suspects for caching in a hash. The following code fragment looks up the IP address of the host named by the $host variable:

```
use Socket;

...

    # Check cache first
    if (exists($address{$host})) {
        # We know the address already
        $thataddr=$address{$host};
    } else {
        # Cache miss, get and remember.
        (my $fqdn, undef, undef, undef, $thataddr) = gethostbyname($host);
        # Hostname lookup failure?  Cache the miss.
        if (defined($fqdn)) {
            $address{$host}=$thataddr;
            $address{$fqdn}=$thataddr if $fqdn ne $host;
        } else {
            $thataddr=$address{$host}=undef;
        }
    }
    if ($thataddr) {
        print "$host resolves to ",inet_ntoa($thataddr),"\n";
    } else {
        print "$host does not resolve\n";
    }
```

This code caches answers, but the caching code does not take the TTL into account. It is not available from the API, but if the program is "alive" for a relatively short time (for hours or less), it is reasonable to ignore the TTL and use the same address throughout the lifetime of the program.

The Net::DNS Module

The module Net::DNS, written by Mike Fuhr, is available on CPAN. It provides a more complete DNS interface, including DNS UPDATE. If you are unfamiliar with CPAN, see the system Perl man pages or http://www.cpan.org/. The Net::DNS home page is at http://www.fuhr.org/~mfuhr/perldns/.

The Net::DNS module enables you to build DNS query packets by calling object methods and then sending and later analyzing the answer. The interfaces are high-level and very powerful, and the documentation is good and filled with examples. This code example is from the man page; it looks up the available records of foo.bar.com and prints any A records returned:

```
use Net::DNS;
$res = new Net::DNS::Resolver;
$query = $res->search("foo.bar.com");
if ($query) {
    foreach $rr ($query->answer) {
        next unless $rr->type eq "A";
        print $rr->address, "\n";
    }
}
else {
    print "query failed: ", $res->errorstring, "\n";
}
```

This module does not use the OS resolver at all. It uses DNS directly and parses your /etc/resolv.conf to obtain the address of your nameservers. Using this library, you also can issue non-blocking, asynchronous DNS queries. See my mresolv2 script for an example (it can be found on the perldns home page).

DNS from Python

Python also includes the gethostbyname and gethostbyaddr calls and puts them in the built-in socket module. The gethostbyname function returns a string containing the IP address of the host:

```
#!/usr/bin/python

from socket import *

...

        "Look up the IP number of the given host"
        try:
                ip = gethostbyname(host)
        except:
                print host,"does not resolve"
        else:
                print "The address of",host,"is",ip
```

Other bindings also exist for Python. Please see the vaults of Parnassus at http://www.vex.net/parnassus/. There you can find bindings for the adns library for asynchronous DNS queries, a DNS server written in Python (!), and a DNS-only interface for resolving names. The latter is not documented, but the test suite documents it quite well. The following is an example:

```python
#!/usr/bin/python

import DNS
# automatically load nameserver(s) from /etc/resolv.conf
# (works on unix - on others, YMMV)
DNS.ParseResolvConf()

r = DNS.DnsRequest(qtype='ANY')

res = r.req("www.microsoft.com",qtype='A')

# res.answers is a list of dictionaries of answers
print len(res.answers),'different A records'

# each of these has an entry for 'data', which is the result.
print map(lambda x:x['data'], res.answers)
```

DNS in Shell Scripts

Some of us still do shell scripting. Name lookups are seldom necessary in shell scripts, but sometimes you do need them. Of course, you can call Perl or some other script language that has gethostbyname (or gethostbyaddr as the case may be), but that is quite expensive. One of the easiest programs to use in shell scripts is the host program that is part of the BIND distribution. Unfortunately, it is not always installed. The reason host is the easiest to use is that its output format is the simplest. Dig and nslookup all provide copious output, most of which is irrelevant if you just want the address of a machine.

With PPP, you usually have an ip-up script, which is run when the PPP interface is configured and up. It is passed a number of parameters, such as the interface name, the device name, the uplink, and your own IP number. To obtain the name belonging to the address you have been assigned, use the following:

```ksh
#!/bin/ksh
interface="$1"
device="$2"
speed="$3"
myip="$4"
upip="$5"

...

$myname = $(host $myip | awk '/name/i { print $(NF) }')
```

This should work with any Korn shell, Bash, and simple adaptations in standard Bourne shells as well. The problem with host is that some variants are available that have different output formats. This ip-up script is the best choice for performing DNS updates when you're getting dynamic addresses from your ISP.

Using Dig or nslookup to look up things in general can get tricky. Dig and nslookup both print many similar lines of output during a normal query:

```
$ nslookup www.amazon.com
Server:   smp.linpro.no
Address:  195.0.166.3


Name:     www.amazon.com
Address:  208.202.218.15
```

Because nslookup is most likely to be available on any given host, it is preferable to Dig (if only for that reason). Detecting errors with nslookup is a bit complicated, however. One way to do this is to count how many Address: lines exist in the output. Another is to note the error message format. In the versions of nslookup I know, error messages always start in ***:

```
address=$(nslookup $host 2>&1 | awk '
               /^Address:/ { a=$(NF); }
               /\*\*\*/    { exit 1; }
               END         { print a; }')
    case $address in
        '') echo error looking up $host;;
        *)  echo $host has address $address;;
    esac
```

The approach is to exit at once if an error message of any kind occurs, and otherwise to print the contents of the last Address: line when the script terminates. In my personal opinion, however, Dig is better.

The Dig output format is quite machine friendly, and little reason should exist for any vendor to change it. Looking for the NOERROR string in its output to check for errors is easy, and adding +pfmin to the command line will take care of trimming down the output amount:

```
$ dig www.amazon.com +pfmin
;; res options: init recurs defnam dnsrch
;; got answer:
;; ->>HEADER<<- opcode: QUERY, status: NOERROR, id: 49781
;; QUERY: 1, ANSWER: 1, AUTHORITY: 2, ADDITIONAL: 2
;; QUERY SECTION:
;;      www.amazon.com, type = A, class = IN

;; ANSWER SECTION:
www.amazon.com.         53S IN A        208.216.182.15
```

This output format reduces the work amount to something acceptable, compared to the following default Dig output format:

```
address=$(dig $host +pfmin 2>/dev/null | awk '
             /IN A/ { print $(NF); exit 0; }
             /NOERROR/ { next; }
             /status:/ { exit 1; }')
    case $address in
        '') echo error looking up $host;;
        *)  echo $host has address $address;;
    esac
```

Asynchronous Resolving

The standard UNIX resolver is *synchronous*, which means it blocks the calling program until the name has been resolved. You make the call, the library issues the DNS query, and any other queries to configured name services such as NIS wait for the reply and then return to your program. This can lead to your application being blocked for several seconds. Depending on the application, this might or might not be acceptable. Under UNIX, though, it's not too hard to find a way around this restriction and implement non-blocking DNS. Some applications, such as Netscape, fork a separate process to perform resolving and use simple IPC mechanisms to communicate with it. Under various flavors of UNIX, the ways to accomplish this with processes, threads, message queues, pipes, shared memory, and semaphores are endless. But of course, you also can use a library that provides asynchronous name lookups.

Several such libraries are available under various licenses. I have not personally programmed with any of these libraries, so apply liberal amounts of your own discretion.

The Perl Net::DNS module is capable of supporting asynchronous requests. See the section "The Net::DNS Module" earlier in this chapter for more information.

GNU adns

GNU adns, written by Ian Jackson and Tony Finch, is in beta as of May 2000. Its authors describe it as "Advanced, easy to use, asynchronous-capable DNS client library and utilities." It not only provides asynchronous DNS, but it also extends beyond the capabilities of the standard UNIX resolver to provide access to all different record types and things such as the TTL of the returned record.

The library home page is at http://www.chiark.greenend.org.uk/~ian/adns/. It is available for FTP from its home site at ftp://ftp.chiark.greenend.org.uk/users/ian/adns/ and also from GNU FTP archives, such as ftp://ftp.gnu.org/gnu/adns/. It is licensed under the GNU GPL and (with some restrictions) the LGPL. These licenses might or might not be compatible with the software you are developing, depending on your licensing. Please read the COPYING file in the distribution carefully if you're not familiar with the GPL and LGPL.

The library is not currently documented except in its header file.

arlib

arlib is part of the BIND contrib bundle, so if you have a complete BIND tar ball, you'll find it there. If not, you will find it at the ISC FTP site (see Chapters 2 and 15). It was designed to be simple so as to attract few bugs and has succeeded in that respect. Because it was written in 1992, it has hardly been maintained; Darren Reed, the author, reports that there have been "no bugs to maintain."

The library is freely available, but you must ask the author for permission to distribute it as part of anything you develop. Reed reports that he has never said no to anyone, but expressly forbids its use in GPLed software. You will find his email address in the software.

In the way of documentation, the bundle includes a pretty complete code sample illustrating its use.

DNScache Library

D.J. Bernstein, the man behind the well-known MTA qmail, has also committed DNScache—a recursive DNS cache server. It includes a resolver library suitable for use in asynchronous resolver implementations. The facilities are basic but perhaps good enough. The DNScache home page is at `http://cr.yp.to/dnscache.html`, and the software is available from there.

13

RESOURCE RECORDS

A lot of Resource Records are documented in RFCs. Finding a definition and user guidelines can be quite a job. DNS was first defined in RFC 882 and RFC 883, which were later updated by RFC 973. These again were later obsoleted by RFC 1034 and RFC 1035 and further expanded in several other RFCs. Please see Appendix B, "Bibliography," for further details about these documents. DNS is a living specification and a very nice database. Changes will occur, though, because people will want to adapt DNS to their own uses. Some of the records listed in this chapter illustrate this.

This chapter contains a lot of general syntax descriptions. In these, all the # suffixed bits are numbers. Also, in all the examples, the record class and TTL specifiers are omitted.

RRs in Current Use

A (Address)

Defined in RFC 1035, section 3.4.1:

```
domainname      A 32-bit-ip-address
```

This defines the IP version 4 Internet address of the domain name. The IP address is written in the usual dotted quad format—for example, 192.168.55.2.

AAAA (IPv6 Address)

Defined in RFC 1886:

```
domainname      A 128-bit-IPv6-address
```

IP version 6 uses 128-bit addresses, which is a lot more bits than in the version of IP currently in use, version 4. With IPv6, reverse lookups are performed in the ip6.int domain instead of in-addr.arpa. In addition, a dot exists between each nibble instead of between each octet, and the nibbles are in reverse order of course.

ATMA (ATM Address)

This record is not defined in any RFC and is not implemented in BIND. It is defined in "ATM Name System Specification Version 1.0." It is, however, present in the Windows 2000 DNS server implementation.

CNAME (Canonical Name of an Alias)

Defined in RFC 1035, section 3.3.1:

```
domainname      CNAME canonical-name
```

The given domain name is an alias for the given canonical name. The domain name can't have any other records associated with it. Earlier, this restriction was not enforced by BIND, so a backward-compatibility setting exists in named.conf:

```
options {
        ...
        multiple-cnames yes-or-no;
        ...
}
```

Additionally MX, NS, and SOA records can't refer to CNAMEs. If they do, the results are "undefined." It might work, it might not work, or it might work for some of the people some of the time. I would not try my luck with it, though.

HINFO (Host Information)

Defined in RFC 1035, section 3.3.2:

```
domainname      HINFO   cpu     os
```

Some people consider host information obsolete, or at least redundant. Both the CPU and OS field must be one word, or quoted. A dated list (anno 1994) of standard CPU names (machine names) and OS names (system names) can be found in RFC 1700. Of course, it may well be considered a security risk to give away this information.

MX (Mail Exchanger)

Defined in RFC 1035, section 3.3.9. Introduced in RFC 973 and defined in RFC 974:

```
domainname    MX preference# mail-server
```

This RR indicates that the given mail server is supposed to handle the mail destined to the given domain name. If multiple MX records with different preference levels exist, the *mail transfer agent (MTA)* tries to deliver to the mail server given the lowest preference value. If it fails, each mail server sorted by preference is tried. In my experience, seldom does any problem occur with MX records; they usually are quite simple. If you do have a mail problem, the problem usually lies in the MTA or its operator, both of which are complex.

The MX record obsoleted the MD and MF records.

NS (Authoritative Nameserver)

Defined in RFC 1035, section 3.3.11:

```
domainname    NS nameserver
```

Specifies the nameserver for the given domain. The nameserver should resolve directly to an address record, not a CNAME.

NSAP

Defined in RFC 1706:

```
domainname    NSAP nsap-address#
```

This record was introduced to support the deployment of CLNP, a OSI connectionless protocol on the Internet. A NSAP is the address of an OSI protocol/transport/connection endpoint. In RFC 1183, an additional record, NSAP_PTR, was defined to accommodate reverse lookups. But in RFC 1706 straight PTR records are used for this. Don't worry if you don't know what OSI is. OSI is on the way out.

PTR (Pointer to Other Name)

Defined in RFC 1035, section 3.3.12:

```
domainname    PTR     name
```

Although this is usually used for reverse lookup zones, it is really meant as an alias mechanism. It's not useful for much else than reverse zones, though. CNAMEs should be used in forward zones. The given domain name, probably in the in-addr.arpa domain, encodes an IP address, or in the classless-delegation case, something a bit more complex than that. The PTR record provides the name belonging to the address. One of the differences between a PTR and CNAME record is that if the nameserver queried knows the address of the host to which the CNAME record points, it will be returned as well, in the additional section of the query (see dig output several places in this book). This will not, normally, happen for a PTR record.

PX (X.400 Mapping)

Defined in RFC 2163:

```
domainname    PX type  X400-address
```

The domain name is an X.400 address in domain format. The X.400 address returned is the equivalent in X.400 format. This is (meant to be) used for mail routing between Internet and X.400 email. X.400 is the OSI email standard.

RP (Responsible Person)

Defined in RFC 1183, section 2.2:

```
domainname    RP mbox txt-domainname
```

For the resource named by the domain name, the responsible person can be reached by mail at the given mailbox. The mailbox address is in the same format as the contact field of the SOA record: *address.host.domain*, with a . (period) instead of the @ (at sign). *txt-domainname* names a TXT record with further information about the person, such as full name, telephone number, and so forth. If no TXT record is defined, specify . (the root domain name).

This record is a good idea, but not very widely used. Of course, publishing email addresses in DNS might not be a good idea in these days of spam.

RT (Route Through)

Defined in RFC 1183, section 3.3:

```
domainname    RT preference# host
```

The specified host will act as an intermediate (router) in reaching the named host. The preference field works as in the MX record. See the X25 record for more information. This is not in wide use.

SOA (Start Of Authority)

Defined in RFC 1035, section 3.3.13:

```
domainname    SOA origin-host contact (
              serial#
              refresh#
```

```
            retry#
            expire#
            minimum#)
```

The SOA record is discussed in Chapter 3, "Maintenance and Enhancements." *origin-host* does not have to be a CNAME.

SRV (Service Locator)

Defined in RFC 2052:

```
 domainname     SRV priority# weight# port# host
```

The SRV record is a very powerful service location facility that went from a good idea to being implemented and used with Windows 2000. Windows 2000 uses SRV records extensively for its active directory service. It could, and should, be used for many other things, too. It is powerful enough to replace the MX and KX records, for example. However, this is not planned.

Using this record, a Web client looking for a server from which to retrieve http://www.penguin.bv/ would look up the SRV record of http.tcp.www.penguin.bv. Likewise for http://penguin.bv/, it would look up the SRV record of http.tcp.penguin.bv. http is the service or protocol name, and tcp is the transport protocol wanted. The rest is the domain name with which the service is associated, the host part of the URL. For mail service in the penguin.bv domain, you would construct a smtp.tcp.penguin.bv SRV record to define the mail server. Note that as of this writing (spring 2000), no HTTP clients or MTAs use the SRV record to find servers, nor is this use planned.

The priority field works as with the MX record, giving rankings to the servers—in which the lowest values are the preferred servers. The weight field is used for a weighted random selection of which server to use. The client is required to select a random SRV record among those returned. This provides a rudimentary load distribution mechanism, but with more control than the current A records in the round robin mechanism BIND offers. The weight can be used to indicate the relative power of each server, giving each server the load it can handle. Statistically, the port field is interesting because it provides the port number on the server host to contact. This port number has usually been specified in RFCs and /etc/services.

When we switch to SRV records, the port numbers used for various services will (or can) become more of a local policy matter than a centralized matter for IANA to decide. Therefore, the used port numbers can be published in DNS instead of in the assigned numbers RFC (STD 2, RFC 1700). I doubt that we will stop using assigned numbers for protocols—in a firewall context, we're dependent on those numbers to be fixed to provide holes or other mechanisms that let traffic through the firewall.

The host must be a hostname, not an IP number. However, the left side of the record is not strictly a domain name; it's a label. Because it's a label, the restrictions on characters used do not really apply to it. However, things are much less chaotic when these labels follow the restrictions for domain names.

TXT (Text Information)

Defined in RFC 1035, section 3.3.14:

```
domainname    TXT "text"
```

This record carries free format text information. No syntax or structure is imposed, and the record can be used for anything you desire. Don't expect to use it as a general database storage mechanism, though. BIND will restrict you to about 2K of data, although DNS implementations exist that don't have this restriction. Also DNS over UDP is restricted to replies of 512 bytes. If the reply string is truncated because of this restriction, a new query (and answer) must be sent using a TCP connection.

If you want a distributed database, try using LDAP or some other directory service. Or, if you must use DNS, use the SINK record (it might finally get us the kitchen sink, which DNS has been without for so long), which is defined for such purposes. However, it is unimplemented at this time.

X25 (X25 Routing Information)

Defined in RFC 1183, section 3.1:

```
domainname    X25    PSDN-address#
```

This record is for routing IP over X25 or X25 over IP (XOI). Cisco supports its use for the latter. It was introduced, together with the ISDN and RT records, in RFC 1183 under the heading "Route Binding." It is apparently meant to be used for IP over X25 over ISDN. The ISDN, RT, and X25 records show which circuits the packets should be routed over. (I'm not well versed in X.25 and should not comment further.)

Experimental RRs

Because DNS is ubiquitous, it is a handy mechanism for many things. Experimental RRs represent suggested uses of DNS, and might make it as an Internet standard in the future. If more appropriate or elegant ways to implement the given mechanisms are developed, they will probably be preferred to the existing RRs.

AFSDB (AFS Database Location)

Defined in RFC 1183:

```
domainname    AFSDB subtype# host
```

The AFSDB record is used for cross-site AFS and DCE/NCA network filesystem mounting. Subtype 1 is used for AFS, and subtype 2 is used for DCE. If you use the AFS or DCE filesystem, the AFSDB record is documented in the accompanying documents.

ISDN

Defined in RFC 1183, section 3.2:

```
domainname    ISDN ISDN-address# sub-address#
```

This RR defines a telephone number and was meant to be used in connection with the X25 record for WAN routing over ISDN/X25 circuits. See the description of the X25 record for more information.

KEY (Public Key)

Defined in RFC 2065.

See the SIG record type.

LOC (Location)

Defined in RFC 1876.

This record is meant to provide DNS with the tool to replace UUCP maps. The LOC record holds a geographical position in latitude, longitude, and altitude, as well as the size of the named entity. The sole use of this record is to draw maps. It would, if employed, enable automatic tools to draw geographically as well as topologically correct maps. I believe that GPS receivers must be more widespread before this record sees wide employment. See also the GPOS record type.

Another proposed name for this record type was ICBM, because of the ease with which high-precision LOC records can be used to automate strategic nuclear attacks.

KX (Key Exchange)

Defined in RFC 2230:

```
domainname    KX preference# host
```

This record defines a key server to be used with IPSEC. It is designed to be used with only DNS-SEC. Otherwise, no chain of trust exists to ensure the authenticity of the retrieved KX record, which would make the information worthless—at least in a security context. The preference field has the same meaning as in the MX record. In addition, the host field must be a hostname that refers to a CNAME, A, or AAAA record.

NULL

Defined in RFC 1035, section 3.3.10.

NULL records are not allowed in zone files, so just forget about them. A NULL record can contain up to 65,536 octets of anything, or nothing.

NAPTR (Name Authority Pointer)

Defined in RFC 2168.

The fact that URLs are not time-resistant is something most of us know only too well. This RFC defines a scheme to resolve URNs, which are similar to URLs but can resist time, in theory. These, combined with SRV records, are part of the framework that will help keep URNs (if they come into use) time resistant.

NXT (Next Valid Name)

Defined in RFC 2065.

See the SIG record type.

SIG (Signature)

Defined in RFC 2065.

Realizing how important and unprotected DNS and the data in DNS is, RFC 2065 suggests security mechanisms for DNS, called DNS-SEC. DNS-SEC defines the facilities necessary to authenticate retrieved data and to verify that DNS answers have not been altered in transit. Implementation of this is being worked on in BIND 9, and it could be the beginning of the end of the security problems DNS has if it becomes widely implemented and employed.

The SIG record provides a crypto signature for each record in a zone. The NXT record would then provide the name of the next record in the zone. By traversing the zone using the NXT records, each signed, you can verify the non-existence of a name in a zone. This provides a secure, authenticated way to retrieve RRs as well as find out that a hostname does not exist in a zone, which are equally significant tasks.

SINK (The Kitchen Sink Record)

Defined in `http://www.ietf.org/internet-drafts/draft-ietf-dnsind-kitchen-sink-02.txt`, which expired in March 2000.

This proposed record specifically enables databases/structured storage (mis)using DNS. The TXT record has been suggested for general storage many times, but the proposals have all disappeared without a trace. Time will tell how the SINK RR fares.

Obsolete RRs

Because DNS is ubiquitous, it is very tempting to use it for many things. Several uses have been suggested, and the following are those uses that have already proven unsuitable.

EID (Endpoint Identifier)

Defined in an Internet Draft, expired as of April 1996.

See the NIMROD record type for further information.

GPOS (Geographical Position)

Defined in RFC 1712.

The RFC has been withdrawn, and the LOC (location) record was defined in RFC 1876. The GPOS record lacks the size and precision fields of the LOC record.

ISDN (ISDN Address)

Defined in RFC 1183, section 3.1.

The ISDN, X25, and RT RRs were meant to hold routing information. They are classified as experimental. In RFC 1183, they appear under the heading "Route Binding." It does not appear to be in use and is not documented in anything but the RFC.

MB (Mailbox)

Defined in RFC 1035:

```
domainname     MB host
```

The named host holds the mailbox named by the domain name. See the MG description for more information.

MD (Mail Destination)

Defined in RFC 1035, section 3.3.4. See RFC 883 for the full, now historical, description:

```
domainname     MD host
```

This record used to name hosts with mail agents willing to handle and deliver mail for the domain. This, along with the MF record, was replaced by the MX record. An MTA would issue a MAILA query and receive the MF and MD records associated with the specified name. As described in RFC 973, the MF and MD records had several problems, including problems with caching. A special query, MAILA, was used to retrieve both MD and MF records.

Unfortunately, cached MD and MF records could originate with MD or MF queries, so the cache server could not know whether it had the complete set of MD and MF records when a MAILA query arrived. Additionally, the mail sender does not need to know whether the agent will forward or deliver the mail so the distinction is redundant.

MF (Mail Forwarder 883)

Defined in RFC 1035, section 3.3.4:

```
domainname    MF host
```

This record defined a host willing to store and forward mail to the named domain, in case the MD host was unavailable. See the MD record for more information.

MG (Mail Group Member)

Defined in RFC 1035:

```
domainname    MG mgname
```

The MG, MR, and MB records make a triad of records described under the heading "Mailbox biding" in RFC 883. They are not really documented in RFC 1035. The MTA would issue a MAILB query. The query could fail, in which case a MAILA query would be issued to find MD and MF records (see the previous description of the MD record). If an MR record was returned, the mailbox name was rewritten as specified by the MR record. If an MB record was retrieved, mail delivery to the named host proceeded. If MG RRs were returned, each mailbox named received a copy of the mail.

The MAILB query had the same problems with caching as the MAILA query, which is explained in the MD RR description and which contributed to replacing MD and MF with the MX RR. These records are not in any wide use and are not implemented by any of the major UNIX-based MTAs. As with the MINFO record, they are all officially classified as experimental, but I'm risking calling them obsolete.

MINFO (Mailbox or Mail-List Info)

Defined in RFC 1035:

```
domainname    MINFO rmailbx emailbx
```

This record specifies additional information about the mailing list named by the domain name—in particular, the request (or administrative) mailbox and the error mailbox. This record is officially marked as experimental, but it is not used or implemented by any mail user agent (MUA) I know or by any popular MTA. It has been ignored since 1984, and the advent of SPAM makes wide implementation unlikely, so I'll risk calling it obsolete. You need to read RFC 883 to find a proper description of this RR.

MR (Mail Rename)

Defined in RFC 1035:

```
domainname    MR mailbox
```

Specifies that the mailbox named by the domain name should be replaced by the mailbox named by the record. See the description of the MG record for further explanation.

NIMLOC (NIMROD Locator)

Defined in an Internet Draft, expired as of April 1996.

NIMROD is a Internet routing architecture. The two RRs proposed in the Internet Draft are not even implemented in BIND. The document is not easily understandable without knowledge of NIMROD.

NSAP_PTR (NSAP Variant of PTR Record)

Defined in RFC 1183.

This was meant to be used for reverse lookups of NSAP addresses. In RFC 1706 this was discontinued and the PTR record used instead.

WKS (Well Known Service)

Defined in RFC 1035:

```
domainname    WKS 32-bit-ip-address protocol service-list
```

This record was used to publish the services a host offered. This was before the practice of giving hosts names or aliases based on their function became widespread (such as one single penguin.bv host answering to both the names ns.penguin.bv and ftp.penguin.bv). Therefore, by examining the WKS records of a zone, you could, in theory, locate the FTP server. No one ever did that, though, and the record fell into disuse. The new SRV RR now enables service location in a much more sensible and powerful manner.

The protocol field must be either TCP or UDP. The service list must be a list of IANA approved TCP or UDP services, which are the services listed in your /etc/services file. The official list is found in the latest "Assigned Numbers" document, known as STD 2. Currently that corresponds to RFC 1700.

PART III

ABOUT BIND

14   A Guide to BIND

15   Compiling and Maintaining BIND

16   BIND 9

17   Miscellany

14

A GUIDE TO BIND 4

BIND 4 is a dead-end, as far as development goes. The ISC is not developing it, and the only possible reason to run it is that some policy, such as "use only vendor supported software," forces you to use a UNIX-vendor supplied version of BIND. In many cases, this means you must use BIND 4. That doesn't necessarily completely limit you to BIND 4, though, because the ISC sells support contracts to BIND users, and you can, in fact, have a vendor-supported BIND 8. See the site at http://www.isc.org/ for more information. If that still is not enough to upgrade to BIND 8, be aware that BIND 4 has security problems that your OS vendor might or might not have done anything to fix in the version you have. (Actually, some people claim that BIND 4.9.7 is more secure than BIND 8. However, there has never been any remote root exploit for BIND 4.9.7, whereas for noncurrent versions of BIND 8, root exploits do exist. For this reason, OpenBSD still ships with BIND 4.9.7. BIND 4.9.7 suffers from some other problems with security impact, though—mainly cache poisoning.) Several UNIX vendor versions of BIND 4 are fixed and patched in some respects, though, so they do not correspond to the information you might find on the Internet about problems with the same version of ISC BIND 4. If you install all available BIND/named and libc/NIS/YP/resolver and related patches from your vendor, it should be reasonably safe.

The latest release of BIND 4 from the ISC is BIND 4.9.7, which was released after BIND 8.1. In it, the ISC fixed bugs (including one important security bug) and memory leaks. Your UNIX-vendor BIND might be based on an older version than that. Still, as mentioned, they might have provided analogous fixes in their patch sets for your UNIX. You should make sure that you install any BIND- and resolver-related (possibly inside libc) patches your vendor supplies. And then hope your vendor fixed all the important problems.

Migrating from BIND 4 to BIND 8

If you have a BIND 4 installation you want to migrate to BIND 8, you might encounter some problems when you attempt the migration. Converting a server from BIND 4 to 8 should not be done without first testing everything under BIND 8; however, a quick test should be sufficient, and the problems should be obvious.

Configuration File Conversion

The zone files BIND 4 uses are identical to BIND 8 zone files, except for the $TTL. As of BIND 8.2.2, you don't have to have $TTLs in your zone files, but you will get several warnings if you don't have them.

The configuration file format is very different, though. Luckily, BIND 8 includes a shell script that converts your `named.boot` file to the `named.conf` file BIND 8 wants. The script is called `named-bootconf` and is installed in the same directory in which named is installed. This `named-bootconf` script is also in the source hierarchy—in the directory called src/bin/named-bootconf. After generating a good `named.conf` file, the only thing left to do is start BIND 8, see which zones are rejected (and for what reasons), and fix all the errors and warnings.

`named-bootconf` is a shell script in BIND 8.2.2P5. It used to be a Perl script, and it is still included in the source tar file in the src/bin/named-bootconf/Grot. Try that if the shell script gives you problems.

CNAME

BIND 8 enforces the rules for CNAME use set forth in the DNS RFCs, which was not enforced in BIND 4. The effect is that users, unwittingly we must assume, have violated the rules. These restrictions, and how to disable them, are detailed in Chapter 3, "Maintenance and Enhancements."

Query Source

BIND 4 uses port 53 to send its queries. A number of firewalls know this, and when rules for letting DNS traffic through are installed, the rules specify source port 53. In contrast, BIND 8 does not use port 53 as the source address of queries unless you specify this in `named.conf`:

```
options {
    ...
    query-source address * port 53;
    ...
};
```

Name Checking

Versions of BIND prior to 4.9.4 perform no checking of the characters used in hostnames. On the other hand, in all BINDs from 4.9.4 on, checking is done. By default, BIND 8 rejects any master zones that do not pass muster and issues warnings about suspect slave zones. You can modify this reaction with the check-names option. The defaults is as follows:

```
options {
    ...
    check-names master fail;
    check-names slave warn;
    check-names response ignore;
    ...
};
```

Setting master to warn cures the immediate problem, but you really should work out a real solution to the problem.

ndc in BIND 4

The very handy ndc program was not added until BIND 4.9.3-beta10, and then it was a shell script. Not all vendors included ndc in their UNIX, so even if your BIND is newer than that, you might not have it. Because it is a relatively simple shell script, you easily can install it by getting the BIND 4.9.7 package and extracting and installing it manually on your DNS servers. A number of %VARIABLE% strings are inside the script; these values can be found in the named/Makefile file. Note that the ndc program in BIND 8 is very different from the one in BIND 4, but it should work because BIND 4 and 8 have at least one signaling mechanism in common—namely, signals such as those sent with the kill shell command.

Configuring BIND 4

Another thing you will find in the 4.9.7 tar ball (it is in the BIND 8 distribution as well) is the BIND Operations Guide (BOG), which might—or might not—be included with your vendor BIND. The BOG is a very complete DNS manual; although it is somewhat abrupt about using new terms and is just a bit dated.

BIND 4 does not have the wealth of configurability that BIND 8 does; it does, however, have more possibilities than you can usually find in the named man page. Zone files used by BIND 4 are identical to the zone files used by BIND 8, except for the $TTL directive that BIND 4 does not support. A BIND 4 slave with a BIND 8 master, which uses $TTL, will give TTL values that are inconsistent with what the BIND 8 master does, if the $TTL value differs from the TTL given in the SOA record. Some registrar zone test scripts have been known to decline validating new zones for this reason.

Zones

The BIND 4 configuration file, which is a flat text file, is called `named.boot`. Each line starts with a keyword, followed by arguments and values. This is a simple file, corresponding roughly to the examples in Chapter 2, "DNS in Practice." Here is an example:

```
directory       /var/named
cache           .                               root.hints
primary         0.0.127.in-addr.arpa            pz/127.0.0
secondary       penguin.bv          192.168.55.2    sz/penguin.bv
secondary       55.168.55.in-addr.arpa 192.168.55.2 sz/192.168.55
stub            walruss.bv          10.1.0.2        sz/walruss.bv
```

As you can see from this example, no quotes are used here. The `directory` line controls in which directory BIND looks for files. The `cache` line is similar to the root hints zone—notice that a dot is in there. The `primary` line has three fields: the keyword, zone name, and zone filename. These are similar to the zones of type master. The `secondary` lines are similar to zones of type slave and have four fields: the keyword, zone name, and as many master IP numbers as you want. The last word on the `secondary` line should be the name of the zone file, which should start with an alphabetic character, not a number, so BIND can tell it from the master IP numbers. `stub` lines have the same format and work the same way as zones of type stub in BIND 8.

Glue Fetching

Glue fetching can cause cache poisoning and is time-consuming. You can disable it with the following command:

```
options         no-fetch-glue
```

If you need the glue for specific zones, you might be better off turning off glue fetching and using the stub zone directive previously described instead.

Forwarders

Forwarding provides the same capabilities as in BIND 8. Here's its syntax:

```
forwarders      10.1.0.2 192.168.55.2
options         forward-only
```

Without the `forward-only` option, it acts as BIND 8's `forward-first`. Old versions of BIND 4 don't understand the `forward-only` option; instead, they implement the following slave directive, which is synonymous:

```
slave
```

This has nothing to do with the slave zones of BIND 8; this only controls forwarding.

Recursive Servers

In BIND 8, you can elect for whom you want to be a recursive server. BIND 4 either is recursive or is not—it can't be controlled with ACLs:

```
options        no-recursion
```

Query Logging

In BIND 8 you can log queries, but only to a file, not via syslogd at all. This is because any server with more than a few clients causes a lot of logging, which bogs down the syslog facility. BIND 4, though, supports query logging only through syslog. So, if you turn it on, expect your syslogd to increase its CPU usage. Here is its syntax:

```
options        query-log
```

Other ways to enable logging are by starting `named` with the `-q` switch, and by sending it the `SIGWINCH` signal with the `kill` command. Please note that this uses a lot of disk space. And I do mean *a lot*, even for a very small server with few clients. Be sure you watch your disk the first few times you try this. According to Murphy's law, it will fill up and cause things to go wrong the moment you look away.

Zone Transfers

You cannot limit who gets to perform zone transfers from you on a zone-by-zone basis—only one access list exists for all zones:

```
xfrnets        172.16.25.66                    ; Illegal
xfrnets        172.16.0.0                      ; Legal, net
xfrnets        172.16.25.66&255.255.255.255    ; Legal, host
```

The interesting part of the previous code is that BIND knows which network class the IP number is in and limits the zone transfer not to the given IP number, but to the implied network. Which class a network has is implied by the first octet in the address. The range 1–127 are A networks and have an implied subnet mask of 255.0.0.0. Networks 128–191 are B networks with a 255.255.0.0 subnet mask. Finally, networks 191–223 are C networks with 255.255.255.0 as the subnet mask. 172.16.25.66 then is a class B network, but BIND requires that you write the host part of the address as 0s, so the first line is illegal. The second line matches

172.16.0.0/255.255.0.0 because 172 networks are B networks. To match a single host, or a classless network, you can specify the mask using the syntax in the third line. (Be sure you don't put a space before or after the ampersand [&].)

This option was called tcplist for a short while. It is still a synonym.

Resource Limits

BIND 4 implements very few, but important, resource limits. All these are 1:1 with the corresponding BIND 8 options:

```
limit           datasize             64m
limit           files                1024
limit           transfers-in         10
limit           transfers-per-ns      2
```

BIND will die, or just act strangely, when the data size and file limits are exceeded; therefore, you probably should raise the limits from the OS defaults. Whether data size and file limits are implemented, and adjustable, is dependent on your OS and the port of BIND to it. The Bourne shell command ulimit -a and the C shell command limit show the limits in force on your OS.

The values shown for limiting zone transfers are the default values. In old versions of BIND 4, the max-fetch directive was used instead of the transfers-in limit:

```
max-fetch      10
```

Address Sorting

BIND 4 has a feature called *address sorting*. When a host has two A records, BIND tries to find out which record is best for the querying party to use, and makes sure that this is the first record in the answer. This feature still exists in BIND 8, but not in the same manner. And in cases in which several A records exist, their order is now randomized, or round-robined, by default. As described in Chapter 3, this can serve as a load distribution mechanism.

BIND easily can make the wrong decision about which address is best, so what BIND thinks can be overridden with the sortlist directive. It has the same syntax as the xfrnets directive, and the same knowledge of network classes:

```
sortlist        10.10.86.0&255.255.255.0
sortlist        192.168.24.0
```

Any address appearing in the sort list is sorted before any address not appearing in the sort list. In some ways, this is worse than what BIND 4 does by default because no way is available to take the source address of the query into account. sortlist makes the sorting static.

In any case, sortlist is potentially useless—the resolver that receives the answer can process the answer in any order it wants. If the resolver needs address sorting, it should do it itself because it has a better chance of knowing its local network topology than the resolver, which might draw incorrect conclusions based on the data available to it. Additionally, an optimal answer today is not optimal tomorrow. The BOG (anno 1993) largely concludes that address sorting should be smarter than it is, but it is probably best left to a device other than the DNS server. Other documentation calls it "useless" outright. In short, you might not want to use, or rely on, this feature. In BIND 8, the answer order is random instead.

A newer use for this feature, and the sort lists, in BIND 4 is that BIND tries to guess which nameserver is closer if several are available to ask. BIND 8 and 9 are switching to measuring the Round Trip Time (RTT) for queries and asking the server with the better RTT record.

Bogus Nameservers

As described in Chapter 8, "Security Concerns," you might not want to use some nameservers. In addition, because the black hole feature is not present in BIND 8, you at least should list the addresses the AUS-CERT advisory discussed in Chapter 8 as bogus. This will enable you to ensure that your server can't be spoofed by those addresses. This is achieved with the bogusns directive, which has the same syntax as xfrnets:

```
bogusns 0.0.0.0&255.0.0.0       ; Null address
bogusns 1.0.0.0&255.0.0.0       ; IANA reserved, popular fakes
bogusns 2.0.0.0&255.0.0.0
bogusns 192.0.2.0&255.255.255.0 ; Test address
bogusns 224.0.0.0&224.0.0.0     ; Multicast addresses

; These may be used internally in your organization, remove them if so.
bogusns 10.0.0.0&255.0.0.0
bogusns 172.16.0.0&255.240.0.0
bogusns 192.168.0.0&255.255.0.0
```

These servers will not be queried, and the answers they might supply would not be used anyway. As with BIND 8, zones for which any real servers that bogusns lists as authoritative will not be reachable. They will not be queried—no matter how authoritative they are—and the domains they serve will not resolve for you. Therefore, use bogusns with care.

Inverse Query

Ancient DNS specified an IQUERY query. It is no longer supported by default, and according to the documentation, only poorly written software ever used it and for no good purpose. BIND 4 can fake IQUERY answers:

```
options fake-iquery
```

Query Domain

The `domain` directive is supported by some very old BIND 4s. If queries for non-FQDN names are made, BIND appends the specified domain to the queried name and tries to resolve it:

```
domain berkeley.edu
```

For example, queries for `ucbvax` would be changed to `ucbvax.berkeley.edu` and then resolved. This feature is now in the resolver where it belongs and is controlled with the `search` and `domain` directives in `resolv.conf`.

Name Checking

BIND 4.9.4 introduced name checking, enforcing the restrictions on which characters can be used in names. This causes some surprises, though—most notably, the slash (/) and underscore (_) are not allowed. Various levels of checking are performed on different types of data. Here are the defaults:

```
check-names primary fail
check-names secondary warn
check-names response ignore
```

If your primary zones contain any illegal names, you can override the primary default—setting it to warn or ignore—and fix it as time allows. See Chapter 17, "Miscellany," for more information about `check-names`.

Miscellaneous

Bind 4 has some additional features. The following sections describe them.

Debugging

Starting `named` with the `-d` command-line option or running `ndc debug` turns on debugging output. If you don't have ndc, sending SIGUSR1 to increment the debug level also accomplishes this. By default, this is written to `/usr/tmp/named.run`. This in addition to, or in place of, query logging can help you figure out whether someone is sending you bogus information or bombarding you with queries, slowing down your system. However, using just query logging might be sufficient. Sending SIGUSR2 disables debugging.

Sending SIGINT to `named` is analogous to the `ndc dumpdb` command. It dumps the entire database and cache contents to a file, probably called `/var/tmp/named_dump.db`. This file then enables you to examine whether the zone data was loaded correctly and whether anything odd is in the cache.

Reloading Zones

If you don't have the ndc program, you can cause a named.boot and zone reload by sending named a SIGHUP. This also forces SOA queries, for serial number comparison, to the master servers. Any updated slave zones are also updated by force when SIGHUP is sent.

Zone Access Lists

BIND 4 has a feature called secure_zone, which lets you define an ACL for a zone. Although secure_zone is implemented by embedding secure_zone records in the zone file, they are in fact not RRs and are not transferred in a zone transfer. So, even if you have secure_zone set up on a master server, none of the slaves will have the necessary information. Additionally, BIND implements no way to distribute them. If you need slave servers and secure_zone to secure the zone(s), you must find some way to distribute them other than traditional zone transfer. The BOG suggests that secure_zone is useful for Hesiod (zone class HS) password zones to restrict the availability of passwords outside local networks. But, secure_zone is perhaps best forgotten. This example is from the BOG:

```
secure_zone    HS    TXT    "130.215.0.0:255.255.0.0"
secure_zone    HS    TXT    "128.23.10.56:H"
```

Similar to xfrnets, BIND knows which class the given network addresses are, and if no subnet mask is given, the class mask is used. In the first line of the previous example, a subnet mask is given. The second line specifies a lone host.

BIND 8 has ACLs for this. ACLs are not transferred by zone transfer either—but at least they are not removed by zone transfers. They stay put in the named.conf file.

15

Compiling and
Maintaining BIND

About BIND

BIND is a cornerstone of your network as well as of the Internet. Some years ago, BIND was seen as uncomplicated when it came to security. No more. If you want to run a tight ship, you must keep your BIND up to date, up to the very latest release.

BIND is maintained and developed by the Internet Software Consortium (ISC). Just like every other software package, BIND has a home page, which can be found at http://www.isc.org/products/BIND/.

BIND is an excellent piece of software that is freely available because ISC spends substantial money to maintain and develop it. ISC gets support from ISPs, software and hardware vendors, companies that use BIND, and BIND users like yourself. The ISC also offers support contracts, which you might consider for your organization. In addition, it develops other software that is frequently used all over the Internet. Its home page is at http://www.isc.org/.

Getting BIND

The latest release of BIND can always be found at ftp://ftp.isc.org/isc/bind/src/. The latest available "current" release is also announced on the Web page.

The src directory holds subdirectories for each recent version of BIND. Each directory in turn contains three .tar.gz files and their corresponding .asc files containing cryptographic PGP signatures. The signatures verify the origin and authenticity of the copy of BIND you get, so you can know that you got an unaltered, trustable version. It also holds a MD5 file with MD5 checksums you can use to verify that you got the files without any problems.

If you want to verify the files you got, you must get hold of the ISC PGP keys, which you can find at http://www.isc.org/ISC/pgpkey.html. You also need PGP software, but I will not get into that here. The MD5 file can be used to verify correct retrieval using the md5sum program. It is included in recent versions of GNUs textutils package, at ftp://ftp.gnu.org/gnu/textutils.

Be sure you get the whole directory of the latest version of BIND.

Keeping It Current

Ensuring that you always have the most current version of BIND is not as hard as it could be. You can keep an eye on the FTP site, of course, but that could grow tedious. Subscribing to the BIND announce list is the most recommended way. Depending on how much time you have for your hostmaster duties, you might also want to peruse newsgroups or their mailing list counterparts. You can learn a lot from the following resources:

Newsgroup	Mailing List	Topic
comp.protocols.dns.bind	bind-users	Using BIND.
N/A	bind-announce	BIND announcements.
comp.protocols.dns.std	namedroppers-request@internic.net	DNS standards.
comp.protocols.dns.ops	N/A	DNS operations.
N/A	bind-bugs@isc.org	Send bug reports here.

The ISC hosts the first two of the previous list. You will find a subscription and un-subscription form on the BIND home page. The announce list is very low volume, but the others are high volume. The address given for the namedroppers list is the subscribe address. If you want to ask a question, it likely has been answered again and again recently. It is polite to use a search engine, such as http://www.deja.com/, to find earlier answers to your question before asking it on the list or newsgroup.

Compiling BIND

Now it's time to get your hands dirty. After you have the tar files, you just need to untar them into a suitable directory. They untar directly as src, doc, and contrib, so you should make an intermediate directory to hold them all. So, to compile BIND, go into the src directory. If you type make, the software will make a (good) guess about your OS and platform and compile BIND according to that.

You might have specific needs, though. On most platforms, the default is to compile with GNU gcc. However, if you have a Solaris machine, you might want to compile BIND with Sun's CC rather than GNU gcc. In that case, you must go into port/solaris and copy Makefile.set.sun over Makefile.set. Platform-specific settings all reside in port/platform, and in many cases, these override the generic makefiles in the source directories.

Installation instructions are provided in the INSTALL file, which also lists the platforms on which this version of BIND is known to work and on which platforms it should work. By default, BIND installs into /usr/local, but this will vary according to your platform. Check the Makefile.set for your platform to find out where it installs. If this default does not suit you, you can override it on the command line as described in the INSTALL file.

In normal cases, BIND should compile without problem. If you get into trouble, check that your compiler and libraries are current because your OS vendor might already have fixed your problem with a patch that you can install on your system. If it still does not work, you should check the newsgroups or mailing lists to see whether anyone is experiencing the same problems as you and whether someone have posted a solution to the problem. If not, you're on your own. You might get help by posting on the Net, but it's best if you try to figure things out for yourself before posting there. If you do post, though, be sure to give a lot of detail and include the error messages because that makes it easier for others to help you.

Installing BIND

As I said earlier, BIND by default installs into /usr/local on most platforms. It installs there so that it's kept out of the way of the vendor versions of BIND you might have installed. Mixing the two can cause many problems.

Unlike GNU software, no easy command-line switch exists to override the installation destination. You must override several makefile variables instead. These are defined in your architecture's port makefile, and a good place to override them is in the Makefile.set file. The following lists the variables:

Variable	Default Value	Use
DESTBIN	/usr/local/bin	User-level commands are installed here.
DESTSBIN	/usr/local/sbin	Administration commands.
DESTEXEC	/usr/local/sbin	named-xfer installs here.
DESTMAN	/usr/local/share/man	Manual pages.
DESTHELP	/usr/local/lib	Built-in help in the software.
DESTETC	/usr/local/etc	Home of named.conf.
DESTRUN	/usr/local/etc	Home of control and pid files.

The default values listed previously are correct for most OSes, The notable exceptions are the free BSDs and Linux, where it's all installed under / and /usr because no vendor BIND exists with which to clash. The ISC BIND is the vendor version. However, the resolver library and header files are still installed under /usr/local because they can still clash with the OS library and header files. Replacing OS libraries and header files can cause no end of grief, so be careful when overriding those install destinations.

Customizing for Chrooted Environments

Before you even start trying to customize chrooted environments, you should set up a working named configuration. This kind of setup complicates things, so you should have a complete, working set of DNS database files and configurations before attempting this.

Chroot is a UNIX security mechanism that insulates the software that is chrooted from the rest of the filesystem. This ensures that even if the software proves to be insecure, a break-in will not compromise more than the insecure software and the other contents of the chroot jail; the rest of the system is protected. You can read more about chroot in your OS man pages chroot(1) and chroot(2). Its use is also the subject of programming and security texts on UNIX.

BIND's -t option is used to activate this feature.

Many ways are available to set this up; you can choose one based simply on personal preference. On the one hand, you can wrap the needed programs in shell scripts that set up everything correctly. On the other hand, you can patch the source code of selected pieces of software to make them do the correct thing themselves. Writing scripts has the disadvantage of the scripts being overwritten each time you reinstall BIND, whereas patching the source code has the disadvantage of tampering with the source. In addition, if you do this manually, you might create problems each time you reinstall BIND. One good argument, though, for modifying the source as well is the fact that you only have to modify the source before compilation. After it's installed, the software will work as needed without further modifications; the modifications are localized to the pre-install-phase. In both cases, you should automate the modification process as far as you can to decrease the likelihood of mistakes.

I like to avoid modifying source code, as well as OS scripts. OSes such as Solaris 2 have a rather monolithic network startup script. If you modify it, you risk the patching of your OS failing. Afterwards, the machine might not boot correctly before you manually intervene and fix the glitch.

I prefer to write shell wrappers for the important pieces and leave the source and the OS scripts alone. This is explained in the following section.

The Chroot Environment

You first must set up the chroot environment so BIND can live in it. As of this writing, it is considered an experimental feature, although it works well. Because it is still experimental, things might have changed by the time you read this. If the requirements described here are not enough to make it work, refer to the INSTALL document that came with your BIND distribution. Follow these steps:

1. Decide where you want the chroot environment (I prefer /var/bind-chroot). Then, create a directory hierarchy under there. The following hierarchy is a "mini" hierarchy to keep the paths short, but you can install a hierarchy that completely mirrors the hierarchy used by named by default:

Path	Use
var/run	pid, log, and control files go here.
var/names	Named databases.
etc	named.conf.
sbin	Copy named-xfer here.
dev	named needs /dev/null.
	Create it with /dev/MAKEDEV or copy it with cp or tar.

2. Next, you must install a configuration file. It should be a normal configuration file, except for two things. The communication mechanism to communicate with syslogd resides in /dev above the chroot environment. Thus, it is unavailable. It also can't be transplanted to the chroot environment. Because BIND likes to use the syslog facility, you must override the default logging. Enter, as a minimum, the following logging configuration at the top of your named.conf file:

    ```
    logging {
            channel the_log {
                    file "/var/run/named.log" versions 20 size 1m;
                    print-time yes;
                    print-category yes;
    ```

```
            print-severity yes;
    };

    category default { the_log; };
    category panic { the_log; };
    category packet { the_log; };
    category event lib { the_log; };
};
```

This replaces the default logging configuration with your own. If you enter it at the bottom of your `named.conf` file, logging will not work until BIND parses it, after loading the zone files. You probably want to see any errors that occur while loading the zones, so this is not a good idea.

3. Next, you need to override the location of `named-xfer` because it probably doesn't match your default location. Enter the following line in the options section of the configuration file:

    ```
    named-xfer "/sbin/named-xfer";
    ```

4. Copy all your database files into `/var/bind-chroot/var/named`.

5. Start `named` with the following command:

    ```
    named -t /var/bind-chroot
    ```

6. Check the logs to see whether everything executed correctly. If it did, check it with `dig` or `nslookup` as well. If not, debug it. Refer to the `named` man page for information about debugging `named`.

The Scripts

After you have a working chroot environment, you can begin to write the scripts to fit everything together. They are easy to write.

named

You should replace `named` first. Copy `named` to `named.bin`, in the same directory, and then save this script as `named`:

```
#!/bin/sh
exec "$0".bin -t /var/bind-chroot "$@"
```

The previous code starts `named.bin` with the correct chroot option. Make it executable and then try it to see whether it works. Then try to create queries.

ndc

The other program you must fix is ndc. Move it to ndc.bin and replace it with the following script:

```
#!/bin/sh
exec "$0".bin -c /var/bind-chroot/var/run/ndc \
    -p /var/bind-chroot/var/run/named.pid "$@"
```

The trick here is to tell it of the nonstandard control-connection and pid-file location with the -c and -p options. Also make it executable and verify that you can stop, start reload, and restart your chrooted named.

Now, remember that every time you install BIND anew, it will overwrite the shell scripts with the binaries from the BIND distribution, and the previous procedure needs to be repeated. It is a good idea to write an automatic procedure for it, or at least document it.

16

BIND 9

The Goals of BIND 9

BIND 9 is a major revision of BIND and will, not too long after it's finished (which is expected sometime in the fall of 2000), be the recommended version of BIND.

BIND 9 addresses some major problems in BIND 8. It became obvious that BIND 8 was not up to the demands of the future. ISC has, on behalf of the Internet community in general, and some named sponsors specifically, undertaken a major rewrite of BIND.

Available when I write this, July 2000, is BIND 9.0.0rc1, the first release candidate release of the BIND 9 code, containing the final set of features slated for BIND 9.0.0. BIND 9 will, when it is released, be available from `ftp.isc.org`. Please see Chapter 15, "Compiling and Maintaining BIND," for more information about getting, compiling, and maintaining BIND. The ISC also has a mailing list for BIND 9 users; email `bind9-users-request@isc.org` to subscribe.

In the words of the ISC, BIND 9 was designed with these goals in mind:

- Scalability
    - Thread safety
    - Multiprocessor scalability
    - Support for very large zones
- Security
    - Support for DNSSEC
    - Support for TSIG
    - Auditability (code and operation)
    - Firewall support (split DNS)
- Portability
- Maintainability
- Protocol Enhancements
    - IXFR, DDNS, Notify, EDNS0
    - Improved standards conformance
- Operational enhancements
    - High availability and reliability
    - Support for alternative backend databases
- IP version 6 support
    - IPv6 resource records (A6, DNAME, and so on)
    - Bitstring labels
    - APIs

Why Use BIND 9?

At some point in the future, the ISC will make BIND 9 the Recommended Version of BIND and stop making bug fix releases of BIND 8. One reason to set up and use BIND 9 on at least one machine is to prepare for that time. Already knowing everything about what it takes to convert your nameservers from BIND 8 to BIND 9 will make the job that much easier, and would make it possible to do quickly if needed by security or other requirements.

The only other reason for using BIND 9 now is that you need some of the functionality present in BIND 9. IPv6 has been cited by some early adopters, and DNSSEC/TSIG on zone transfers is another thing some people like. Other key features is the new view feature (see the following), which makes split DNS setups easier, and the scalability.

The support for alternative backend databases is not what you might hope at present because no implementations of alternative backend databases are available. Also, BIND is exceedingly fast at performing lookups in its own memory-resident database. It has been reported to handle upwards of 15,000–20,000/second, and to be restricted by the speed of the IP stack rather than the lookup engine. A unpublished MySQL-based database backend has been reported to perform 1000+ of lookups/second.

All this was discussed in July of 2000 on the ISC BIND 9 users mailing list. The author of the backend cannot release the source code because it is the property of one of his customers.

Replacing BIND's own database with your own can give you two things: instant startup even with multitudes of zones and smaller memory footprint. At least BIND won't be using up memory; your database, on the other hand, might. Similarly, if your database takes five minutes to start, a one-second startup time for BIND might not help you.

Two ways are available to replace zone files with a database. One is to replace the zone-loading mechanism and load zones into BIND's own fast database from something other than a zone file. This is easy to do, but BIND will still use the same amount of memory. Plus, doing this any faster than BIND 9 can perform simple reads from a zone file is difficult. The other method is to replace BIND's database engine and create something using some other database store, such as MySQL, DB2, or Oracle. BIND's database access and search methods are complex and numerous (23 exist), so this can be quite a large task. However, if you have the resources to develop such a backend, BIND 9 can be used—which was not the case with BIND 4 or 8. Of course, in a security-minded environment, the database needs to have security features similar to BIND. Adding a complex, networked RMDBMS securely might prove difficult.

Compiling BIND 9

BIND 9 is both harder and easier to compile than BIND 8. It's harder because it requires an ANSI C compiler (and not all UNIX versions come with one). BIND 9 also uses threads, as implemented with pthreads, and supports IPv6. The quality of the OS thread libraries can vary, and I would expect a shakedown phase both in BIND 9 and the OSs concerned. On the other hand BIND 9 is easier to compile because it is GNU-autoconfigurable. Therefore, if it has already been ported and tested on your OS, everything should be as easy to get working as GNU software usually is. BIND 9.0.0tr5 is reported to build on a number of platforms, as found in the README file:

- AIX 4.3
- COMPAQ Tru64 UNIX 4.0D
- COMPAQ Tru64 UNIX 5 (with IPv6 EAK)
- FreeBSD 3.4-STABLE
- HP-UX 11

- IRIX64 6.5
- NetBSD-current (with unproven-pthreads-0.17)
- Red Hat Linux 6.0, 6.1, 6.2
- Solaris 2.6, 7, 8 (beta)

The README file also contains the compilation instructions. In most cases, it will be this familiar sequence:

```
$ ./configure
$ make
$ make install
```

It accepts the usual GNU autoconf options and variables, of course, and some BIND 9–specific options. See ./configure --help and in the README file for more information about that.

If you have one of the platforms previously listed, you are now quite likely to have BIND 9 installed. It is started, stopped, and configured identically to BIND 8. But ndc has been replaced with rndc, which requires configuration. I will return to that later in this chapter. You might want to take a look at the CHANGES file, where you will find the added and changed functionality, as well as fixed bugs.

The Documentation

In the doc subdirectory, several new documents describe BIND 9.0.0. For the somewhat experienced administrator, the doc/misc/migration document is perhaps the most interesting document of all. The main README file, or the CHANGES file, is likely to be the best place to find succinct information if any changes occurred in the BIND 9 you're dealing with as compared to 9.0.0rc1.

Administrator Reference Manual

In doc/arm you will find the BIND 9 Administrator Reference Manual. This is the replacement for the BOG (Bind Operations Guide) of BIND 4. This is a very extensive document, and reading it is highly recommended. If for no reason other than because it will give you an alternative presentation of what you find in this book, which can clarify things for you, or alternatively reassure you that you already know everything.

New Configuration Options

In the doc/misc directory, you will find a summary of the supported options in BIND 9's named.conf file. Here are the highlights.

The old `maintain-ixfr-base`, `support-ixfr`, and `ixfr-base` options are now obsolete. BIND 9 maintains an incremental database whenever it can. Instead, you can use the `provide-ixfr` option inside the `options`, `server`, and `view` clauses. This controls whether incremental zone transfers will be available at all to the given server or for the given view. The `request-ixfr` option can be used to control whether you want to ask for incremental transfers at all, with a given server or for a given view. Normally, you would want to use incremental transfers—the only reason I can think of to not use it is if it's buggy. If IXFR is not available from a server, BIND falls back to AXFR.

In BIND 9 the named-xfer program is built in and not an external program. This makes the `named-xfer` option obsolete and adds some previously unavailable controls to zone transfers:

```
max-transfer-time-in number;
max-transfer-idle-in number;
max-transfer-time-out number;
max-transfer-idle-out number;
```

All these go either in the options, zone, or view sections of the conf file. `number` is the number of minutes. `max-transfer-time-in` controls how long inbound zone transfers can run, in total, before they time out; the default is two hours. In contrast, `max-transfer-idle-in` limits how long BIND will wait on a stalled zone transfer before it is abandoned; the default is one hour. `max-transfer-time-out` and `max-transfer-idle-out` do the same thing for outbound transfers, and both have the same timeouts. If you serve many zones, these timeouts (or the number of simultaneous transfers) might need to be adjusted. However, if you're in that situation, you probably already did this.

In Chapter 3, "Maintenance and Enhancements," I described the CNAME rules that BIND 8 (may) enforce. BIND 9 does not enforce these, for the time being. Thus, the `multiple-cnames` option is inactive. The checks might be reintroduced at any time, though, and they are enforced for dynamic updates. So, violating the CNAME rules is a definite no-no.

The `deallocate-on-exit` option is now always on for debugging reasons, so the option is obsolete.

The `has-old-clients` functionality in BIND 8 was incorrectly implemented, and the option is ignored in BIND 9. To get BIND 9 to be old-client compatible use the following instead:

```
options {
  auth-nxdomain yes;
  rfc2308-type1 no;
};
```

Running BIND 9

Some differences exist when running BIND 9.

named

You can use your existing BIND 8 `named.conf` file. Providing your BIND 9 was compiled with the same --`prefix` option as your BIND 8, it will be found and loaded without problems. Read your log file carefully, noting warnings and error messages. The unimplemented options in BIND 9 will result in warnings in the log. If you have read the migration guide in doc/misc/ migration, you will probably get no surprises. To control BIND 9, you use rndc (remote name demon control), not ndc as you're used to from BIND 4 and 8.

Note that named has a new command-line syntax:

```
named [-c conffile] [-d debuglevel] [-f|-g] [-n number_of_cpus]
           [-p port] [-s] [-t chrootdir] [-u username]
```

rndc

rndc communicates with BIND 9 by network, not filesystem sockets or signals, as ndc in BIND 4/8 does. To make this secure, it must use crypto keys for authentication. Therefore, a configuration file is required. `/etc/rndc.conf` is a subset of `named.conf`, it is limited to the `options`, `key`, and `server` statements. The `key` statement works the same as in `named.conf`; the `server` statement can associate each server you need to control with its key. The `options` statement takes two options: `default-server` and `default-key`, which identify the default server and the default key, respectively. Here is an example from the ARM:

```
key rndc_key {
    algorithm "hmac-md5";
    secret "c3Ryb25nIGVub3VnaCBmb3IgYSBtYW4gYnV0IG1hZGUgZm9yIGEgd29tYW4K";
};

options {
    default-server localhost;
    default-key    rndc_key;
};
```

I describe how to generate keys later in this chapter, in the section "Security Enhancements."

Correspondingly, you need to configure your named to accept the given key by defining the same key and a `controls` statement in `named.conf`:

```
key rndc_key {
    algorithm "hmac-md5";
```

```
        secret "c3Ryb25nIGVub3VnaCBmb3IgYSBtYW4gYnV0IG1hZGUgZm9yIGEgd29tYW4K";
};

controls {
    inet 127.0.0.1 allow { localhost; } keys { rndc_key; };
};
```

These keys are shared secrets, equivalent to passwords. The `named.conf` and `rndc.conf` files must not be readable for the world, so take care when read-protecting them.

When running rndc, the default server is contacted unless you specify a different server with the `-s` option. You also can specify a different key with the `-y` option, but using the `server` statement is probably better for that.

The command line of rndc is as follows:

```
rndc [-c config] [-s server] [-p port] [-y key] command [command ...]
```

lwresd

The lwresd is used by lwresd-enabled resolving libraries. That means your OS resolver will not use lwresd, unless you replace it with one that does. Software linked with the BIND 9 resolver, on the other hand, will. lwresd is required to pursue the kinds of resolution complexities that DNAME and A6 records cause. The stub OS resolver is too simple, and using the site-wide caching server has the potential of site-wide denial of service (DoS) attacks. Both A6 and DNAME require a recursive resolution process that can be far more complex, and exponential, than the process used earlier.

lwresd acts as a caching-only resolver for the localhost. It takes its configuration from `/etc/resolv.conf`, using the servers named there as forwarders. Because lwresd must be capable of being trusted by the localhost, it runs on a sub-1024 port, and because of that, it must be run by root at bootup. But it, like named, can be run chrooted and as nobody, dropping the root privileges when they are not needed anymore. All that is described in Chapters 8, "Security Concerns," and 15, "Compiling and Maintaining BIND."

lwresd is a bit of a misnomer. It is not lightweight, but it enables the OS stub resolver to remain lightweight. As of 9.0.0rc1, lwresd is in fact identical to named, and it can't in any way be considered lightweight. If it ever becomes autonomous, it is likely to borrow most of the code in named.

New Resource Limits

`max-cache-ttl` is a new option that sets the maximum TTL for caching of ordinary (positive) records. This overrides whatever might be set in the SOA record for the record, if it's higher than this value. This helps limit the size of the cache to some degree, but it also enables you to override excessively high TTL values. The default value is one week.

recursive-clients, defaulting to 1000, limits how many recursive queries can be in progress at any one time. If you have several clients, this might have to be increased. In fact, it has already proven to be too low, so the default might be much higher by the time you read this.

tcp-clients, defaulting to 100, limits how many simultaneous client connections over TCP named can keep. TCP connections eat file handles and possibly free i-nodes in the OS tables, possibly causing starvation on the system. 100 is a very low value, but some older UNIX versions need this value set well below 64, so don't laugh. Most modern UNIX versions will work even if the number of simultaneous TCP connections in BIND passes 255, but check your OS documentation.

max-cache-size is, alas, not implemented in BIND 9.0.0. It will, when implemented, enable you to limit the memory consumption of the cache in your server. BIND 8 can control the total size of its data structures with the datasize option, but when the size is passed, BIND dies. max-cache-size, then, is a much better idea. Of course, the amount of memory used by BIND is also determined by other dynamic things, but mainly by the number and size of the zones for which the server is authoritative.

Views

In Chapter 8, I discussed split DNS and internal and external views of zones. BIND 8 requires different instances of BIND serving the different zone data. BIND 9 (and, in fact, 8.2) enables implementation of split DNS more easily with the view option. With a view set up, different clients can be answered from different zone data. So, an internal client can be answered from the full internal zone data, and an external client can be answered from the limited, externally available zone data—all from one instance of BIND, instead of the two different BINDs required in the setup described in Chapter 8. The setup is as follows:

```
view "internal" {
    // This is the internal network, and the host itself:
    match-clients { 192.168.70.0/24; 127.0.0.1; };
    recursion yes;  // Provide recursion to internal hosts

    zone "penguin.bv" {
        type master;
        file "pz/full-penguin.bv";
    };
};

view "external" {
    match-clients { any; };
    recursion no;  // No recursion to foreign cretins

    zone "penguin.bv" {
        type master;
```

```
        file "pz/limited-penguin.bv";
    };
};
```

The order of the view options is significant, as you might imagine. When the client address is matched, no further views are checked, and the zone data available in the matched view is presented to the client. The following is the full (implemented) syntax for views:

```
view "view_name" [ ( in | hs | hesiod | chaos ) ] {
  match-clients { address_match_list };
  [ zone ... ]
  [ auth-nxdomain yes_or_no; ]
  [ notify yes_or_no; ]
  [ recursion yes_or_no; ]
  [ also-notify { ip_addr; [ ip_addr; ... ] }; ]
  [ forward ( only | first ); ]
  [ forwarders { [ in_addr ; [ in_addr ; ... ] ] }; ]
  [ allow-query { address_match_list }; ]
  [ allow-transfer { address_match_list }; ]
  [ allow-recursion { address_match_list }; ]
  [ query-source ... ]
  [ query-source-v6 ... ]
  [ max-transfer-time-out number; ]
  [ max-transfer-idle-out number; ]
  [ max-cache-ttl number; ]
  [ max-ncache-ttl number; ]
  [ transfer-format ( one-answer | many-answers ); ]
  [ transfer-source ip_addr; ]
  [ transfer-source-v6 ip_addr; ]
  [ request-ixfr yes_or_no; ]
  [ provide-ixfr yes_or_no;]
  [ cleaning-interval number; ]
  [ key ... ]
  [ server ... ]
  [ trusted-keys ... ]
};
```

As you can see, this gives you quite a few possibilities in the way of differentiated service based on the client address. I for one have been missing this.

New RRs

BIND 9 implements two new RRs, discussed in the following sections.

DNAME, Domain Alias

RFC2672 specifies the DNAME record. The RFC is titled "Non-Terminal DNS Name Redirection," which means that DNAME is similar to CNAME but does not alias a single name. Instead, it aliases a whole domain. It is non-terminal in the sense that when a DNAME is found, a new name is computed and then resolved. CNAME, on the other hand, is terminal in the sense that when the CNAME record has been found, the job is done.

DNAME is a simple enough record:

```
[domainname]      DNAME [target]
```

The effect of this is that the entire subtree of DNS identified by the domain name can be mapped onto the target domain. The main purpose of this is to create a mechanism to help with network renumbering, but the result can also be used for domain renaming. And doubtless it can be abused in other new and exciting ways. Considering the work needed to be done by the lightweight resolver when using DNAME, I recommend using DNAME only when necessary and for the intended purposes only—and then only for a limited, well-defined period of time.

Let's imagine that the good folks at Penguin Industries got venture capital and decided to buy Walruss. They decide to make Walruss a subsidiary of Penguin, and to make walruss.bv a subdomain of penguin.bv—to create walruss.penguin.bv, in other words. In the interest of keeping things working and compatible, walruss.bv must be kept working while walruss.penguin.bv is phased in, announced, and made a part of everyday life. In the penguin.bv zone, the hostmaster would simply enter this command:

```
walruss         DNAME walruss.bv.
```

From this point on, the lookup of names, such as www.walruss.penguin.bv, will result in a DNAME record being returned for walruss.penguin.bv. Additionally, the lightweight resolver will then translate the name to www.walruss.bv and then proceed to resolve that instead. This is shown in Figure 16.1. The answer returned consists of a CNAME record mapping the name asked for to the name arrived at by following DNAME records. A resolver that is not aware of DNAME will see this.

```
$ dig www.walruss.penguin.bv any
...
;; ANSWER SECTION:
walruss.penguin.bv.     1H IN 39        \#(                 ; unknown RR type
        07 77 61 6c 72 75 73 73 02 62 76 00 )               ; .walruss.bv.
www.walruss.penguin.bv.   1H IN CNAME  www.walruss.bv.
www.walruss.bv.         1D IN A         10.1.0.3
www.walruss.bv.         1D IN MX        10 mail.walruss.bv.
www.walruss.bv.         1D IN MX        20 mail.penguin.bv.
www.walruss.bv.         1D IN HINFO     "i86" "Debian Linux"
...
```

1. Query for
   www.walruss.penguin.bv's
   A record

2. www.walruss.penguin.bv
   is DNAME for
   walruss.bv

3. Query for www.walruss.bv
   as well

4. Return sysnthesized
   answer saying that
   www.walruss.penguin.bv
   is a CNAME for
   www.walruss.bv, and the
   A record found for it.

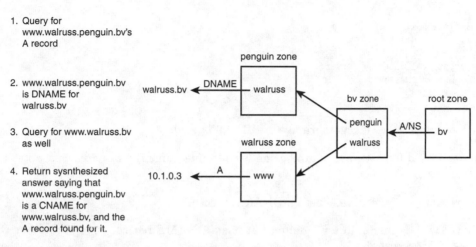

Figure 16.1   Making walruss.bv a subdomain of penguin.bv with a DNAME record, and
resolving it.

The unknown record is the DNAME record, and the 39 is the DNAME RR type. As you can see,
dig deciphers the contents, and the comment shows it as being .walruss.bv. A DNAME-aware
dig shows this:

```
$ dig www.walruss.penguin.bv any
...
;; ANSWER SECTION:
walruss.penguin.bv.       3600    IN      DNAME   walruss.bv.
www.walruss.penguin.bv. 3600    IN      CNAME   www.walruss.bv.
www.walruss.bv.           86400   IN      A       10.1.0.3
www.walruss.bv.           86400   IN      MX      10 mail.walruss.bv.
www.walruss.bv.           86400   IN      MX      20 mail.penguin.bv.
www.walruss.bv.           86400   IN      HINFO   "i86" "Debian Linux"
...
```

If an A record is requested, the resolver still returns a DNAME record, a CNAME record, and
finally the A record, as shown in the previous code. The returned DNAME record does not
have any detrimental effect on other DNS tools, such as nslookup and host, either. Consider
the following example:

```
$ host -t A www.walruss.penguin.bv 127.0.0.1
Using domain server 127.0.0.1:
walruss.penguin.bv 39 ???
www.walruss.penguin.bv is a nickname for www.walruss.bv
www.walruss.bv has address 10.1.0.3
www.walruss.bv has address 10.1.0.3
$ nslookup www.walruss.penguin.bv 127.0.0.1
Answer crypto-validated by server:
```

```
Server:  localhost
Address:  127.0.0.1

Answer crypto-validated by server:
Name:    www.walruss.bv
Address:  10.1.0.3
Aliases:  www.walruss.penguin.bv
```

In the nslookup, the use of cryptography in BIND 9 is evident.

The approach used for network renumbering is the same, alias the in-addr.arpa zones for the affected networks.

Some restrictions do, of course, exist on DNAME records:

- There can be other data for a name that has a DNAME record, but not another DNAME or a CNAME record.
- There must not be any data for any subdomain of a DNAME record. This does not apply to data of classes other than the DNAME record. (Recall that IN [Internet] is a class, as is Chaos and Hesiod.)
- This restriction is not found in the RFC, but avoid having DNAME aliased hostnames in SOA, MX, NS and records, as well as other places where CNAME is forbidden. This is because the DNAME results in a CNAME answer to the client and can have results you don't want.

A6, IPv6 Address

The A6 record is described in RFC 2874. It is an address record for IPv6 and is meant to replace the AAAA record. It has provisions, with the help of DNAME, for supporting network renumbering. A6 is intimately tied to IPv6 addressing schemes and hierarchies, and I refer the eager reader to the RFC for the details and use of this RR.

Scalability

Scalability in BIND 9 is better in several ways. One is that it can be used for zone storage methods other than zone files. Thus, on-demand loading of zone data from databases of your choice will be possible in the future. This is especially beneficial for those who run name-servers with thousands of zones that take a long time to restart (nameservers taking more than 30 minutes to restart is not unheard of).

Another scalability issue is zone transfers for such massive nameservers. A built-in `named-xfer` helps solve that problem.

Use of lightweight threading in the application programming helps make all this easy within one instance of named. The use of threads also enables named to take advantage of multi-processor systems, such that the main resolver can be split in several threads—each running on different CPUs on the system. The single-threaded model of BIND 4 and BIND 8 did not allow this; at best, `named-xfer` would run on a separate CPU.

Security Enhancements

BIND 9 has several security enhancements.

TSIG

TSIG is how BIND signs transactions. In Chapter 9, "Dynamic DNS," I explained how TSIG is used to sign dynamic update requests. BIND 9 supports TSIG for queries, the NOTIFY protocol, and zone transfers. It enables you to know who sent the information and that it has not been changed in transit.

BIND 9's software for creating keys has been renamed and changed somewhat. Whereas the BIND 8 version of the key generator required a FQDN for host keys, the BIND 9 documentation recommends naming keys after both the hosts that share it. Say I want to make a shared key for ns.penguin.bv and ns.walruss.bv. However, because the names are identical, I use the next part of their names, which makes sense in this context:

```
$ dnssec-keygen -a hmac-md5 -b 512 -n HOST penguin-walruss
Kns-rms.+157+02485
```

In the file `Kpenguin-walruss.+157+02485.private`, you will find the key (broken in two to fit the page):

```
Private-key-format: v1.2
Algorithm: 157 (HMAC_MD5)
Key: EVYYnfezPJnaVhs3arhHFeyhVuSzzYrAtySpIEG4HfL8IvPqGqZ6
     iQxg1FzffnL1RXXn66e51WTJmOr+5tLDuw==
```

This is suitable for inclusion in a `named.conf` key statement (also broken in two, so you must concatenate the line):

```
key penguin-walruss {
    algorithm "hmac-md5";
    secret "EVYYnfezPJnaVhs3arhHFeyhVuSzzYrAtySpIEG4HfL8IvPqGqZ6
            iQxg1FzffnL1RXXn66e51WTJmOr+5tLDuw==";
};
```

Because these are shared secrets, don't store them in world-readable files!

Using keys for dynamic updates is the same as before. But for server-to-server communication, more configuration is necessary. On ns.penguin.bv, to configure signed communication with ns.walruss.bv, I set up the following:

```
server 10.1.0.2 {
    keys { penguin-walruss; };
};
```

In BIND 8, the keys option for the server statement was available, but not active. After setting up the symmetric statement on ns.walruss.bv, we're ready to let named use TSIG on communication between the two servers.

DNSSEC

The basic DNSSEC is described in RFC2535. With BIND 9, you'll see DNSSEC fully implemented. Although DNSSEC is available in the BIND 9.0.0rc1 release, DNSSEC is still very much a work in progress, both on the specification and the implementation sides. For now, DNSSEC is not for general consumption. Look for further documentation in the ARM, or in the next edition of this book.

IPv6 Support

Currently, the Internet builds on IPv4. Several problems exist with IPv4, though. Some problems affecting the security design of the Internet are proving hard to beat, but more importantly, the address space offered by the 32-bit addresses is almost exhausted. IPv6 is the answer. IPv6 has been tested on the Internet for a number of years in a organization called the 6Bone and on the research network known as Internet2. It's not quite certain when IPv6 will be in wide deployment across the ordinary Internet, but it is in experimental use at more and more sites. Meanwhile, BIND needs to support IPv6 in two ways: It stores IPv6 addressing information in A6 and AAAA records, and, with BIND 9, it can also speak IPv6 with clients and other DNS servers (as long as your platform supports IPv6). Special IPv6 versions of BIND options are available. Here's a summary:

```
options {
  [ listen-on-v6 [ port ip_port ] { address_match_list }; ]
  [ query-source-v6 ... ]
  [ transfer-source-v6 ip_addr; ]
}

zone "domain_name" [ ( in | hs | hesiod | chaos ) ] {
  type slave;
  [ transfer-source-v6 ip_addr; ]
}

view "view_name" [ ( in | hs | hesiod | chaos ) ] {
  [ transfer-source-v6 ip_addr; ]
}
```

## 17

MISCELLANY

There are a few last things I want to tell you before this book ends.

How ncd Works

Before ndc there was the kill command. In the beginning, sending HUP to named caused files to be re-read, as is usual for UNIX daemons. As time passed, other signals were added to do other things. The first versions of ndc, as found in BIND 4, were shell scripts that simply provided a handy tool to send all these signals to named. ndc in BIND 8, however, can use a named pipe to communicate with BIND and get messages back about how and what BIND is doing. But it also can still use signals to deliver the message to BIND. In BIND 9, the evolution is complete, and ndc is called *rndc* for *remote* ndc. It uses an encrypted network connection to send commands and a shared secret or key to authenticate itself to named.

However, it is still handy to be able to send signals to a named to control it. These are the signals:

INT	Dump database; ndc dumpdb
ABRT	Dump statistics (BIND 4); ndc stats. Also known as IOT
ILL	Dump statistics (BIND 8)
HUP	Reload database; ndc reload
USR1	Increment debug level; ndc trace

USR2	Reset debug level; ndc notrace
WINCH	Enable/disable query logging; ndc querylog
TERM	Exit, stop, quit; ndc stop

Admittedly, this is most handy when you're struggling with a setup problem that has stopped named from using the normal communications channel.

ndc in BIND 8 prefers to use a named socket—a *channel* in ndc terms—usually named /var/run/ndc. A security issue exists with named sockets because some versions of UNIX do not permit, or enforce, permission bits on sockets. This allows anyone to access the socket and control your named. The fix is to create a directory that is available to only the users meant to control your named. The name of the socket is controlled by the controls statement in named.conf:

```
controls {
    ...
    unix "/var/ndc/ndc"
      perm 0600
      owner 0          // root
      group 0;         // wheel
    ...
};
```

As this example should make obvious, on OSs that enforce access permissions on named sockets, you can set the permission bits the socket is supposed to have. The benefit of this is that a user with the correct file group membership can use ndc to control named, so the user doesn't have to be root to do the job. This is a big advantage. Of course, ndc does not read named.conf, and when you change the path, you must give it an option so it can find the socket:

```
$ ndc -c /var/ndc/ndc reload
Reload initiated.
```

BIND 8 can also be controlled by network sockets, although I would not recommend that. The only way to access-control it would be to restrict access to the hosts allowed to use the network socket. By default, BIND does not listen for ndc messages on any network socket.

In addition to the old tricks, ndc can now perform a number of new tricks through the socket.

status

The last line of output from ndc status can be a bit disconcerting:

```
$ ndc status
named 8.2.2-P5 Mon Feb 28 10:17:53 EST 2000  \
        root@lookfar:/usr/src/bind-8.2.2_P5/src/bin/named
number of zones allocated: 64
debug level: 0
```

```
xfers running: 0
xfers deferred: 0
soa queries in progress: 0
query logging is OFF
server is DONE priming
server IS NOT loading its configuration
```

The last line means that named is not reading the configuration right now. It is not an error; your configuration file will be quite big before you will get to see it still loading. The number of zones allocated has nothing to do with how many zones are loaded; it simply indicates how large the zone data structure is. It is enlarged in chunks of 64 zones as necessary. The debug level is for dynamic logging, as discussed in Chapter 3, "Maintenance and Enhancements." xfers running, xfers deferred, and SOA queries in progress have to do with the mechanics of zone transfers. If the number of deferred xfers keeps growing, you might have a problem that bears looking into. The parameters controlling this are described later in this chapter. priming refers to loading the hints zone.

Address Sorting

This is a somewhat arcane subject simply because few people need features related to the address sorting functions in BIND. While address sorting was the default in older versions of BIND 4, newer versions of BIND 4 and BIND 8 use the address round-robin scheme described in Chapter 3 in the section "DNS Round Robin and Load Distribution."

Address sorting in BIND is the process in which, if the host being queried about has several addresses and one address is closer to the client, that address should be returned first. This is based on the theory that using the address closer to the client is more optimal, which it usually is. This, of course, assumes that the client does not hash the answer, parse it backward, or sort it—as it is allowed to do. That would ruin the whole scheme. Additionally, the nameserver does not really have any knowledge of the network topology; it can only make guesses based on (possibly incorrect) assumptions about subnetting and so on. Because of this, sorting by the server has been found to be somewhat lacking in merit, and the round-robin scheme is seen as more desirable (so it is the default). Instead, new stub resolvers now support a sorting option in /etc/resolv.conf. This makes more sense because the administrator of the host does know things about the network topology and can set up the correct sorting options if necessary. Please see your resolv(5) or resolver(5) man page for more information about the resolv.conf sortlist option.

Of course, installing a sortlist on each and every client in your network can be a lot of work. Therefore, the old sorting behavior in BIND can still be achieved through the sortlist and topology options, enabling you to perform centralized address sorting instead of decentralized sorting in the stub resolvers.

Sortlist

A sortlist defines the preferred addresses for addresses or subnets. This example is from the named.conf man page:

```
sortlist {
    { localhost; localnets; };
        { localnets; };
};
```

The sortlist consists of pairs. First in the pair is a list of addresses to match, and second is a list of addresses to prefer. In the previous example, one pair exists. When a query comes in from a host matching the predefined ACLs localhost or localnets, any A records matching the localnets ACL is sorted before any other A records matching the query. Queries from anyone else are sorted according to the rrset-ordering for the records (round-robin by default). The previous sortlist is quite reasonable for a small network of one subnet. If penguin.bv has two www.penguin.bv servers, one at an ISP and one on its own network, this sortlist ensures that when the penguin employees type http://www.penguin.bv/, they will use their local server, and not their Internet line. In addition, it ensures that users outside penguin.bv get a round-robined random address as usual. If you want to pursue this subject, please see Appendix A, "named.conf Man Page," which has a much more elaborate, commented example.

Topology

Topology overrides your nameserver's preferences for remote nameservers. BIND bases its choice of which remote nameservers to use on the RTT—servers with good RTT records get chosen over servers with worse RTT records. This is exactly what we want in most cases. But in some cases, such as when one line costs more to put traffic on, one line is more liable to be overloaded, or a nameserver is more likely to be down, it makes sense to prefer nameservers based on another metric.

The topology statement assigns distances based on the order in the topology list. A negated element gets assigned the maximum distance. Here is an example for ns.penguin.bv:

```
topology {
    192.168.55/24;      // Local net is preferred
    !192.168.56.0/25;   // But the emperor-net is overloaded
    192.168.226/24;     // Walruss-net
};
```

The local net is preferred before the walruss net, and the emperor.penguin.bv net is least preferred, being negated. This is the default topology list in BIND 8:

```
topology {
    localhost;
    localnets;
};
```

Sorting Is Out of Band

All record sorting configuration is out of band. BIND does not communicate sorting requirements to caching or slave servers. Most often, slave and cache servers round robin the records. If they are to sort addresses, the same (or at least analogous) `sortlist` and `rrset-order` options have to be installed on them as on the master.

Checknames, Legal Hostnames

Formally, a domain name consists of labels connected with periods (.). For example, www.penguin.bv consists of three labels—the leftmost label is also a hostname. Hostnames are more restricted than labels.

RFC 952 defines hostnames as consisting of the letters A–Z, the numbers 0–9, the minus sign or dash (-), and the period. Periods are allowed as delimiters only in domain style names. The first character must be a letter, and the last character can't be a   or .. It also does not allow single-character names. RFC 1035 recommends following RFC 952 for hostname strings.

RFC 1123 changes one rule. It allows a digit as the first character. The obvious example here is 3com.com. It also sets the maximum length of labels to 63 characters, but says that names up to 255 characters should be handled. Modern versions of this say that a label part should be restricted to 63 characters and that the complete FQDN of a host should not be longer than 255 characters.

RFC 1912 has its own opinions and adds, "Labels may not be all numbers." However, because RFC 1912 is an informational RFC, not a standards RFC, this has been largely ignored.

The trick then is to remember what a label is and what hostnames are. The restriction is on hostnames. Hostnames are on the left side of A and MX records, and on the right side of NS, SOA, PTR, SRV, and some other records. The left side of an SRV record is a label. This is why Windows 2000 can place SRV records with a slash (/) in their names into DNS, and why reverse zones for classless networks often have names with slashes in them. Slashes and underscores are not legal in hostnames.

As mentioned, BIND now enforces these restrictions. Earlier versions of BIND 4 did not enforce them, and a lot of interesting names were found in DNS at the time.

BIND 8 has an option to control these checks and how fatal they are. The default configuration is

```
options {
    ...
    check-names master fail;
    check-names slave warn;
    check-names response ignore;
    ...
};
```

This means, of course, that if any illegal hostnames are found in your master zones, they will not be loaded. However, any illegal hostnames found in your slave zones result in warnings. This is good because you do not control the contents of your slave zones—not always, anyway. You should send a friendly note to the master server administrator saying that illegal names exist in his (or her) zones, which are in need of fixing. Not checking the composition of what DNS returns to us when we query it is a good idea. It enables us to resolve names even if they are illegal.

It is, in spite of the option to allow everything, a good idea to stay on the right side of the RFCs. If you use illegal characters in hostnames, you risk people on the Internet (or even in your own company) being unable to resolve names because their resolver implementations are less graceful than yours. So, just say no to illegal names.

The Limits of BIND

BIND does not have many implementation limits, or at least not limits you easily bump into. Most of these limits are not explicitly documented, and for that reason, I might easily have missed or misinterpreted some in spite of my best efforts. These are some of the limits in BIND 8.2.2P5:

- A slave zone can have only 16 masters.
- BIND will try only up to 16 NS records when making queries about a zone.
- The maximum concurrent inbound zone transfers is 20.
- BIND handles only 65,536 zones.
- BIND will issue only 20 queries to recursively resolve a name.
- The maximum SOA refresh interval is 2,419,200 seconds, or 4 weeks.
- The maximum retry interval is 1,209,600 seconds, or 2 weeks.
- Only 20 additional records in a query answer are handled.
- Domain names can be only 1,024 characters long in total.

    Software such as dig apparently thinks that 255 is a more reasonable limit, and this is in line with assumptions made other places, so stick to 255. Your kernel might also limit you to setting FQDN hostnames shorter than 255 characters.

- UDP DNS packets are restricted to 512 bytes. Under some new protocol extensions implemented in BIND 9, this is no longer true, though.

These limits are encoded in various parts of the source code. Some of them are design limits, which are hard to get around. Some are protocol limits that you shouldn't try to get around (and if you do, you face interoperability issues), and some are just limits you can change by simply changing a #define in the source code and recompiling. If you want to change the source, you must be able to distinguish them from each other first.

The Housekeeping of BIND

BIND has a few housekeeping routines. The dial-up heartbeat-interval has already been covered in Chapter 10, "DNS and Dial-Up Connections," and the cleaning-interval was covered in Chapter 8, "Security Concerns."

Interface Scanning

Every 60 minutes BIND scans your system for new interfaces, and if it finds any, it starts listening on port 53 (TCP and UDP) on the interfaces. If your machine takes interfaces up and down often, 1 hour might be too long to wait for this. The `interface-interval` option can help:

```
options {
    ...
    interface-interval 0;
    ...
};
```

The interval is measured in minutes. If `interface-interval` is set to 0, as in this example, the interfaces are scanned only each time the `named.conf` file is read—at reload or reconfig. At the interface scanning, any deleted interfaces also are cleaned up. If you use the `query-source` option and the interface identified by it is deleted, named panics and exits.

Of course, all this is moot if you use `listen-on` options or don't take network interfaces up and down frequently.

Zone Transfers

The main points of zone transfers are covered earlier in this book, but some things were left out.

BIND 8 performs zone transfers with the help of the external program, named-xfer. You can set the path of named-xfer with the `named-xfer` option. BIND 9, in contrast, performs zone transfers internally in named.

Faster Zone Transfers

Old zone transfers used a format now called *one-answer*, meaning one answer per network packet. This is not quite optimal, but is necessary for compatibility with old versions of BIND and named-xfer. *many-answers* packs each message with resource records but is understood only by BIND 8.1 or later, as well as special patched versions of BIND 4.9.5. The option is `transfer-format`, and it can be used globally or per server:

```
options {
    ...
```

```
    transfer-format many-answers;
    ...
};

server 192.168.0.2 {
    transfer-format one-answer; // Old server
};
```

Zone Transfer Limits

Options are available to adjust quite a few other things about zone transfers. This code shows the default values, except for the server clause:

```
options {
    ...
    transfers-in 10;
    transfers-out ?;
    transfers-per-ns 2;
    transfer-source 0.0.0.0;
    max-transfer-time-in 120;
    serial-queries 4;
    ...
};

server 192.168.0.2 {
    transfers 10;        // Really super server!
};
```

transfers-in defaults to 10 and cannot be set higher than 20. transfers-out, on the other hand, is not implemented. transfers-per-ns is 2 by default. Setting the maximum number of transfers higher, globally or per server, enables the zones to be copied more quickly. This is possible only if enough bandwidth is available, but it also can use a lot of resources on both hosts. Recall that BIND 8 uses an external program to perform zone transfers. Executing the external program is quite expensive, and it uses some memory.

transfer-source is similar to the query source option. By default, zone transfer requests appear to be coming from the interface closest to the master server. If the master server uses an allow-transfer option to limit who gets to make transfers, you must perform zone transfers from the correct interface.

max-transfer-time-in is measured in minutes and sets how long named will wait for a zone to transfer before aborting it. Almost any reasonable zone should be capable of transferring in two hours, even over a 9600bps modem. Temporary network problems, such as packet loss, routing loops, back-hoe operator errors, and so on, can cause a zone transfer to fail and then revert to its usual snappy self when the network is restored. If network problems affect enough of the zone transfers, 10 halted incoming transfers can block all other zone transfers for many hours. Setting transfers-in high and transfers-per-ns low (as is the default) helps this by letting a downed network link block only 2 (by default, that is) of the incoming transfer slots.

serial-queries controls how many concurrent SOA queries a slave server will leave outstanding when checking whether zone transfers are necessary. Each outstanding query uses a small amount of memory. If the server is slave to many (hundreds or thousands) of zones, you should raise this; otherwise, it won't get enough SOA queries out to even discover that the zones have been outdated.

Manual Zone Transfers

Few reasons exist to perform manual zone transfers, but should you need to, it is quite simple:

```
$ named-xfer
Usage error: no domain
Usage: named-xfer
        -z zone to transfer
        -f db_file
        [-i ixfr_file]
        [-s serial_no]
        [-d debug_level]
        [-l debug_log_file]
        [-t trace_file]
        [-p port]
        [-S] [-Z]
        [-C class]
        [-x axfr-src]
        [-T tsig_info_file]
        servers [-ixfr|-axfr]...
$ named-xfer -z penguin.bv -f sz/penguin.bv ns.penguin.bv
named-xfer[3814]: send AXFR query 0 to 192.168.55.2
```

Afterward, the zone is in sz/penguin.bv, just as if named did it itself. To get the zone loaded, restart your named. The normal way to reload slave zones is to perform a zone transfer.

You can use other methods to copy zone files, such as rcp, scp (an ssh utility), rdist, or rsync. If this is your mode of zone transfer, you must not have any masters for each zone. In addition, it might even be easiest to tell your slave server that it is master for the zones. Using tools such as scp, rdist, or rsync combined with scp provides a very secure method of transferring zones. However, BIND 9 can use TSIG for zone transfers—you can't get more secure than that. On the other hand, scp does use private/public key pairs, which can make key management easier.

Incremental Zone Transfers

IXFR was introduced in RFC 1995. It allows the DNS servers to transfer the changes made to a zone instead of the whole zone, which saves time and bandwidth and is an excellent idea.

BIND 8 can maintain an IXFR database, if and only if you maintain your zones by dynamic DNS protocol, such as is achieved with the command-line tool nsupdate.

IXFR is a new protocol and a new feature in BIND. Unfortunately, the code associated with IXFRs in BIND 8.2.2P5 is too buggy to use and was not even meant to keep an IXFR database—but it does, due to a bug. However, I trust that the code will mature.

The reason the IXFR database is maintained only if you manage your zone by dynamic DNS is that finding the changes between two versions of a zone is easier if you are told what the changes are. This is what we tell named with DDNS. Finding the difference between two versions of the zone file, on the other hand, is more subtle and harder to do.

The following are options to control IXFR issues:

```
options {
    ...
    maintain-ixfr-base yes;
    max-ixfr-log-size ?;
    ...
};
```

I can't think of a reason to disable keeping IXFR databases, unless they are known to be buggy. The max-ixfr-log-size option is not implemented but will limit the size of the IXFR database, which is beneficial because transferring an IXFR database larger than the zone itself is useless. BIND 8.2.2P5 does implement a limit on the IXFR database, but it's undocumented and not user-tunable.

The default for maintain-ixfr-base in BIND 8.2.2P5 was supposed to be no.

Statistics

BIND computes statistics. BIND injects three lines of statistics into the log every statistics interval (the lines have been wrapped to fit on the page):

```
Aug 13 07:16:09 ns named[17871]: USAGE 966143769 965983563
        CPU=25.27u/16.68s CHILDCPU=4.05u/2.83s
Aug 13 07:16:09 ns named[17871]: NSTATS 966143769 965983563 A=64872
        CNAME=51 SOA=1641 PTR=24273 MX=1773 TXT=33 AAAA=365 SRV=7
        AXFR=5 ANY=1494
Aug 13 07:16:09 ns named[17871]: XSTATS 966143769 965983563 RR=11076
        RNXD=766 RFwdR=6192 RDupR=9 RFail=74 RFErr=0 RErr=14 RAXFR=5
        RLame=191 ROpts=0 SSysQ=4112 SAns=90404 SFwdQ=5214 SDupQ=2864
        SErr=1 RQ=97527 RIQ=24 RFwdQ=5214 RDupQ=19 RTCP=3110 SFwdR=6192
        SFail=204 SFErr=0 SNaAns=18049 SNXD=3216
```

Each line starts with two timestamps: The first is now (or at least when the log line was written), in seconds since the epoch. The second is the time when named started. Subtracting the second from the first yields the wall-clock time named has been running, which is about 44 hours in this case.

The USAGE line tells how much CPU time named has used: 25.27 user seconds and 16.68 system seconds. CHILDCPU shows how much of that time was used by named children; named-xfer is the only child named runs, so it's the CPU usage for zone transfers.

The NSTATS line indicates the how many of each query type your server has received. Any query types not received are not listed.

The XSTATS line is more difficult to decipher. This is the meaning of the fields:

Field	Number of
RR=11076	Responses received.
RNXD=766	Received NXDOMAIN (no existent domain) responses.
RFwdR=6192	Received and forwarded responses. In other words, the response was sent back to the original querier.
RDupR=9	Received duplicate responses. When a query times out because of network problems, for example, it is sent again. If the original query, or the answer, was delayed—not lo—and the original answer then arrives (followed by the answer to the retried query), a duplicate response results.
RFail=74	Received SERVFAIL responses. A server sends this when it thinks it should have managed to answer the query but couldn't.
RFErr=0	Received FORMERRs. The remote server thought our query had a format error.
RErr=14	Received errors that were not SERVFAIL or FORMERR.
RAXFR=5	Received AXFRs.
RLame=191	Lame delegations found.
ROpts=0	Received packets with IP options set. This should be 0.
SSysQ=4112	Sent system queries. A *system* query is a query initiated by the server itself. For example, when the server starts, it asks around for the root servers and to measure the RTT.
SAns=90404	Sent answers. How many queries answers were sent for.
SFwdQ=5214	Sent forwarded queries. Queries received that we have forwarded.
SDupQ=2864	Sent duplicate queries. As mentioned earlier, after a timeout, the query is sent again.
SErr=1	Send errors. The number of sendto() calls that have failed.
RQ=97527	Received queries.
RIQ=24	Received inverse queries. Inverse queries are obsolete and unsupported, but some old versions of nslookup still use them. When this stays at 0 for lengthy periods, the world will be a better place.
RFwdQ=5214	The number of RQs received that needed further processing. This reflects the number of recursive clients the server has.

Field	Number of
RDupQ=19	Received duplicate queries. This happens when the recursive clients times out and retries the query.
RTCP=3110	Received TCP queries. Some of these are AXFRs; the rest are probably reissued, truncated UDP queries.
SFwdR=6192	Number of responses forwarded to queriers.
SFail=204	Sent SERVFAIL responses.
SFErr=0	Sent FORMERR responses.
SNaAns=18049	Sent non-authoritative answers.
SNXD=3216	Sent NXDOMAIN answers.

That is a lot of statistics. But wait, there is more. You can dump this to a file, as well. `ndc stats` dumps the file `named.stats` to named's directory. If you have enabled `host-statistics`, it will show statistics about each and every host it has ever answered a query from, or sent a query to, since it was (re)started. A statistics file should be capable of being put into a statistics package or a performance analysis tool, to track the server's performance—not that I know of any such tools. You can override the name of this file with the `statistics-file` option.

These host statistics can be used to track down problems with specific clients or servers. Together with a cache dump (ndc dumpdb, see Chapter 6, "Troubleshooting DNS"), this is a lot of information, perhaps too much, to base detective work on.

One statistic that is easy to understand and keep an eye on is the RQ. It gives you a way to track the query rate on your server. However, it is, perhaps, more important to track the load on your server.

Memory Statistics

If you enable `deallocate-on-exit`, named will want to write some memory statistics to file. The default name for this file is `named.memstats`. It can be overridden with the `memstatistics-file` option. This is most useful if you're trying to debug a memory leak in named.

The Rest of the Options

There are some named.conf options left that should be presented.

`fake-iquery`

IQUERY is an obsolete DNS query type. It was meant to perform reverse lookups, much the way the in-addr.arpa domain is used for reverse lookups now. In some quite old RFCs, IQUERY clients were talked about to the effect of "the result is never used for anything useful." Newer documentations claim that old versions of nslookup are the only remaining applications using IQUERY. By default, BIND does not support IQUERYs. However, IQUERY can be enabled with the `fake-iquery` option, in which case the response for an IQUERY for 192.168.0.2 is the hostname [129.168.0.2] (with the brackets). This is clearly fake.

treat-cr-as-space

If you generate your zone files on a DOS/Windows/NT and then transfer them to UNIX in binary format, the files will have CR-NL newlines instead of NL, as expected on UNIX machines. This option, should you choose to enable it, makes named treat the superfluous CR as space, rendering it harmless.

min-roots

This is the minimum number of root servers the server must know about before answering any query about the root servers. The default is 2. In that case, if the server knows only one root server, it won't answer any queries about it. The theory is that if the server knows fewer than this number of root servers, it knows nothing about the root servers worth passing on to other servers. If you're on the Internet, do not lower this number. If you're on a closed network, you should have at least two internal root servers, and you won't have to adjust it in any case.

has-old-clients

This is an alias for

```
auth-nxdomain yes;
maintain-ixfr-base yes;
rfc2308-type1 no;
```

If you combine any of those options with `has-old-clients`, the result is order-dependent. These are all the default values in BIND 8.2.2P5.

auth-nxdomain

The documentations simply state to not change this from the default, which is yes. I'm afraid I don't know the reasons behind this.

rfc2308-type1

RFC2308 specifies to send the NS record along with the SOA record for negative answers. Old forwarding servers will not understand this; therefore, the default is no. If you know you don't have any old servers forwarding queries to you (due to forwarder options), you can enable this.

## PART IV

APPENDIXES

A named.conf Man Page

B Bibliography

NAMED.CONF MAN PAGE

NAMED.CONF(5) System Programmer's Manual NAMED.CONF(5)

NAME

named.conf—configuration file for named(8)

Overview

BIND 8 is much more configurable than previous releases of BIND. There are entirely new areas of configuration, such as access control lists and categorized logging. Many options that previously applied to all zones can now be used selectively. These features, plus a consideration of future configuration needs led to the creation of a new configuration file format.

General Syntax

A BIND 8 configuration consists of two general features, statements and comments. All statements end with a semicolon. Many statements can contain substatements, which are each also terminated with a semicolon.

The following statements are supported:

logging	Specifies what the server logs, and where the log messages are sent
options	Controls global server configuration options and sets defaults for other statements
zone	Defines a zone
acl	Defines a named IP address matching list for access control and other uses
key	Specifies key information for use in authentication and authorization
trusted-keys	Defines DNSSEC keys that are preconfigured into the server and implicitly trusted
server	Sets certain configuration options for individual remote servers
controls	Declares control channels to be used by the ndc utility
include	Includes another file

The logging and options statements may only occur once per configuration, while the rest may appear numerous times. Further detail on each statement is provided in individual sections following.

Comments may appear anywhere that whitespace may appear in a BIND configuration file. To appeal to programmers of all kinds, they can be written in C, C++, or Shell/Perl constructs.

C-style comments start with the two characters /* (slash, star) and end with */ (star, slash). Because they are completely delimited with these characters, they can be used to comment only a portion of a line or to span multiple lines.

C-style comments can't be nested. For example, the following is not valid because the entire comment ends with the first */:

```
/* This is the start of a comment.
This is still part of the comment.
/* This is an incorrect attempt at nesting a comment. */
This is no longer in any comment. */
```

C++-style comments start with the two characters // (slash, slash) and continue to the end of the physical line. They can't be continued across multiple physical lines; to have one logical comment span multiple lines, each line must use the // pair. For example

```
// This is the start of a comment. The next line
// is a new comment, even though it is logically
// part of the previous comment.
```

Shell-style (or Perl-style, if you prefer) comments start with the character # (hash or pound or number or octothorpe or whatever) and continue to the end of the physical line, like C++ comments. For example

```
# This is the start of a comment. The next line
# is a new comment, even though it is logically
# part of the previous comment.
```

WARNING

You cannot use the ; (semicolon) character to start a comment such as you would in a zone file. The semicolon indicates the end of a configuration statement, so whatever follows it will be interpreted as the start of the next statement.

Converting from BIND 4.9.x

BIND 4.9.x configuration files can be converted to the new format by using src/bin/named/named-bootconf, a shell script that is part of the BIND 8.2.x source kit.

Documentation Definitions

Described in the following list are elements used throughout the BIND configuration file documentation. Elements which are only associated with one statement are described only in the section describing that statement:

acl_name	The name of an address_match_list as defined by the acl statement.
address_match_list	A list of one or more ip_addr, ip_prefix, key_id, or acl_name elements, as described in the ADDRESS MATCH LISTS section.
dotted-decimal	One or more integers valued 0 through 255 separated only by dots (.), such as 123, 45.67, or 89.123.45.67.
domain_name	A quoted string which will be used as a DNS name, for example my.test.domain.
path_name	A quoted string which will be used as a pathname, such as zones/master/my.test.domain.
ip_addr	An IP address with exactly four elements in dotted-decimal notation.
ip_port	An IP port number. The number is limited to 0 through 65535, with values below 1024 typically restricted to root-owned processes. In some cases an asterisk (*) character can be used as a placeholder to select a random high-numbered port.
ip_prefix	An IP network specified in dotted-decimal form, followed by / and then the number of bits in the netmask. E.g. 127/8 is the network 127.0.0.0 with netmask 255.0.0.0. 1.2.3.0/28 is network 1.2.3.0 with netmask 255.255.255.240.

key_name	A string representing the name of a shared key, to be used for transaction security.
number	A non-negative integer with an entire range limited by the range of a C language signed integer (2,147,483,647 on a machine with 32-bit integers). Its acceptable value might further be limited by the context in which it is used.
size_spec	A number, the word unlimited, or the word default.
	The maximum value of size_spec is that of unsigned long integers on the machine, unlimited requests, unlimited use, or the maximum available amount. Default uses the limit that was in force when the server was started.
	A number can optionally be followed by a scaling factor: K or k for kilobytes, M or m for megabytes, and G or g for gigabytes, which scale by 1024, 1024*1024, and 1024*1024*1024, respectively.
	Integer storage overflow is currently silently ignored during conversion of scaled values, resulting in values less than intended, possibly even negative. Using unlimited is the best way to safely set a really large number.
yes_or_no	Either yes or no. The words true and false are also accepted, as are the numbers 1 and 0.

Address Match Lists

Syntax

```
address_match_list    = 1*address_match_element

   address_match_element = [ "!" ] ( address_match_list /
                                     ip_address / ip_prefix /
                                     acl_name / "key " key_id ) ";"
```

Definition and Usage

Address match lists are primarily used to determine access control for various server operations. They are also used to define priorities for querying other nameservers and to set the addresses on which named will listen for queries. The elements which constitute an address match list can be any of the following:

- An ip-address (in dotted-decimal notation)
- An ip-prefix (in the /-notation)
- A key_id, as defined by the key statement
- The name of an address match list previously defined with the acl statement
- Another address_match_list

Elements can be negated with a leading exclamation mark (!), and the match list names any, none, localhost, and localnets are predefined. More information on those names can be found in the description of the acl statement.

The addition of the key clause made the name of this syntactic element something of a misnomer, since security keys can be used to validate access without regard to a host or network address. Nonetheless, the term address match list is still used throughout the documentation.

When a given IP address or prefix is compared to an address match list, the list is traversed in order until an element matches. The interpretation of a match depends on whether the list is being used for access control, defining listen-on ports, or as a topology, and whether the element was negated.

When used as an access control list, a non-negated match allows access and a negated match denies access. If there is no match at all in the list, access is denied. The clauses allow-query, allow-transfer, allow update, allow-recursion, and blackhole all use address match lists like this. Similarly, the listen-on option will cause the server to not accept queries on any of the machine's addresses which do not match the list.

When used with the topology option, a non-negated match returns a distance based on its position on the list (the closer the match is to the start of the list, the shorter the distance is between it and the server). A negated match will be assigned the maximum distance from the server. If there is no match, the address will get a distance which is further than any non-negated list element, and closer than any negated element.

Because of the first-match aspect of the algorithm, an element that defines a subset of another element in the list should come before the broader element, regardless of whether either is negated. For example, in 1.2.3/24; !1.2.3.13 the 1.2.3.13 element is completely useless, because the algorithm will match any lookup for 1.2.3.13 to the 1.2.3/24 element. Using !1.2.3.13; 1.2.3/24 fixes that problem by having 1.2.3.13 blocked by the negation but all other 1.2.3.* hosts fall through.

The Logging Statement

Syntax

```
logging {
  [ channel channel_name {
    ( file path_name
       [ versions ( number | unlimited ) ]
       [ size size_spec ]
    | syslog ( kern | user | mail | daemon | auth | syslog | lpr |
              news | uucp | cron | authpriv | ftp |
```

```
                  local0 | local1 | local2 | local3 |
                  local4 | local5 | local6 | local7 )
      | null );

     [ severity ( critical | error | warning | notice |
                    info  | debug [ level ] | dynamic ); ]
     [ print-category yes_or_no; ]
     [ print-severity yes_or_no; ]
     [ print-time yes_or_no; ]
   }; ]

   [ category category_name {
     channel_name; [ channel_name; ... ]
   }; ]
   ...
};
```

Definition and Usage

The logging statement configures a wide variety of logging options for the nameserver. Its channel phrase associates output methods, format options and severity levels with a name that can then be used with the category phrase to select how various classes of messages are logged.

Only one logging statement is used to define as many channels and categories as are wanted. If there are multiple logging statements in a configuration, the first defined determines the logging, and warnings are issued for the others. If there is no logging statement, the logging configuration will be

```
logging {
    category default { default_syslog; default_debug; };
    category panic { default_syslog; default_stderr; };
    category packet { default_debug; };
    category eventlib { default_debug; };
};
```

The logging configuration is established as soon as the logging statement is parsed. If you want to redirect messages about processing of the entire configuration file, the logging statement must appear first. Even if you do not redirect configuration file parsing messages, we recommend always putting the logging statement first so that this rule need not be consciously recalled if you ever do need or want the parser's messages relocated.

The Channel Phrase

All log output goes to one or more *channels*; you can make as many of them as you want.

Every channel definition must include a clause that says whether messages selected for the channel go to a file, to a particular syslog facility, or are discarded. It can optionally also limit the message severity level that will be accepted by the channel (default is info), and whether to include a time stamp generated by named, the category name, or severity level. The default is not to include any of those three.

The word null as the destination option for the channel will cause all messages sent to it to be discarded; other options for the channel are meaningless.

The file clause can include limitations both on how large the file is allowed to become, and how many versions of the file will be saved each time the file is opened.

The size option for files is simply a hard ceiling on log growth. If the file ever exceeds the size, then named will just not write anything more to it until the file is reopened; exceeding the size does not automatically trigger a reopen. The default behavior is to not limit the size of the file.

If you use the version logfile option, then named will retain that many backup versions of the file by renaming them when opening. For example, if you choose to keep 3 old versions of the file lamers.log then just before it is opened lamers.log.1 is renamed to lamers.log.2, lamers.log.0 is renamed to lamers.log.1, and lamers.log is renamed to lamers.log.0. No rolled versions are kept by default; any existing log file is simply appended. The unlimited keyword is synonymous with 99 in current BIND releases. Example usage of size and versions options:

```
channel an_example_level {
    file "lamers.log" versions 0 size 20m;
    print-time yes;
    print-category yes;
};
```

The argument for the syslog clause is a syslog facility as described in the syslog(3) manual page. How syslogd will handle messages sent to this facility is described in the syslog.conf(5) manual page. If you have a system which uses a very old version of syslog that only uses two arguments to the openlog()() function, then this clause is silently ignored.

The severity clause works like syslog's priorities, except that they can also be used if you are writing straight to a file rather than using syslog. Messages which are not at least of the severity level given will not be selected for the channel; messages of higher severity levels will be accepted.

If you are using syslog, then the syslog.conf priorities will also determine what eventually passes through. For example, defining a channel facility and severity as daemon and debug but only logging daemon.warning via syslog.conf will cause messages of severity info and notice to be dropped. If the situation were reversed, with named writing messages of only warning or higher, then syslogd would print all messages it received from the channel.

The server can supply extensive debugging information when it is in debugging mode. If the server's global debug level is greater than zero, then debugging mode will be active. The global debug level is set either by starting the named server with the -d flag followed by a positive integer, or by sending the running server the SIGUSR1 signal (for example, by using ndc trace). The global debug level can be set to zero, and debugging mode turned off, by sending the server the SIGUSR2 signal (as with ndc notrace). All debugging messages in the server have a debug level, and higher debug levels give more detailed output. Channels that specify a specific debug severity, for example

```
channel specific_debug_level {
    file "foo";
    severity debug 3;
};
```

will get debugging output of level 3 or less any time the server is in debugging mode, regardless of the global debugging level. Channels with dynamic severity use the server's global level to determine what messages to print.

If print-time has been turned on, then the date and time will be logged. print-time may be specified for a syslog channel, but is usually pointless since syslog also prints the date and time. If print-category is requested, then the category of the message will be logged as well. Finally, if print-severity is on, then the severity level of the message will be logged. The print-options may be used in any combination, and will always be printed in the following order: time, category, severity. Here is an example where all three print-options are on:

```
28-Apr-1997 15:05:32.863 default: notice: Ready to answer queries.
```

There are four predefined channels that are used for named's default logging as follows. How they are used is described in the next section, "The Category Phrase."

```
channel default_syslog {
    syslog daemon;        # send to syslog's daemon facility
    severity info;        # only send priority info and higher
};

channel default_debug {
    file "named.run";     # write to named.run in the working directory
                          # Note: stderr is used instead of "named.run"
                          # if the server is started with the -f option.
    severity dynamic;     # log at the server's current debug level
};

channel default_stderr { # writes to stderr
    file "<stderr>";      # this is illustrative only; there's currently
                          # no way of specifying an internal file
                          # descriptor in the configuration language.
    severity info;        # only send priority info and higher
};

channel null {
    null;                 # toss anything sent to this channel
};
```

Once a channel is defined, it cannot be redefined. Thus you cannot alter the built-in channels directly, but you can modify the default logging by pointing categories at channels you have defined.

The Category Phrase

There are many categories, so you can send the logs you want to see wherever you want, without seeing logs you don't want. If you don't specify a list of channels for a category, then log messages in that category will be sent to the default category instead. If you don't specify a default category, the following "default default" is used:

```
category default { default_syslog; default_debug; };
```

As an example, let's say you want to log security events to a file, but you also want keep the default logging behavior. You'd specify the following:

```
channel my_security_channel {
    file "my_security_file";
    severity info;
};
category security { my_security_channel;
                    default_syslog; default_debug; };
```

To discard all messages in a category, specify the null channel:

```
category lame-servers { null; };
category cname { null; };
```

The following categories are available:

Default	The catch-all. Many things still aren't classified into categories, and they all end up here. Also, if you don't specify any channels for a category, the default category is used instead. If you do not define the default category, the following definition is used:
	`category default { default_syslog; default_debug; };`
config	High-level configuration file processing.
Parser	Low-level configuration file processing.
Queries	A short log message is generated for every query the server receives.
lame-servers	Messages like "Lame server on ..."
statistics	Statistics.
Panic	If the server has to shut itself down due to an internal problem, it will log the problem in this category as well as in the problem's native category. If you do not define the panic category, the following definition is used:
	`category panic { default_syslog; default_stderr; };`

update	Dynamic updates.
Ncache	Negative caching.
xfer-in	Zone transfers the server is receiving.
xfer-out	Zone transfers the server is sending.
Db	All database operations.
Eventlib	Debugging info from the event system. Only one channel may be specified for this category, and it must be a file channel. If you do not define the eventlib category, the following definition is used:

```
category eventlib { default_debug; };
```

packet	Dumps of packets received and sent. Only one channel may be specified for this category, and it must be a file channel. If you do not define the packet category, the following definition is used:

```
category packet { default_debug; };
```

notify	The NOTIFY protocol.
Cname	Messages like "... points to a CNAME."
Security	Approved/unapproved requests.
Os	Operating system problems.
Insist	Internal consistency check failures.
Maintenance	Periodic maintenance events.
Load	Zone loading messages.
response-checks	Messages arising from response checking, such as "Malformed response ...," "wrong ans. name ...," "unrelated additional info ...," "invalid RR type ...," and "bad referral ...."

The Options Statement

Syntax

```
options {
  [ version version_string; ]
  [ directory path_name; ]
  [ named-xfer path_name; ]
  [ dump-file path_name; ]
  [ memstatistics-file path_name; ]
  [ pid-file path_name; ]
  [ statistics-file path_name; ]
  [ auth-nxdomain yes_or_no; ]
  [ deallocate-on-exit yes_or_no; ]
  [ dialup yes_or_no; ]
  [ fake-iquery yes_or_no; ]
```

```
    [ fetch-glue yes_or_no; ]
    [ has-old-clients yes_or_no; ]
    [ host-statistics yes_or_no; ]
    [ multiple-cnames yes_or_no; ]
    [ notify yes_or_no; ]
    [ recursion yes_or_no; ]
    [ rfc2308-type1 yes_or_no; ]
    [ use-id-pool yes_or_no; ]
    [ treat-cr-as-space yes_or_no; ]
    [ also-notify yes_or_no; ]
    [ forward ( only | first ); ]
    [ forwarders { [ in_addr ; [ in_addr ; ... ] ] }; ]
    [ check-names ( master | slave | response ) ( warn | fail | ignore); ]
    [ allow-query { address_match_list }; ]
    [ allow-recursion { address_match_list }; ]
    [ allow-transfer { address_match_list }; ]
    [ blackhole { address_match_list }; ]
    [ listen-on [ port ip_port ] { address_match_list }; ]
    [ query-source [ address ( ip_addr | * ) ]
                   [ port ( ip_port | * ) ] ; ]
    [ lame-ttl number; ]
    [ max-transfer-time-in number; ]
    [ max-ncache-ttl number; ]
    [ min-roots number; ]
    [ serial-queries number; ]
    [ transfer-format ( one-answer | many-answers ); ]
    [ transfers-in  number; ]
    [ transfers-out number; ]
    [ transfers-per-ns number; ]
    [ transfer-source ip_addr; ]
    [ maintain-ixfr-base yes_or_no; ]
    [ max-ixfr-log-size number; ]
    [ coresize size_spec ; ]
    [ datasize size_spec ; ]
    [ files size_spec ; ]
    [ stacksize size_spec ; ]
    [ cleaning-interval number; ]
    [ heartbeat-interval number; ]
    [ interface-interval number; ]
    [ statistics-interval number; ]
    [ topology { address_match_list }; ]
    [ sortlist { address_match_list|fR }; ]
    [ rrset-order { order_spec ; [ order_spec ; ... [ [ };
};
```

Definition and Usage

The options statement sets up global options to be used by BIND. This statement may appear only once in a configuration file; if more than one occurrence is found, the first occurrence determines the actual options used, and a warning will be generated. If there is no options statement, an options block with each option set to its default will be used.

Pathnames

Version	The version the server should report via the ndc command or via a query of name version.bind in class chaos. The default is the real version number of the server, but some server operators prefer the string (surely you must be joking).
Directory	The working directory of the server. Any non-absolute pathnames in the configuration file will be taken as relative to this directory. The default location for most server output files (for example, named.run) is this directory. If a directory is not specified, the working directory defaults to ., the directory from which the server was started. The directory specified should be an absolute path.
named-xfer	The pathname to the named-xfer program that the server uses for inbound zone transfers. If not specified, the default is system dependent (for example, /usr/sbin/named-xfer).
dump-file	The pathname of the file the server dumps the database to when it receives SIGINT signal (as sent by ndc dumpdb). If not specified, the default is named_dump.db.
memstatistics-file	The pathname of the file the server writes memory usage statistics to on exit, if deallocate-on-exit is yes. If not specified, the default is named.memstats.
pid-file	The pathname of the file the server writes its process ID in. If not specified, the default is operating system dependent, but is usually /var/run/named.pid or /etc/named.pid. The pid-file is used by programs like ndc that want to send signals to the running nameserver.
statistics-file	The pathname of the file the server appends statistics to when it receives SIGILL signal (from ndc stats). If not specified, the default is named.stats.

Boolean Options

auth-nxdomain	If yes, then the AA bit is always set on NXDOMAIN responses, even if the server is not actually authoritative. The default is yes. Do not turn off auth-nxdomain unless you are sure you know what you are doing, as some older software won't like it.
deallocate-on-exit	If yes, then when the server exits it will painstakingly deallocate every object it allocated, and then write a memory usage report to the memstatistics-file. The default is no, because it is faster to let the operating system clean up. deallocate-on-exit is handy for detecting memory leaks.

Dialup	If yes, then the server treats all zones as if they are doing zone transfers across a dial on demand dialup link, which can be brought up by traffic originating from this server. This has different effects according to zone type and concentrates the zone maintenance so that it all happens in a short interval, once every heartbeat-interval and hopefully during the one call. It also suppresses some of the normal zone maintenance traffic. The default is no. The dialup option may also be specified in the zone statement, in which case it overrides the options dialup statement.
	If the zone is a master then the server will send out NOTIFY request to all the slaves. This will trigger the zone up to date checking in the slave (providing it supports NOTIFY) allowing the slave to verify the zone while the call is up.
	If the zone is a slave or stub then the server will suppress the zone regular zone up to date queries and only perform the when the heartbeat-interval expires.
fake-iquery	If yes, the server will simulate the obsolete DNS query type IQUERY. The default is no.
fetch-glue	If yes (the default), the server will fetch "glue" resource records it doesn't have when constructing the additional data section of a response. fetch-glue no can be used in conjunction with recursion no to prevent the server's cache from growing or becoming corrupted (at the cost of requiring more work from the client).
has-old-clients	Setting the option to yes, is equivalent to setting the following three options: auth-nxdomain yes, maintain-ixfr-base yes, and rfc2308-type1 no; has-old-clients with auth-nxdomain, maintain-ixfr-base, and rfc2308-type1 is order dependent.
host-statistics	If yes, then statistics are kept for every host that the nameserver interacts with. The default is no. Note: turning on host-statistics can consume huge amounts of memory.
maintain-ixfr-base	If yes, statistics are kept for every host that the nameserver interacts with. The default is no. Note: turning on host-statistics can consume huge amounts of memory.
multiple-cnames	If yes, then multiple CNAME resource records will be allowed for a domain name. The default is no. Allowing multiple CNAME records is against standards and is not recommended. Multiple CNAME support is available because previous versions of BIND allowed multiple CNAME records, and these records have been used for load balancing by a number of sites.

Notify

If yes (the default), DNS NOTIFY messages are sent when a zone the server is authoritative for changes. The use of NOTIFY speeds convergence between the master and its slaves. Slave servers that receive a NOTIFY message and understand it will contact the master server for the zone and see if they need to do a zone transfer, and if they do, they will initiate it immediately. The notify option may also be specified in the zone statement, in which case it overrides the options notify statement.

Recursion

If yes, and a DNS query requests recursion, then the server will attempt to do all the work required to answer the query. If recursion is not on, the server will return a referral to the client if it doesn't know the answer. The default is yes. See also fetch-glue above.

rfc2308-type1

If yes, the server will send NS records along with the SOA record for negative answers. You need to set this to no if you have an old BIND server using you as a forwarder that does not understand negative answers which contain both SOA and NS records or you have an old version of sendmail. The correct fix is to upgrade the broken server or send-mail. The default is no.

use-id-pool

If yes, the server will keep track of its own outstanding query ID's to avoid duplication and increase randomness. This will result in 128KB more memory being consumed by the server. The default is no.

treat-cr-as-space

If yes, the server will treat CR characters the same way it treats a space or tab. This may be necessary when loading zone files on a UNIX system that were generated on an NT or DOS machine. The default is no.

Also-Notify

also-notify

Defines a global list of IP addresses that also get sent NOTIFY messages whenever a fresh copy of the zone is loaded. This helps to ensure that copies of the zones will quickly converge on "stealth" servers. If an also-notify list is given in a zone statement, it will override the options also-notify statement. When a zone notify statement is set to no, the IP addresses in the global also-notify list will not get sent NOTIFY messages for that zone. The default is the empty list (no global notification list).

Forwarding

The forwarding facility can be used to create a large site-wide cache on a few servers, reducing traffic over links to external nameservers. It can also be used to allow queries by servers that do not have direct access to the Internet, but wish to look up exterior names anyway. Forwarding occurs only on those queries for which the server is not authoritative and does not have the answer in its cache.

Forward

This option is only meaningful if the forwarders list is not empty. A value of first, the default, causes the server to query the forwarders first, and if that doesn't answer the question the server will then look for the answer itself. If only is specified, the server will only query the forwarders.

Forwarders	Specifies the IP addresses to be used for forwarding. The default is the empty list (no forwarding).

Forwarding can also be configured on a per-zone basis, allowing for the global forwarding options to be overridden in a variety of ways. You can set particular zones to use different forwarders, or have different forward only/first behavior, or to not forward at all. See THE ZONE STATEMENT section for more information.

Future versions of BIND 8 will provide a more powerful forwarding system. The syntax described above will continue to be supported.

Name Checking	The server can check domain names based upon their expected client contexts. For example, a domain name used as a hostname can be checked for compliance with the RFCs defining valid hostnames.

Three checking methods are available:

Ignore	No checking is done.
Warn	Names are checked against their expected client contexts. Invalid names are logged, but processing continues normally.
Fail	Names are checked against their expected client contexts. Invalid names are logged, and the offending data is rejected.

The server can check name's three areas: master zone files, slave zone files, and in responses to queries the server has initiated. If check-names response fail has been specified, and answering the client's question would require sending an invalid name to the client, the server will send a REFUSED response code to the client.

The defaults are:

check-names master fail;

check-names slave warn;

check-names response ignore;

check-names may also be specified in the zone statement, in which case it overrides the options check-names statement. When used in a zone statement, the area is not specified (because it can be deduced from the zone type).

Access Control	Access to the server can be restricted based on the IP address of the requesting system or via shared secret keys. See ADDRESS MATCH LISTS for details on how to specify access criteria.
allow-query	Specifies which hosts are allowed to ask ordinary questions. allow-query may also be specified in the zone statement, in which case it overrides the options allow-query statement. If not specified, the default is used.

allow-recursion	Specifies which hosts are allowed to ask recursive questions. allow-recursion may also be specified in the zone statement, in which case it overrides the options allow-recursion statement. If not specified, the default is to allow recursive queries from all hosts.
allow-transfer	Specifies which hosts are allowed to receive zone transfers from the server. allow-transfer may also be specified in the zone statement, in which case it overrides the options allow-transfer statement. If not specified, the default is to allow transfers from all hosts.
Blackhole	Specifies a list of addresses that the server will not accept queries from or use to resolve a query. Queries from these addresses will not be responded to.
Interfaces	The interfaces and ports that the server will answer queries from may be specified using the listen-on option. listen-on takes an optional port, and an address match list. The server will listen on all interfaces allowed by the address match list. If a port is not specified, port 53 will be used.
	Multiple listen-on statements are allowed. For example,
	listen-on { 5.6.7.8; };
	listen-on port 1234 { !1.2.3.4; 1.2/16; }; will enable the nameserver on port 53 for the IP address 5.6.7.8, and on port 1234 of an address on the machine in net 1.2 that is not 1.2.3.4.
	If no listen-on is specified, the server will listen on port 53 on all interfaces.
Query Address	If the server doesn't know the answer to a question, it will query other nameservers. query-source specifies the address and port used for such queries. If address is * or is omitted, a wildcard IP address (INADDR_ANY) will be used. If port is * or is omitted, a random unprivileged port will be used. The default is query-source address * port *.

Note

query-source currently applies only to UDP queries; TCP queries always use a wildcard IP address and a random unprivileged port.

Zone Transfers	max-transfer-time-in
	Inbound zone transfers (named-xfer processes) running longer than this many minutes will be terminated. The default is 120 minutes (2 hours).
transfer-format	The server supports two zone transfer methods. one-answer uses one DNS message per resource record transferred. many-answers packs as many resource records as possible into a message. many-answers is more efficient, but is only known to be understood by BIND 8.1 and patched versions of BIND 4.9.5. The default is one-answer. transfer-format may be overridden on a per-server basis by using the server statement.

transfers-in	The maximum number of inbound zone transfers that can be running concurrently. The default value is 10. Increasing transfers-in may speed up the convergence of slave zones, but it also may increase the load on the local system.
transfers-out	This option will be used in the future to limit the number of concurrent outbound zone transfers. It is checked for syntax, but is otherwise ignored.
transfers-per-ns	The maximum number of inbound zone transfers (named-xfer processes) that can be concurrently transferring from a given remote nameserver. The default value is 2. Increasing transfers-per-ns may speed up the convergence of slave zones, but it also may increase the load on the remote nameserver. transfers-per-ns may be overridden on a per-server basis by using the transfers phrase of the server statement.
transfer-source	transfer-source determines which local address will be bound to the TCP connection used to fetch all zones transferred inbound by the server. If not set, it defaults to a system controlled value which will usually be the address of the interface "closest to" the remote end. This address must appear in the remote end's allow-transfer option for the zones being transferred, if one is specified. This statement sets the transfer-source for all zones, but can be overridden on a per-zone basis by including transfer-source statement within the zone block in the configuration file.

Resource Limits

The server's usage of many system resources can be limited. Some operating systems don't support some of the limits. On such systems, a warning will be issued if the unsupported limit is used. Some operating systems don't support limiting resources, and on these systems a set resource limits on this system message will be logged.

Scaled values are allowed when specifying resource limits. For example, 1G can be used instead of 1073741824 to specify a limit of one gigabyte. unlimited requests unlimited use, or the maximum available amount. default uses the limit that was in force when the server was started. See the definition of size_spec in the DOCUMENTATION DEFINITIONS section for more details.

Coresize	The maximum size of a core dump. The default value is default.
Datasize	The maximum amount of data memory the server may use. The default value is default.
Files	The maximum number of files the server may have open concurrently. The default value is unlimited. Note that on some operating systems the server cannot set an unlimited value and cannot determine the maximum number of open files the kernel can support. On such systems, choosing unlimited

will cause the server to use the larger of the rlim_max from getrlimit(RLIMIT_NOFILE) and the value returned by sysconf(_SC_OPEN_MAX). If the actual kernel limit is larger than this value, use limit files to specify the limit explicitly.

max-ixfr-log-size   The max-ixfr-log-size will be used in a future release of the server to limit the size of the transaction log kept for Incremental Zone Transfer.

Stacksize   The maximum amount of stack memory the server may use. The default value is default.

Periodic Task Intervals

cleaning-interval   The server will remove expired resource records from the cache every cleaning-interval minutes. The default is 60 minutes. If set to 0, no periodic cleaning will occur.

heartbeat-interval   The server will perform zone maintenance tasks for all zones marked dialup yes whenever this interval expires. The default is 60 minutes. Reasonable values are up to 1 day (1440 minutes). If set to 0, no zone maintenance for these zones will occur.

interface-interval   The server will scan the network interface list every interface-interval minutes. The default is 60 minutes. If set to 0, interface scanning will only occur when the configuration file is loaded. After the scan, listeners will be started on any new interfaces (provided they are allowed by the listen-on configuration). Listeners on interfaces that have gone away will be cleaned up.

statistics-interval   Nameserver statistics will be logged every statistics-interval minutes. The default is 60. If set to 0, no statistics will be logged.

Topology

All other things being equal, when the server chooses a nameserver to query from a list of nameservers, it prefers the one that is topologically closest to itself. The topology statement takes an address match list and interprets it in a special way. Each top-level list element is assigned a distance. Non-negated elements get a distance based on their position in the list, where the closer the match is to the start of the list, the shorter the distance is between it and the server. A negated match will be assigned the maximum distance from the server. If there is no match, the address will get a distance which is farther than any non-negated list element, and closer than any negated element. For example,

```
topology {
    10/8;
    !1.2.3/24;
    { 1.2/16; 3/8; };
};
```

will prefer servers on network 10 the most, followed by hosts on network 1.2.0.0 (netmask 255.255.0.0) and network 3, with the exception of hosts on network 1.2.3 (netmask 255.255.255.0), which is preferred least of all.

The default topology is

```
topology { localhost; localnets; };
```

Resource Record Sorting

When returning multiple RRs, the nameserver will normally return them in Round Robin, i.e. after each request, the first RR is put to the end of the list. As the order of RRs is not defined, this should not cause any problems.

The client resolver code should re-arrange the RRs as appropriate, i.e. using any addresses on the local net in preference to other addresses. However, not all resolvers can do this, or are not correctly configured.

When a client is using a local server, the sorting can be performed in the server, based on the client's address. This only requires configuring the nameservers, not all the clients.

The sortlist statement takes an address match list and interprets it even more specially than the topology statement does.

Each top level statement in the sortlist must itself be an explicit address match list with one or two elements. The first element (which may be an IP address, an IP prefix, an ACL name or nested address match list) of each top level list is checked against the source address of the query until a match is found.

Once the source address of the query has been matched, if the top level statement contains only one element, the actual primitive element that matched the source address is used to select the address in the response to move to the beginning of the response. If the statement is a list of two elements, the second element is treated like the address match list in a topology statement. Each top level element is assigned a distance and the address in the response with the minimum distance is moved to the beginning of the response.

In the following example, any queries received from any of the addresses of the host itself will get responses preferring addresses on any of the locally connected networks. Next most preferred are addresses on the 192.168.1/24 network, and after that either the 192.168.2/24 or 192.168.3/24 network with no preference shown between these two networks. Queries received from a host on the 192.168.1/24 network will prefer other addresses on that network to the 192.168.2/24 and 192.168.3/24 networks. Queries received from a host on the 192.168.4/24 or the 192.168.5/24 network will only prefer other addresses on their directly connected networks.

```
sortlist {
          { localhost;          // IF    the local host
            { localnets;         // THEN first fit on the
              192.168.1/24;      //       following nets
              { 192,168.2/24; 192.168.3/24; }; }; };
          { 192.168.1/24;        // IF    on class C 192.168.1
            { 192.168.1/24;      // THEN use .1, or .2 or .3
              { 192.168.2/24; 192.168.3/24; }; }; };
          { 192.168.2/24;        // IF    on class C 192.168.2
            { 192.168.2/24;      // THEN use .2, or .1 or .3
              { 192.168.1/24; 192.168.3/24; }; }; };
          { 192.168.3/24;        // IF    on class C 192.168.3
            { 192.168.3/24;      // THEN use .3, or .1 or .2
              { 192.168.1/24; 192.168.2/24; }; }; };
          { { 192.168.4/24; 192.168.5/24; }; // if .4 or .5, prefer that net
          };
};
```

The following example will give reasonable behavior for the local host and hosts on directly connected networks. It is similar to the behavior of the address sort in BIND 4.9.x. Responses sent to queries from the local host will favor any of the directly connected networks. Responses sent to queries from any other hosts on a directly connected network will prefer addresses on that same network. Responses to other queries will not be sorted.

```
sortlist {
          { localhost; localnets; };
          { localnets; };
};
```

RRset Ordering

When multiple records are returned in an answer it may be useful to configure the order the records are placed into the response. For example the records for a zone might be configured to always be returned in the order they are defined in the zone file. Or perhaps a random shuffle of the records as they are returned is wanted. The rrset-order statement permits configuration of the ordering made of the records in a multiple record response. The default, if no ordering is defined, is a cyclic ordering (round robin).

An order_spec is defined as follows:

```
[ class class_name ][ type type_name ][ name "FQDN" ] order ordering
```

If no class is specified, the default is ANY. If no Ictype is specified, the default is ANY. If no name is specified, the default is "*".

The legal values for ordering are:

Fixed	Records are returned in the order they are defined in the zone file.
Random	Records are returned in some random order.
Cyclic	Records are returned in a round-robin order.

For example,

```
rrset-order {
    class IN type A name "rc.vix.com" order random;
    order cyclic;
};
```

will cause any responses for type A records in class IN that have "rc.vix.com" as a suffix, to always be returned in random order. All other records are returned in cyclic order.

If multiple rrset-order statements appear, they are not combined—the last one applies.

If no rrset-order statement is specified, a default one of

```
rrset-order { class ANY type ANY name "*" order cyclic ; };
```

is used.

Tuning

lame-ttl	Sets the number of seconds to cache a lame server indication. 0 disables caching. Default is 600 (10 minutes). Maximum value is 1800 (30 minutes).
max-ncache-ttl	To reduce network traffic and increase performance the server store negative answers. max-ncache-ttl is used to set a maximum retention time for these answers in the server is seconds. The default max-ncache-ttl is 10800 seconds (3 hours). max-ncache-ttl cannot exceed the maximum retention time for ordinary (positive) answers (7 days) and will be silently truncated to 7 days if set to a value which is greater that 7 days.
min-roots	The minimum number of root servers that is required for a request for the root servers to be accepted. Default is 2.

The Zone Statement

Syntax

```
zone domain_name [ ( in | hs | hesiod | chaos ) ] {
  type master;
  file path_name;
  [ check-names ( warn | fail | ignore ); ]
  [ allow-update { address_match_list }; ]
```

```
    [ allow-query { address_match_list }; ]
    [ allow-transfer { address_match_list }; ]
    [ forward ( only | first ); ]
    [ forwarders { [ ip_addr ; [ ip_addr ; ... ] ] }; ]
    [ dialup yes_or_no; ]
    [ notify yes_or_no; ]
    [ also-notify { ip_addr; [ ip_addr; ... ] };
    [ pubkey number number number string; ]
};

zone domain_name [ ( in | hs | hesiod | chaos ) ] {
    type ( slave | stub );
    [ file path_name; ]
    masters [ port ip_port ] { ip_addr; [ ip_addr; ... ] };
    [ check-names ( warn | fail | ignore ); ]
    [ allow-update { address_match_list }; ]
    [ allow-query { address_match_list }; ]
    [ allow-transfer { address_match_list }; ]
    [ forward ( only | first ); ]
    [ forwarders { [ ip_addr ; [ ip_addr ; ... ] ] }; ]
    [ transfer-source ip_addr; ]
    [ max-transfer-time-in number; ]
    [ notify yes_or_no; ]
    [ also-notify { ip_addr; [ ip_addr; ... ] };
    [ pubkey number number number string; ]
};

zone domain_name [ ( in | hs | hesiod | chaos ) ] {
    type forward;
    [ forward ( only | first ); ]
    [ forwarders { [ ip_addr ; [ ip_addr ; ... ] ] }; ]
    [ check-names ( warn | fail | ignore ); ]
};

zone "." [ ( in | hs | hesiod | chaos ) ] {
    type hint;
    file path_name;
    [ check-names ( warn | fail | ignore ); ]
};
```

Definition and Usage

The zone statement is used to define how information about particular DNS zones is managed by the server. There are five different zone types.

Master	The server has a master copy of the data for the zone and will be able to provide authoritative answers for it.
Slave	A slave zone is a replica of a master zone. The masters list specifies one or more IP addresses that the slave contacts to update its copy of the zone. If a port is specified then checks to see if the zone is current and zone transfers will be

	done to the port given. If file is specified, then the replica will be written to the named file. Use of the file clause is highly recommended, since it often speeds server startup and eliminates a needless waste of bandwidth.
Stub	A stub zone is like a slave zone, except that it replicates only the NS records of a master zone instead of the entire zone.
Forward	A forward zone is used to direct all queries in it to other servers, as described in The Options Statement section. The specification of options in such a zone will override any global options declared in the options statement.
	If either no forwarders clause is present in the zone or an empty list for forwarders is given, then no forwarding will be done for the zone, canceling the effects of any forwarders in the options statement. Thus if you want to use this type of zone to change only the behavior of the global forward option, and not the servers used, then you also need to respecify the global forwarders.
Hint	The initial set of root nameservers is specified using a hint zone.
	When the server starts up, it uses the root hints to find a root nameserver and get the most recent list of root nameservers.

NOTE

Previous releases of BIND used the term primary for a master zone, secondary for a slave zone, and cache for a hint zone.

Classes

The zone's name may optionally be followed by a class. If a class is not specified, class in (for "internet") is assumed. This is correct for the vast majority of cases.

The hesiod class is for an information service from MIT's Project Athena. It is used to share information about various systems databases, such as users, groups, printers and so on. More information can be found at ftp://athena-dist.mit.edu/pub/ATHENA/usenix/athena_changes.PS. The keyword hs is a synonym for hesiod.

Another MIT development was CHAOSnet, a LAN protocol created in the mid-1970s. It is still sometimes seen on LISP stations and other hardware in the AI community, and zone data for it can be specified with the chaos class.

Options

check-names	See the subsection on Name Checking in The Options Statement.
allow-query	See the description of allow-query in the Access Control subsection of The Options Statement.
allow-update	Specifies which hosts are allowed to submit Dynamic DNS updates to the server. The default is to deny updates from all hosts.

allow-transfer	See the description of allow-transfer in the Access Control subsection of The Options Statement.
transfer-source	transfer-source determines which local address will be bound to the TCP connection used to fetch this zone. If not set, it defaults to a system controlled value which will usually be the address of the interface "closest to" the remote end. This address must appear in the remote end's allow-transfer option for this zone if one is specified.
max-transfer-time-in	See the description of max-transfer-time-in in the Zone Transfers subsection of The Options Statement.
Dialup	See the description of dialup in the Boolean Options subsection of The Options Statement.
Notify	See the description of notify in the Boolean Options subsection of The Options Statement.
also-notify	also-notify is only meaningful if notify is active for this zone. The set of machines that will receive a DNS NOTIFY message for this zone is made up of all the listed nameservers for the zone (other than the primary master) plus any IP addresses specified with also-notify. also-notify is not meaningful for stub zones. The default is the empty list.
Forward	forward is only meaningful if the zone has a forwarders list. The only value causes the lookup to fail after trying the forwarders and getting no answer, while first would allow a normal lookup to be tried.
Forwarders	The forwarders option in a zone is used to override the list of global forwarders. If it is not specified in a zone of type forward, no forwarding is done for the zone; the global options are not used.
Pubkey	The DNSSEC flags, protocol, and algorithm are specified, as well as a base-64 encoded string representing the key.

The acl Statement

Syntax

```
acl name {
  address_match_list
};
```

Definition and Usage

The acl statement creates a named address match list. It gets its name from a primary use of address match lists: Access Control Lists (ACLs).

Note that an address match list's name must be defined with acl before it can be used elsewhere; no forward references are allowed.

The following ACLs are built-in:

Any   Allows all hosts.

None   Denies all hosts.

Localhost   Allows the IP addresses of all interfaces on the system.

Localnets   Allows any host on a network for which the system has an interface.

The key Statement

Syntax

```
key key_id {
  algorithm algorithm_id;
  secret secret_string;
};
```

Definition and Usage

The key statement defines a key ID which can be used in a server statement to associate a method of authentication with a particular name server that is more rigorous than simple IP address matching. A key ID must be created with the key statement before it can be used in a server definition or an address match list.

The algorithm_id is a string that specifies a security/authentication algorithm. secret_string is the secret to be used by the algorithm, and is treated as a base-64 encoded string. It should go without saying, but probably can't, that if you have secret_string's in your named.conf, then it should not be readable by anyone but the superuser.

The trusted-keys Statement

Syntax

```
trusted-keys {
  [ domain_name flags protocol algorithm key; ]
};
```

Definition and Usage

The trusted-keys statement is for use with DNSSEC-style security, originally specified in RFC 2065. DNSSEC is meant to provide three distinct services: key distribution, data origin authentication, and transaction and request authentication. A complete description of DNSSEC and its use is beyond the scope of this document, and readers interested in more information should start with RFC 2065 and then continue with the Internet Drafts available at http://www.ietf.org/ids.by.wg/dnssec.html.

Each trusted key is associated with a domain name. Its attributes are the non-negative integral flags, protocol, and algorithm, as well as a base-64 encoded string representing the key.

Any number of trusted keys can be specified.

The server Statement

Syntax

```
server ip_addr {
  [ bogus yes_or_no; ]
  [ transfers number; ]
  [ transfer-format ( one-answer | many-answers ); ]
  [ keys { key_id [ key_id ... ] }; ]
};
```

Definition and Usage

The server statement defines the characteristics to be associated with a remote name server.

If you discover that a server is giving out bad data, marking it as bogus will prevent further queries to it. The default value of bogus is no.

The server supports two zone transfer methods. The first, one-answer, uses one DNS message per resource record transferred. many-answers packs as many resource records as possible into a message. many-answers is more efficient, but is only known to be understood by BIND 8.1 and patched versions of BIND 4.9.5. You can specify which method to use for a server with the transfer-format option. If transfer-format is not specified, the transfer-format specified by the options statement will be used.

The transfers will be used in a future release of the server to limit the number of concurrent in-bound zone transfers from the specified server. It is checked for syntax but is otherwise ignored.

The keys clause is used to identify a key_id defined by the key statement, to be used for transaction security when talking to the remote server. The key statement must come before the server statement that references it.

The keys statement is intended for future use by the server. It is checked for syntax but is otherwise ignored.

The controls Statement

Syntax

```
controls {
  [ inet ip_addr
    port ip_port
    allow { address_match_list; }; ]
  [ unix path_name
    perm number
    owner number
    group number; ]
};
```

Definition and Usage

The controls statement declares control channels to be used by system administrators to affect the operation of the local name server. These control channels are used by the ndc utility to send commands to and retrieve non-DNS results from a name server.

A unix control channel is a FIFO in the file system, and access to it is controlled by normal file system permissions. It is created by named with the specified file mode bits (see chmod(1)), user and group owner. Note that, unlike chmod, the mode bits specified for perm will normally have a leading 0 so the number is interpreted as octal. Also note that the user and group ownership specified as owner and group must be given as numbers, not names. It is recommended that the permissions be restricted to administrative personnel only, or else any user on the system might be able to manage the local name server.

An inet control channel is a TCP/IP socket accessible to the Internet, created at the specified ip_port on the specified ip_addr. Modern telnet clients are capable of speaking directly to these sockets, and the control protocol is ARPAnet-style text. It is recommended that 127.0.0.1 be the only ip_addr used, and this only if you trust all non-privileged users on the local host to manage your name server.

The include Statement

Syntax

```
include path_name;
```

Definition and Usage

The include statement inserts the specified file at the point that the include statement is encountered. It cannot be used within another statement, though, so a line such as acl internal_hosts { include internal_hosts.acl; }; is not allowed.

Use include to break the configuration up into easily-managed chunks.

For example,

```
include "/etc/security/keys.bind";
include "/etc/acls.bind";
```

could be used at the top of a BIND configuration file in order to include any ACL or key information.

Be careful not to type "#include", like you would in a C program, because "#" is used to start a comment.

Examples

The simplest configuration file that is still realistically useful is one which simply defines a hint zone that has a full path to the root servers file:

```
zone "." in {
        type hint;
        file "/var/named/root.cache";
};
```

Here's a more typical real-world example:

```
/*
 * A simple BIND 8 configuration
 */

logging {
        category lame-servers { null; };
        category cname { null; };
};

options {
        directory "/var/named";
};

controls {
        inet * port 52 allow { any; };                  // a bad idea
        unix "/var/run/ndc" perm 0600 owner 0 group 0;  // the default
};

zone "isc.org" in {
        type master;
        file "master/isc.org";
};

zone "vix.com" in {
        type slave;
```

```
        file "slave/vix.com";
        masters { 10.0.0.53; };
};

zone "0.0.127.in-addr.arpa" in {
        type master;
        file "master/127.0.0";
};

zone "." in {
        type hint;
        file "root.cache";
};
```

Files

```
/etc/named.conf
```
   The BIND 8 named configuration file.

See Also

■ named(8), ndc(8)

B

BIBLIOGRAPHY

Books

Droms, Ralph and Ted Lemon. *The DHCP Handbook*. Indianapolis: Macmillan Technical Publishing, 1999. (ISBN: 1-57870-137-6)

Menezes, Alfred J., Paul C. van Oorschot, and Scott A. Vanstone. *Handbook of Applied Cryptography*. CRC Press, 1996. (ISBN: 0-8493-8523-7) This book is also available electronically at http://www.cacr.math.uwaterloo.ca/hac/. It is known for being complete and rigorous, as well as cool.

Schneir, Bruce. *Applied Cryptography: Protocols, Algorithms, and Source Code in C, 2nd Edition*. John Wiley and Sons, 1995. (ISBN: 0-4711-1709-9) Also available in soft cover. This is probably the best book about cryptography if you're not all that interested in the math.

Stevens, W. Richard. *UNIX Network Programming*. Prentice Hall, 1990. (ISBN: 0-13-949876-1) A very good and extensive text on network service programming.

RFCs

Notes

An *RFC* is a Request For Comments document. RFCs can be standards-in-the-making, notes about problems and possible solutions, notes about practices, prescriptions of policies, and anything else that needs to be published to the technical Internet community at large. After being debated and commented, an RFC can become an STD or perhaps a BCP. An *STD* is an Internet standard, and a *BCP* is documentation of a Best Current Practice. These documents are a goldmine when it comes to understanding the more technical sides of the Internet. You can read more about STDs in STD 1 and BCPs in BCP 1. The official RFC, STD, and BCP archive is at `ftp://ftp.isi.edu/in-notes/`, but you also should see `http://www.rfc-editor.org/`. My favorite RFC archive is `ftp://sunsite.uio.no/pub/rfc`. It has all these documents.

Current

RFC 952. K. Harrenstien, M. Stahl, and E. Feinler. "DOD Internet Host Table Specification." October 1985. Obsoletes RFC 810 and RFC 608. This restricts names to A–Z, 0–9, "-" (dash, minus), and "." (period), and sets a number of other restrictions.

RFC 974, STD 14. Craig Partridge. "Mail Routing and the Domain System." January 1986.

RFC 1032. M. Stahl. "Domain Administrators Guide." November 1987. Explains how to register a domain with (now defunct) NIC and DDN and gives guidelines for establishing and administrating a domain.

RFC 1033. M. Lottor. "Domain Administrators Operations Guide." November 1987. This explains DNS for administrators; familiarity with the concepts is assumed.

RFC 1034. P. Mockapetris. "Domain Names—Concepts and Facilities." November 1987. Obsoletes RFCs 882, 883, and 973. *Recommended reading.*

RFC 1035. STD 13. P. Mockapetris, "Domain Names—Implementation and Specification." November 1987. This is the base DNS standard. It has been amended and updated in other documents.

RFC 1123. R. Braden, editor. "Requirements for Internet Hosts—Application and Support." October 1989.

RFC 1183. C. Everhart, et al. "New DNS RR Definitions." October 1990. Updates RFCs 1034 and 1035. Quite a few new RRs were introduced in this RFC.

RFC 1321. R. Rivest and RSA Data Security. "The MD5 Message-Digest Algorithm." April 1992. MD5 is a cryptographic hash, or "fingerprint," function. It is, among other things, used in conjunction with HMAC; see RFC 2104.

RFC 1535. E. Gavron. "A Security Problem and Proposed Correction With Widely Deployed DNS Software." October 1993.

RFC 1591. J. Postel. "Domain Name System Structure and Delegation." March 1994.

RFC 1597. V. Rekhter, et. al. "Address Allocation for Private Internets." March 1994. This is the RFC that specifies which address ranges can be used for internal, private networks.

RFC 1700, STD 2. J. Reynolds and J. Postel. "Assigned Numbers." October 1994. Obsoletes RFCs 1340, 1060, 1010, 990, 960, 943, 923, 900, 870, 820, 790, 776, 770, 762, 758, 755, 750, 739, 604, 503, 433, and 349, and IENs 127, 117, and 93. This document summarizes all the numbers assigned to various things by IANA (Internet Assigned Numbers Authority)— numbers such as the well-known port number of services, (http is on port number 80), the IP protocol numbers of TCP (6) and UDP (17), and so on.

RFC 1706. B Manning and R. Colella. "DNS NSAP Resource Records." October 1994. Obsoletes RFC 1637 and 1348.

RFC 1713, FYI 27. A. Romao. "Tools for DNS Debugging." November 1994.

RFC 1876. C. Davis, et. al. "A Means for Expressing Location Information in the Domain Name System." January 1996. Updates RFCs 1034 and 1035.

RFC 1886. S. Thomson and C. Huitema. "DNS Extensions to Support IP Version 6." December 1995.

RFC 1912. D. Barr. "Common DNS Operational and Configuration Errors." February 1996. Obsoletes RFC 1537.

RFC 1995. M. Ohta. "Incremental Zone Transfer in DNS." August 1996. Updates RFC 1035. This introduces the IXFR mechanism.

RFC 1996. P. Vixie. "A Mechanism for Prompt Notification of Zone Changes." August 1996. This is the DNS NOTIFY standard.

RFC 2010. B. Manning and P. Vixie. "Operational Criteria for Root Name Servers." October 1996. Covers running root nameservers in the year 1996.

RFC 2050, BCP 12. K. Hubbard, et. al. "Internet Registry IP Allocation Guidelines." November 1996. Obsoletes RFC 1466.

RFC 2052. A. Gulbrandsen and P. Vixie. "A DNS RR for Specifying the Location of Services (DNS SRV)." October 1996.

RFC 2065. D. Eastlake III and C. Kaufman. "Domain Name System Security Extensions." January 1997. Obsoleted by RFC 2535. Updates RFCs 1034 and 1035. Describes the DNS records needed to implement DNS security, DNSSEC, and the procedures and practices associated with it.

RFC 2104. H. Krawczyk. "HMAC: Keyed-Hashing for Message Authentication." February 1997. TSIG is based on this.

RFC 2136. P. Vixie, editor. "Dynamic Updates in the Domain Name System (DNS UPDATE)." April 1997. Updates RFC 1035.

RFC 2137. D. Eastlake. "Secure Domain Name System Dynamic Update." April 1997. Updates RFC 1035.

RFC 2163. C. Allocchio. "Using the Internet DNS to Distribute MIXER Conformant Global Address Mapping (MCGAM)." January 1998. Obsoletes RFC 1664. This RFC defines the PX RR.

RFC 2181. Elz and Bush. "Clarifications to the DNS Specification." July 1987. Updates RFCs 1034, 1035, and 1123. This RFC clarifies several problematic areas in RFCs 1034 and 1035. See also RFC 1123. *Recommended reading.*

RFC 2182, BCP 16. R. Elz, et. al. "Selection and Operation of Secondary DNS Servers." July 1997. *Recommended reading.*

RFC 2219, BCP 17. M. Hamilton and R. Wright. "Use of DNS Aliases for Network Services." October 1997. Recommendations about CNAME use. *Recommended reading.*

RFC 2230. R. Atkinson. "Key Exchange Delegation Record for the DNS." November 1997. This RFC defines a mechanism for IP-SEC to locate key servers.

RFC 2308. M. Andrews. "Negative Caching of DNS Queries." March 1998. Updates RFCs 1034 and 1035. This RFC is the basis for negative caching and the $TTL zone file directive.

RFC 2317, BCP 20. H. Eidnes, et. al. "Classless IN-ADDR.ARPA Delegation." March 1998. *Recommended reading.*

RFC 2403. C. Madson and R. Glenn. "The Use of HMAC-MD5-96 within ESP and AH." November 1998. This discusses the use of HMAC-MD5, used in DNS-SEC/TSIG, for IP-SEC.

RFC 2535. D. Eastlake. "Domain Name System Security Extensions." March 1999. Updates RFCs 2181, 1035, and 1034. Obsoletes 2065.

RFC 2671. P. Vixie. "Extension Mechanisms for DNS (EDNS0)." August 1999. This extension overcomes some limitations in the DNS network protocol and provides a way for resolvers to announce their capabilities to servers.

RFC 2672. M. Crawford. "Non-Terminal DNS Name Redirection." August 1999. This RFC specifies the DNAME RR, which pretty much amounts to a symbolic link from one domain to another domain, creating a powerful alias mechanism.

RFC 2874. M. Crawford and C. Huitema. "DNS Extensions to Support IPv6 Address Aggregation and Renumbering." July 2000. This introduces the A6 RR.

Related

RFC 1101. P. Mockapetris. "DNS Encoding of Network Names and Other Types." April 1989. Updates RFCs 1034 and 1035. Outlines different methods for using DNS to encode various local information. These methods do not appear to be in use.

RFC 1122. R. Branden, editor. "Requirements for Internet Hosts—Communication Layers." October 1989.

Historical Documents

Here are some obsolete but still interesting documents:

RFC 799. D.L. Mills. "Internet Name Domains." September 1981. The problems with the HOSTS.TXT file is discussed, and domains are discussed in the context of internet mail. Here, domains are seen as associated with the various network types, such as ARPANET, DCENET, and MIT's CHAOSNET.

RFC 805. J. Postel. "Computer Mail Meeting Notes." February 1982. Notes from a meeting where the use of domain names, rather than a completely flat space of hostnames, was the conclusion. The need for nameservers was seen, and the general requirements of such a service were discussed. One of the action items from this meeting was "Host Name Server Description."

RFC 819. Z. Su and J. Postel. "The Domain Naming Convention for Internet User Applications." August 1982. The domain name scheme is discussed in more detail. The initial TLD is revealed to be ARPA.

RFC 830. Zaw-Sing Su. "A Distributed System for Internet Name Service." October 1982. This proposes SINS (System for Internet Name Service) with DNS as an element.

RFC 882. P. Mockapetris. "Domain Names—Concepts and Facilities." November 1983. This RFC describes DNS as we know it. It discusses the problems with the hosts.txt file and the design goals and considerations that went into the solution: DNS. The overall design is still the same.

RFC 883. P. Mockapetris. "Domain Names—Implementation and Specification." November 1983. This memo discusses the implementation in more detail, including additional problems it has to solve in heterogeneous internets. It then goes into detail about the query and response formats and how names resolve.

RFC 920. J. Postel and J. Reynolds. "Domain Requirements." October 1984. The end of the ARPA TLD is announced, and the new, now familiar TLDs of GOV, EDU, COM, MIL, and ORG, as well as the use of ISO-3166 country codes for national entities, are introduced.

RFC 953. K. Harrenstien, M. Stahl, and E. Feinler. "Hostname Server." October 1985. Obsoletes RFC 811. This specifies a hostname server implemented at SRI.

RFC 973. P. Mockapetris. "Domain System Changes and Observations." January 1986. This updates RFCs 882 and 883 based on the experience with DNS thus far.

RFC 1010. J. Reynolds and J. Postel. "Assigned Numbers." May 1987. A frequently referenced RFC, since replaced by RFC 1700.

RFC 1032. M. Stahl. "Domain Administrators Guide." November 1987. Covers how to register a domain with the NIC.

RFC 1367. C. Topolcic. "Schedule for IP Address Space Management Guidelines." October 1992. Obsoleted by RFC 1467. This and RFC 1467 provide a historical perspective on the use of classless subnets.

RFC 1467. C. Topolcic. "Status of CIDR Deployment in the Internet." August 1993. Obsoletes RFC 1367. Obsoleted by RFC 2050.

RFC 1664. Allocchio, et. al. "Internet DNS for Mail Mapping Tables." August 1994. Obsoleted by RFC 2163.

INDEX

SYMBOLS

! (exclamation mark), negating elements, 261

$ (dollar sign), listings, 1

. (period), RP resource records, 198

(pound), Shell-style comments, 1, 259

; (semicolon), comments, 259

// (slash, slash) C++-style comments, 258

/* (slash, star) C-style comments, 258

*/ (star, slash), C-style comments, 258

799 RFC, 291

805 RFC, 291

819 RFC, 291

830 RFC, 291

833 RFC, 292

882 RFC, 291

920 RFC, 292

952 RFC, 245, 288

953 RFC, 292

973 RFC, 292

974 RFC, 288

1010 RFC, 292

1032 RFC, 288, 292

1033 RFC, 288

1034 RFC, 288

1035 RFC, 288

1101 RFC, 291

1122 RFC, 291

1123 RFC, 245, 288

1183 RFC, 288

1321 RFC, 288

1367 RFC, 292

1467 RFC, 292

1535 RFC, 289

1591 RFC, 289

1597 RFC, 289

1664 RFC, 292

1700 RFC, 289

1706 RFC, 289

1713 RFC, 289

1876 RFC, 289

1886 RFC, 289

1912 RFC, 97, 245, 289

1995 RFC, 289

1996 RFC, 289

2010 RFC, 289

2050 RFC, 289

2052 RFC, 289

2065 RFC, 290

2104 RFC, 290

2136 RFC, 290

2137 RFC, 290

2181 RFC, 90, 290

2182 RFC, 290

2219 RFC, 290

2230 RFC, 290

2308 RFC, 253, 290

2317 RFC, 290

2403 RFC, 290

2535 RFC, 153, 290

2671 RFC, 290

2672 RFC, 291

2874 RFC, 291

A

A (Address) resource record
dig commands, finding, 13
RFC 1035, 195

A6 resource record, 238

aa flags, 91

AAAA (IPc6 Address) resource record, RFC 1886, 196

AARNet2 (Australian Academic and Research Network), 70
resolving Internet congestion, 70-71

ACLs (Access Control Lists)
BIND, 144
statements, syntax, 280-281
zones (BIND 4), 217

actions (zone updates), 169

activating chroot (BIND), 222

adding
domains (BIND), 67
resolving servers, 160
resource records, 169
slave servers, 49-50

Address resource record. See A resource record

addresses
blackholing, 145
DNS names, looking up from, 18
Ipv6, 106
match lists, elements, 260
nslookup, finding, 93-94
obtaining (DHCP), 173
PTR records, mapping, 18
sorting
BIND, 243-244
BIND 4, 214
BIND 8, 214
sortlists, 244

Administrators Reference Manual (BIND 9 documenta- tion), 230

Advisories (AUS-CERT), 145

AFSDB (AFS Database Location) resource record, RFC 1183, 200

Allocchio, C.
RFC 1664, 292
RFC 2163, 290

allow-query option, 144

allow-transfer option, 149, 248

AlterNIC attack, 143

analog connections, 176

Andrews, M., RFC 2308, 290

answers (IQUERY), 215

API calls (UNIX resolver)
gethostbyaddr, 187-188
gethostbyname, 187-188

application proxies, 161

Applied Cryptography: Protocols, Algorithms, and Source Code in C, 2nd Edition **by Bruce Schneir, 165, 287**

arlib (BIND), 194

Ask Mr. DNS Web site, 97

asynchronous
DNS, 193
name lookups, 193
resolving, 193

Atkinson, R., RFC 2230, 290

ATM Address (ATMA) resource record, 196

ATM Name System Specification Version 1.0, ATMA resource record, 196

ATMA (ATM Address) resource record, 196

attacks
AlterNIC, 143
chroot, 150-151
least privilege, 150

AUS-CERT advisory, 145
  Web site, 145

Australian Academic and Research Network. *See* **AARNet2**

auth-nxdomain option, 253

authentication (TSIG), 166

Authoritative Nameserver resource record. *See* **NS**

auto-dial function, disabling, 178

B

bad servers, security, 146

bad ttl messages, 139

bands, sorting records, 245

Barr, D., RFC 1912, 289

batch files, dig, 89-90

BCP (Best Common Practice), 288

Berkeley Internet Name Daemon. *See* **BIND**

Bernstein, D.J., DNScache library, 194

Best Common Practice (BCP), 288

BIND (Berkeley Internet Name Daemon)
  ACLs (Access Control Lists), 144
  address sorting, 243-244
  arlib, 194

BSD vendors, 22
cache cleaning, 148-149
chroot, activating, 222
chrooted environments, customizing, 222
comments, 258
    C++-style, 258
    C-style, 258
    Shell-style, 259
compiling, 22-23, 221
configuring, 23
distribution LICENSE file, 21
domains, adding, 67
elements configuration, 259-260
heartbeat intervals, 176
in class, 35
installing, 221-222
interface scanning, 247
Internet, disconnecting, 176-178
ISC, 219
ISC Web site, 22
limits, 246
Linux, 22
logging
    categories, 64-65
    default configurations, 65-66
    directives, 62
    facilities, 64
logs, 62
    severity, 63
moderating names.conf option, 176
named.conf, configuring, 23-24
ndc command, starting, 26-27

newsgroups, 220
obtaining, 219
overriding global forwarding policies, 161-162
poisoning, 142
pz/127.0.0m configuring, 25-26
query ID numbers, 151-152
roots.hints, configuring, 24-25
security, 23, 142-144
spoofing, 142-144
src directory, 220
statistics, 250-252
testing, 26-29
topology, 244
traffic, 176
UNIX, 22
versions, 2
    hiding, 152-153
Web site, 219
zone transfers, 247-250

BIND 4, 209
  address sorting, 214
  configuring, 211
  debugging, 216
  forwarders, 213
  migrating to BIND 8
    CNAME configuration, 210
    file conversion configuration, 210
    name checking, 211
    ndc, 211
    query source, 210
  secure_zone, 217
  zone access control lists, 217
  zones, configuring, 212

BIND 4.9.7, 209

BIND 4.9x, converting files, 259

BIND 8
  address sorting, 214
  forwarders, 213
  migrating from BIND 4
    CNAME, 210
    file conversion configuration, 210
    name checking, 211
    ndc, 211
    query source, 210
  resource limits, 214
  statements, 258

BIND 9, 227-228
  compiling, 229-230
  database, replacing, 229
  documentation
    Administrators Reference Manual, 230
    named.conf file, 230-231
  IP version 6, 228
    support, 240
  lookups, 229
  lwresd, 233
  named.conf file, 232
  operational enhancements, 228
  options, 231
  protocol enhancements, 228
  README file, 230
  resource limits, 233-234
  resource records, 235-238
  rndc, 232-233
  scalability, 228, 238-239

  security, 228
  views, 234-235

bind-announce mailing list, 141

blackholing
  addresses, 145
  security, 146

bogus nameservers, 215

bogusns directive, 215

books, resources, 287

Boolean options, 268-273

Bouvet code, 184-185

BSD vendors (BIND), 22

Bugtraq security mailing list, 141

Bush and Elz, RFC 2181, 290

C

-c <query-class> dig option, 89

C++-style comments (BIND), 258

C-style comments, nesting BIND, 258

cache
  cleaning (BIND), 148-149
  corruption, 102-103
  servers, 184
  sizes, 234

cache/database dump listing, 103

caching
  DNS, 9, 29-30
  name daemon, resolving names, 29

  negative, 102
  TTL, 34

Canonical Name of an Alias resource record. *See* **CNAME**

categories logging statement, 265-266

changing
  IP numbers (hosts), 167
  Zones, NOTIFY
    extension, 50-51

channels
  debug, controlling
    logging, 66-67
  logging method, 63,
    262-265
  ncd, 242
  options, 263

checking names, 216
  migrating BIND 4 to
    BIND 8, 211

chroot (BIND)
  activating, 222
  attacks, 150-151

chroot environments
  customizing (BIND), 222
  setting up, 223-224

cl flag, 104

classes zone statement, 279

classless nets, reverse delegations, 47-49

clauses
  files, 263
  logging statements, 263
  severity, 263
  syslog, 263

**cleaning caches (BIND),
148-149**

clients
OS resolvers, configuring,
34
recursive, 234
tcp, 234
updates (DNS), 168

**closed networks (DNS),
179-180**

**CNAME (Canonical Name
of an Alias) resource
records, 18, 60**
migrating BIND 4 to
BIND 8, 210
problems using, 60
RFC 1035, 196

codes, Bouvet, 184-185

Colella, R., RFC 170, 289

**combining stub zones
and root zones, 183**

**command-line terms
(dig)**
%comment, 86
-dig-option, 86
domain, 86
query-class, 86
+query-option, 86
query-type, 86
@server, 86

**command-line tools,
nsupdate, 168**

commands
dig
finding records, 13
recursion, 14-15
fwhois, 77
passing queries, 77-78

help, whois database, 77
kill, 241
lserver, nslookup, 95
makefile, variables,
221-222
ndc
errors, 27
starting BIND, 26-27
nslookup, help, 95
whois, 77-79

**%comment dig command-
line term, 86**

comments
BIND, 258
C++-style, 258
C-style, 258
Shell-style, 259
semicolon (;), 259

compiling
BIND, 22-23, 221
BIND 9, 229-230

**concentrations (queries),
160**

**conditions, troubleshoot-
ing networks, 98-99**

configurations
BIND elements, 259-260
named.conf, 23-24
pz/127.0.0, 25-26
roots.hints, 24-25
zones, 212
clients (OS resolvers), 34
errors, 106-130
file, 285
file conversion, 210
file listings Web site, 1
logging, 262
BIND default, 65-66
rootservers, 180
UNIX resolvers, 32-33

**congestion, diagnosing
networks, 98**

connections
analog, 176
dial-up (DNS), 175
DNS, testing, 99
masters and slaves, 175

**controlling logging
(debug channel), 66-67**

controls statement, 283
syntax, 283

converting
BIND 4.9 files, 259
migration files, 210

cp clients, 234

CPAN Web site, 190

Cr flag, 104

Crawford, M.,
RFC 2182, 291
RFC 2672, 291

**cryptography (HMAC-
MD5), 165**

**customizing BIND,
chrooted environments,
222**

D

data
slave servers, 101
zones, mistakes, 104-105

**database/cache dump
listing, 103**

databases
BIND 9, replacing, 229
whois, 76-77
help command, 77

dates, logging, 264

Davis, C., RFC 1876, 289

db.linpro file, 133

debug channel, control-ling logging, 66-67

debugging
BIND 4, 216
servers, 263

default logging configu-rations (BIND), 65-66

defining
domains, 31-32
nameservers, 31

Deja.com Web site, 131

delegating
domains, 10, 46, 99
troubleshooting, 99
lame, 121
reverse, 99
classless nets, 47-49

deleting resource records, 169

Demon Web site, 132

DHCP
addresses, obtaining, 173
DNS, 173
obtaining, 172
servers, 168, 174

DHCP Handbook by **Ralph Droms and Ted Lemon, 173, 287**

diagnosing network con-gestion, 98

dial-up connections (DNS), 175

dig, 85, 92
batch files, 89-90
command
finding A records, 13
recursion, 14-15
command-line terms
%comment, 86
-dig-option, 86
domain, 86
query-class, 86
+query-option, 86
query-type, 86
@server, 86
flags, 91
options
-c <query-class>, 89
-envsav, 89
-envset, 89
-f <file>, 88
-k <keydir:keyname>, 89
-[no]stick, 89
-P [<ping-string>], 89
-p <port>, 89
-t <query-type>, 89
-T <time>, 89
-x <dotted.address>, 88
output, 90-91
queries, processing, 89
shell scripting, 192

-dig-option dig command-line term, 86

DigIt
troubleshooting domain
delegation, 99
Web site, 132
Web tool, 132

directives
bogusns, 215
domain, 216

logging (BIND), 62
sortlist, 214
xfrnets, 214

directories (BIND), 220

disabling
auto-dial function, 178
external interfaces, 178
glue fetching, 212

disconnecting Internet (BIND), 176-178

displaying errors (nsup-date), 170

distributing
DNS hierarchy, 7
loads
DNS round robin,
58-59
Eddie, 59
zones, 11

DNAME resource record, 235-237
restrictions, 238

DNS (Domain Naming Service)
asynchronous, 193
caching, 9, 29-30
closed networks, 179-180
connections, testing, 99
DHCP, 173
dial-up connections, 175
domains, setting up,
34-41
edges, 8
firewalls, 154-155
packet filtering,
154-155
split DNS, 158-160

hierarchy
  distribution, 7
  domain names, 7
  TLDs, 7
information security,
  155-158
Internet, 2-3, 131
large corporate networks,
  160-161
logs, 62
names, looking addresses
  up from, 18
networks, setting up,
  34-41
OS resolver, 30
Perl, 189
poisoning, 47, 102
Python, 191
queries, forwarding,
  70-72
Resource Directory Web
  site, 131
RFC 882, 195
RFC 883, 195
RFC 973, 195
root nodes, 8
round robin, distributing
  loads, 58-59
scalability, 8
servers
  *determining amount
    internally, 68*
  myths about, 67-68
  updates, 164
shell scripting, 191
SOA resource records, 53
split, 155
tree structure, 20
Tricks and Tips Web site,
  97

troubleshooting
  network conditions, 98
  resources, 97
update clients (DHCP
  servers), 168
zone transfer, 12
***DNS and Bind* by Liu
Cricket, 132**
***DNS cache library* by
D.J. Bernstein, 194**
  Web site, 194
DNSRD Web site, 97
DNSSEC
  BIND 9 security enhance-
    ment, 240
  security, 153
dnswalk
  quality control tool,
    136-137
  software, 97
  troubleshooting domain
    delegation, 99
  Web site, 136
**DOC (Domain Obscenity
Control), 137-138**
  quality control tool,
    137-138
  troubleshooting domain
    delegation, 99
  Web site, 137
documentation (BIND 9)
  Administrators Reference
    Manual, 230
  names.conf file, 230-231
dollar sign ($), 1
**domain dig command-
line term, 86**
domain directive, 216

**Domain Obscenity
Control.** *See* **DOC**
domains
  BIND, adding, 67
  defining, 31-32
  delegating, 10, 46, 99
    troubleshooting, 99
  DNS, setting up, 34-41
  ISO, 7
  names
    DNS hierarchy, 7
    records resolution, 13
  nameservers, 80
  obtaining, 80
  registering, 81
    IANA, 76
  registration, expiring, 99
  top-level, establishing,
    75-76
  unavailability, 80
  vanishing, 99
  zones, 10
**Droms, Ralph and Ted
Lemon,** *The DHCP
Handbook*, **287**
duplicating
  nameservers, 11
  rootservers, 11-12
  zones, 11
**dynamic updates (DHCP
servers), 174**
**dynamic zones, seeding,
167**

E

Eastlake, D.
  RFC 2065, 290
  RFC 2137, 290
  RFC 2182, 290

Eddie
loads, distributing, 59
Web site, 59

edges (DNS), 8

editing
serial numbers, 101
zones, 168

**EID (Endpoint Identifier)
resource record, 203**

Eidnes, H., RFC 2317, 290

elements
address match lists, 260
BIND configuration,
259-260
negating, 261
*! (exclamation mark),
261*
ordering, 261

**Elz and Bush, RFC 2181,
290**

Elz, R., RFC 2182, 290

**Endpoint Identifier (EID)
resource record, 203**

**environments (chroot),
setting up, 223-224**

-envsav dig option, 89

-envset dig option, 89

errors
configuration, 106-130
messages, 179
ndc command, 27
nslookup, 192
nsupdate, displaying, 170
troubleshooting, 106-130

**establishing top-level
domains (ISPs), 75**

**/etc/resolv.conf (OS
resolvers), 31-33**

**ethereal network traffic,
99**

**Everhart, C., RFC 1183,
288**

**examining reverse zones,
42**

**exclamation mark (!),
negating elements, 261**

expiring
domain registration, 99
zones, 36

**extended outages, using
SOA resource records,
69**

**external interfaces, dis-
abling, 178**

**externally redundant
nameservers, 69**

F

-f <file> dig option, 88

-f switch, 136

fake-iquery option, 253

Feinler, E.
RFC 952, 288
RFC 953, 292

**fields (first), primary
masters, 164**

file clause, 263
options, 263

**file conversion configu-
ration, migrating BIND
4 to BIND 8, 210**

files
batch, dig, 89-90
BIND 4.9, converting,
259

configurations, 285
db.linepro, 133
LICENSE, BIND distri-
bution, 21
log, 106
Web site, 106
names.conf
BIND 9, 232
*BIND 9 documen-
tation, 230-231*
README (BIND 9), 230
root.hints, maintaining,
72-74
root.zone, 181
zone, 106

**filtering packets, discon-
necting BIND, 177**

**Finch, Tony and Ian
Jackson, *GNU adns*, 193**

finding
A records, dig command,
13
addresses, nslookup,
93-94
reverse zone owners, 76
top-level domain owners,
76

firewalls
DNS, 154-155
*packet filtering,
154-155*
split DNS, 158-160
network conditions, 98

**first fields primary mas-
ters, 164**

flags
aa, 91
CL, 104
CR, 104
dig, 91

qr, 91

ra, 91

rd, 91

tc, 91

forward lookups, 18

forward resolution. *See* **forward lookup**

forward zones, 34-41

forward-only option, 213

forwarders, 158
BIND 4, 213
BIND 8, 213

forwarding queries (DNS), 70-72

FQDN (fully qualified domain name), 7

Fuhr, Mike, *Net:DNS*, **190**

fully qualified domain name (FQDN), 7

functions, gethostby* (Perl), 189

fwhois command, 77
queries, passing, 77-78

G

gateways, NATing Internet, 155

Gavron, E., RFC 1535, 289

Geographical Position. *See* **GPOS**

gethostby* function (Perl), 189

gethostbyaddr API call (UNIX resolvers), 187-188

gethostbyaddr call (Python), 190

gethostbyname API call (UNIX resolvers), 187-188

gethostbyname call (Python), 190

Glenn, R., RFC 2403, 290

global forwarding policies, overriding, 161-162

glue fetching, disabling, 212

GNU adns **by Ian Jackson and Tony Finch, 193**
Web site, 193

GNU textutils package Web site, 220

GPOS (Geographical Position) resource record, RFC 1712, 203

Gulbrandsen, A., RFC 2052, 289

H

-h option whois tool, 77-79

h2n maintenance tools, 132-133

Hamilton, M., RFC 2182, 290

Handbook of Applied Cryptography, **165, 287**

Harrenstein
RFC 952, 288
RFC 953, 292

has-old clients option, 253

hash symbol (#), 1

heartbeat intervals (BIND), 176

help command
nslookup, 95
whois database, 77

Hesiod zone, 217

hiding
BIND version security, 152-153
networks, 158

hierarchy (DNS)
distribution, 7
domain names, 7
TLDs, 7

HINFO (Host Information) resource record, 38
RFC 1035, 196

HMAC, RFC 2104, 165

HMAC-MD5
cryptography, 165
IP-SEC, 165
RFC 2403, 165
TSIG updates, 165

Host Information resource record. *See* **HINFO**

hostnames, 245
illegal, 246
labels, 245

hosts, changing IP numbers, 167

housing services, moving Web servers, 54-55

Hubbard, K., RFC 2050, 289

Huitema, C.
RFC 1886, 289
RFC 2874, 291

I

IANA (Internet Assigned Numbers Authority)
registering domains, 76
Web site, 76

ID numbers, query (BIND), 151-152

illegal hostnames, 246

implementing internal rootservers, 180

IN class (BIND), 35

include statement, 283

incremental zone transfers, 249-250

inspecting zones, 40

installing BIND, 221-222

interactive mode, nslookup, 93

interface scanning (BIND), 247

interfaces, disabling external, 178

internal rootservers
implementing, 180
Internet, 180

internally redundant nameservers, 68

International Standards Organization (ISO), domains, 7

Internet
BIND, disconnecting, 176-178
congestion, resolving, 70-71
DNS, 2-3, 131
internal rootservers, 180
InterNIC, 2

Internet Assigned Numbers Authority. *See* IANA

Internet Query Tools, 132

"Internet Registry IP Allocation Guidelines" RFC 2050, 289

Internet Service Providers. *See* ISPs

Internet Software Consortium. *See* ISC

Internet Standard (STDs), 288

InterNIC (Internet), 2

intervals, periodic task, 274

IP numbers, changing hosts, 167

IP version 6 support (BIND 9), 228, 240

IP-SEC, HMAC-MD5, 165

Iptraf, network traffic, 99

IPv6 address, 106

IPv6 Address (AAAA) resource record, 196

IQUERY
answers, 215
queries, 215

ISC (Internet Software Consortium), 21
BIND, 219
BIND Web site, 22
PGP Web site, 22, 219
Web site, 22, 172, 219

ISDN (ISDN Address) resource record, RFC 1183, 201-203

ISO (International Standards Organization), domains, 7

ISPs (Internet service providers), establishing top-level domains, 75

J-K

Jackson, Ian and Tony Finch, *GNU adns*, 193

-k <keydir:keyname> dig option, 89

Kaufman, C., RFC 2065, 290

KEY (Public Key) resource record, RFC 2065, 201

Key Exchange Routing Information resource record. *See* KX

key statement, 281
syntax, 281

keys, securing, 166

keywords, query options, 87-88

kill command, 241

Kitchen Sink Record (SINK) resource record, 202

Krawcsyk, H., RFC 2104, 290

KX (Key Exchange) resource record, RFC 2230, 201

L

labels, hostnames, 245

lame delegations, 121

lame servers, 62, 94, 100

lame-ttl tuning, 277

lamer logging, 121

large corporate networks (DNS), 160-161

least privilege (attacks), 150

Lemon, Ted and Ralph Droms, *The DHCP Handbook*, 287

libresolv, 189

LICENSE file (BIND distribution), 21

limiting zone transfers, 214

limits
  BIND, 246
  resources, values, 273-274
  server resources, 273-274

LinPro, whois, 78-79

Linux (BIND), 22

listing multiple servers, semicolon (;), 50

listings
  database/cache dump, 103
  dollar sign ($), 1
  hash symbol (#), 1
  mail header, 156
  Web site, 1

Liu, Cricket, *DNS and Bind*, 132

loads
  distributing, DNS round robin, 58-59
  Eddie, distributing, 59

LOC (Location) resource record, RFC 1876, 201

log files, 106
  Web site, 106

logging
  BIND
    categories, 64-65
    facilities, 64
  configurations, BIND
    default, 65-66, 262
  dates, 264
  debug channel, controlling logging, 66-67
  directives (BIND), 62
  lamer, 121
  methods (channels), 63
  queries, 213
  statement, 98, 106, 263
    categories, 265-266
    channels, 263-265
    clauses, 263
    configurations, 262
    syntax, 261
  time, 264

logs
  BIND, 62
    severity, 63
  DNS, 62
  reading, 98

lookups
  BIND 9, 229
  DNS names, addresses, 18
  forward, 18
  reverse, 18-19
    troubleshooting, 100

Lottor, M., RFC 1033, 288

lserver command, nslookup, 95

lwresd (BIND 9), 233

M

Madson, C., RFC 2403, 290

Mail Destination (MD) resource record, RFC 1035, 203

Mail Exchanger (MX) resource record, 37, 61
  RFC 973, 197
  RFC 974, 197
  RFC 1035, 197

Mail Forwarder (MF) resource record 883, RFC 1035, 205

Mail Group Number (MG) resource record, RFC 1035, 204

Mail Rename (MR) resource record, RFC 1035, 205

Mail-List Info (MINFO) resource record, RFC 1035, 204

Mailbox (MB) resource record, RFC 1035, 203

mailing lists
bond-announce, 141
Bugtraq, 141

maintaining
root.hints files, 72-74
zones, 165-168

maintenance tools
h2n, 132-133
mkrdns, 134-135
Webmin, 133

makefile command, variables, 221-222

Manning, B.
RFC 1706, 289
RFC 2010, 289

manual zone transfers, 249

mapping addresses (PTR records), 18

master servers, 12
defined, 164

master zone, 25

masters
primary
first fields, 164
zone updaters, 164
slaves, connecting to, 175

max-cache-ttl, 233

max-ncache-ttl tuning, 277

max-transfer-time-in option, 248

MB (Mailbox) resource record, RFC 1035, 203

MD (Mail Destination) resource record, RFC 1035, 203

MD5, RFC 1321, 165

memory statistics (BIND), 252

Menezes, Alfred J., *Handbook of Applied Cryptography*, 287

messages (ttl), bad, 139

methods, logging, 63

MF (Mail Forwarder 883) resource record, RFC 1035, 204

MG (Mail Group Number) resource record, RFC 1035, 204

migrating BIND 4 to BIND 8
file conversion configuration, 210
name checking, 211
NAME configuration, 210
ndc, 211
query source, 210

Mills, D.L., RFC 799, 291

min-roots
option, 253
tuning, 277

MINFO (Mail-List Info) resource record, RFC 1035, 204

mkrdns maintenance tools, 134-135

Mockapetris, P.
RFC 833, 292
RFC 882, 291
RFC 973, 292
RFC 1035, 204
RFC 1101, 291

moderating BIND, names.conf option, 176

modifying routing tables, 178

moving
nameservers, 56-57
Web servers housing services, 54-55

MR (Mail Rename) resource record, RFC 1035, 205

MX (Mail Exchanger) resource record, 37, 61
RFC 973, 197
RFC 974, 197
RFC 1035, 197

N

NA stub query, 182

Name Authority Pointer (NAPTR) resource record, RFC 2168, 202

name checking, 216

name daemon, 21
caching, resolving names, 29

Name Daemon Control. *See* ndc

name lookups, asynchronous, 193

named
configuration, working, 222
script, writing, 224
sockets
ncd, 242
ndc, 242

named-bootconf script, 210

named.conf, 196
BIND, configuring, 23-24
BIND 9, 230-232
options, 253

names
caching name daemon, resolving, 29
checking, migrating BIND 4 to BIND 8, 211

names.conf option, moderating BIND, 176

nameservers, 8
bogus, 215
defining, 31
domains, 80
duplicating, 11
moving, 56-57
querying, 15-17
redundant
external, 69
internal, 68
root, 24
setting up, 80

NAPTR (Name Authority Pointer) resource record, RFC 2168, 202

NATing Internet gateway, 155

ncd
channels, 242
named sockets, 242
signals, 241

ndc
command, starting BIND, 26-27
migrating BIND 4 to BIND 8, 211
named sockets, 242
script, writing, 225
signals, 242
status, 242-243

negating elements, 261
! (exclamation mark), 261

negative caching, 102

nesting BIND C-style comments, 258

Net:DNS by Mike Fuhr, **190**
Web site, 190

nets (classless), reverse delegations, 47-49

netstat, network traffic, 99

networks
closed (DNS), 179-180
conditions, troubleshooting DNS, 98-99
congestion, diagnosing, 98
DNS, setting up, 34-41
hiding, 155-158
large corporate (DNS), 160-161
traffic, 99

newsgroups (BIND), 220

Next Valid Name (NXT) resource record, RFC 2065, 202

NIMLOC (NIMROD Locator) resource record, 205

NIMROD Locator. *See* **NIMLOC**

-[no]stick dig option, 89

NOTIFY
extension, zone changes, 50-51
request, transferring zones, 55-56
slave servers, updating, 171

NPlex, 156

NS (Authoritative Nameserver) resource record, 15-17
RFC 1035, 197

NSAP resource record, RFC 1706, 197

NSAP_PTR (NSAP Variant of PTR Record) resource record, RFC 1183, 205

nslint
quality control tool, 138-139
Web site, 138

nslookup, 92
addresses, finding, 93-94
errors, 192
help command, 95
interactive mode, 93
lserver command, 95
shell scripting, 192

nsping
  quality control tool, 139
  Web site, 139

NSTATS line (BIND statistics), 251

nsupdate
  command-line tool, 168
  errors, displaying, 170
  testing, 170
  using, 170-171

NULL resource record, RFC 1035, 202

numbers
  query, BIND, 151-152
  serial, editing, 101

NXT (Next Valid Name) resource record, RFC 2065, 202

O

O'Neil, Kevin, log messages, 106

obsolete resource records
  EID, 203
  GPOS, 203
  ISDN, 203
  MB, 203
  MD, 203
  MF, 204
  MG, 204
  MINFO, 204
  MR, 205
  NIMLOC, 205
  NSAP_PTR, 205
  WKS, 205

obtaining
  addresses (DHCP), 173
  BIND, 219
  DHCP, 172
  domains, 80

Ohta, M., RFC 1995, 289

operational enhancements (BIND 9), 228

options
  allow transfer, 149
  allow-query, 144
  BIND 9, 231
  Boolean, 268-273
  channels, 263
  dig
    -c <query-class>, 89
    -envsav, 89
    -envset, 89
    -f <file>, 88
    -k <keydir:keyname>, 89
    -[no]stick, 89
    -P [<ping-string>], 89
    -p <port>, 89
    -t <query-type>, 89
    -T <time>, 89
    -x <dotted.address>, 88
  file clause, 263
  forward-only, 213
  -hwhois option, 77-79
  min-roots, 253
  named.conf, 253
  queries, 87
    keywords, 87-88
  tcp list, 214
  zone statement, 279-280
  zone transfers, 248-249

options statement
  Boolean options, 268-273
  pathnames, 268

  periodic task intervals, 274
  resource limits, 273-274
  syntax, 266-267

ordering
  elements, 261
  RRsets, 276
  values, 277

OS resolvers
  clients, configuring, 34
  DNS, 30
  /etc/host.conf, 33
  /etc/resolv.conf, 31
  searches, 32

outages (extended), using SOA resource records, 69

output, dig, 90-91

P

-P [<ping-string>] dig option, 89

-p <port> dig option, 89

packet filters
  BIND, disconnecting, 177
  firewalls (DNS), 154-155
  network conditions, 98

packets (UDP), 98

Parnassus Web site, 191

Partridge, Craig, RFC 974, 288

passing queries, fwhois command, 77-78

pathnames, options statement, 268

Peckman, Chris, 97

period (.), RP resource records, 198

periodic task intervals, 274

Perl
DNS, 189
gethostby* functions, 189

Perl-style. *See* **Shell-style**

ping, diagnosing network congestion, 98

Pointer to Other Name resource record. *See* **PTR**

poisoning, 142
BIND, 142
DNS, 47, 102

Postal, Su and J., RFC 819, 291

Postel, J.
RFC 805, 291
RFC 920, 292
RFC 1010, 292
RFC 1591, 289
RFC 1700, 289

pound (#), Shell-style comments, 259

prerequisites, zone updates, 169

primary masters
first fields, 164
zone updaters, 164

primary zone. *See* **master zone**

processing queries, dig, 89

protocol enhancements (BIND 9), 228

proxies, application, 161

pseudo rootservers, 182

PTR (Pointer to Other Name) resource record
addresses, mapping, 18
RFC 1035, 197

Public Key (KEY) resource record, RFC 2065, 201

PX (X.400 Mapping) resource record, RFC 2163, 198

Python
DNS, 191
gethostbyaddr, 190
gethostbyname call, 190

pz/127.0.0, configuring BIND, 25-26

Q

qr flags, 91

quality control tools
dnswalk, 136-137
DOC (Domain Obscenity Control), 137-138
nslint, 138-139
nsping, 139

queries
concentration, 160
dig, processing, 89
DNS, forwarding, 70-72
fwhois command, passing, 77-78
ID numbers (BIND), 151-152
IQUERY, 215
logging, 213
nameservers, 15-17

options, 87-88
source, migrating BIND 4 to BIND 8, 210
stub
NA, 182
SOA, 182
wildcard resource records, 61

query-class dig command-line term, 86

+query-option dig command-line term, 86

query-type dig command-line term, 86

quoting values, 104

R

ra flags, 91

rd flags, 91

reading logs, 98

README file (BIND 9), 230

records. *See* **resource records**

recursion
dig command, 14-15
turning off, 14-15

recursive clients, 234

recursive servers, 213

redundant nameservers
external, 69
internal, 68

Reed, Darren, arlib, 194

registering domains, 81
expiring, 99
IANA, 76

Rekhter, V., RFC 1597, 289

remote name demon control. *See* **rndc**

replacing databases (BIND 9), 229

Request For Comments. *See* **RFCs**

requests (NOTIFY), transferring zones, 55-56

resolution
record domain names, 13
reverse, 19-20
RR, 13

resolvers
OS
configuring for clients, 34
DNS, 30
/etc/host.conf, 33
searches, 32
UNIX, 31
API calls, 187-188
configuring, 32-33
synchronous, 193

resolving
asynchronous, 193
Internet congestion (AARNet2), 70-71
names, caching name daemon, 29
problems, 121
servers, adding, 160

resource limits
BIND 8, 214
BIND 9, 233-234
values, 273-274

resource records, 86
A, 195
A6, 238
AAAA, 196
adding, 169
AFSDB, 200
ATMA, 196
CNAME, 18, 60, 196
problems using, 60
deleting, 169
DNAME, 235-237
restrictions, 238
domain name resolutions, 13
HINFO, 38, 196
ISDN, 201
KEY, 201
KX, 201
LOC, 201
MX, 37, 61, 197
NAPTR, 202
NS, 15-17, 197
NSAP, 197
NULL, 202
NXT, 202
obsolete
EID, 203
GPOS, 203
ISDN, 203
MB, 203
MD, 203
MF, 204
MG, 204
MINFO, 204
MR, 205
NIMLOC, 205
NSAP_PTR, 205
WKS, 205
PTR, 18, 197
PX, 198
RP, 198

RT, 198
SIG, 202
SINK, 202
SOA, 101
DNS, 53
extended outages, 69
sorting, 275-276
SRV, 198-199
TXT, 200
wildcards
errors, 62
querying, 61
restrictions, 61
X25, 200

resources
books, 287
servers, limits, 273-274
troubleshooting DNS, 97
usage, security, 147-148

Responsible Person (RP) resource record, RFC 1183, 198

reverse delegations, 99
classless nets, 47-49

reverse lookups, 18-19
troubleshooting, 100

reverse resolution, 19-20

reverse zones, 11, 41-42
examining, 42
owners, locating, 76
updating, 171
zone/206.6.177, 45

Reynolds, J.
RFC 920, 292
RFC 1010, 292
RFC 1700, 289

RFCs (Request for Comments), 288-292
799, 291
805, 291

819, 291
830, 291
882, 291
  DNS, 195
883, 292
  DNS, 195
920, 292
952, 245, 288
953, 292
973, 292
  DNS, 195
  MX resource record,
  197
974, MX resource record,
  197
1010, 292
1032, 288, 292
1033, 288
1034, 288
1035, 164, 288
  A resource record, 195
  CNAME resource
  record, 196
  Host Information
  resource record, 196
  Mail Destination
  resource record, 203
  Mail Exchanger
  resource record, 197
  Mail Forwarder 883
  resource record, 204
  MB resource record,
  203
  MG resource record,
  204
  MINFO resource
  record, 204
  MR resource record,
  205
  NS resource record,
  197

NULL resource record,
  202
PTR resource record,
  197
SOA resource record,
  198-199
TXT resource record,
  200
WKS resource record,
  205
1101, 291
1122, 291
1123, 245, 288
1183, 288
  AFSDB resource
  record, 200
  ISDN resource record,
  201-203
  NSAP_PTR resource
  record, 205
  RP resource record,
  198
  RT resource record,
  198
  X25 resource record,
  200
1321, 288
  MD5, 165
1367, 292
1467, 292
1535, 289
1591, 289
1664, 292
1700, 289
1706, 289
  NSAP resource record,
  197
1712, GPOS resource
  record, 203
1713, 289

1876, 289
  LOC resource record,
  201
1886, 289
  AAAA resource record,
  196
1912, 97, 104, 245, 289
1995, 289
1996, 289
2010, 289
2050, 289
2052, 289
  SRV resource record,
  199
2063, NXT resource
  record, 202
2065, 290
  KEY resource record,
  201
  SIG resource record,
  202
2104, 290
  HMAC, 165
2136, 163-164, 290
2137, 290
2163, PX resource record,
  198
2168, NAPTR resource
  record, 202
2181, 97, 164, 290
2182, 69, 290
  secondary servers, 49
2219, 290
2230, 290
  KX resource record,
  201
2308, 253, 290
2317, 290
2403, 290
  HMAC-MD5, 165
2535, 153, 290

2671, 290
2672, 291
2874, 291

Rivest, R., "MD5 Message-Digest Algorithm", 288

rndc (Remote name demon control), 232
BIND 9, 232-233

Romao, A., RFC 1713, 289

root, 8

root domain, 8

root nameservers, 24

root nodes, 8

root zones
files, 181
stub zones, combining, 183

root.hints file
BIND, configuring, 24-25
maintaining, 72-74

rootservers
configuration, 180
duplicating, 11-12
internal
implementing, 180
Internet, 180
pseudo, 182

round robin (DNS), distributing loads, 58-59

Round Trip Time. *See* RTT

Route Through (RT) resource record, RFC 1183, 198

routing tables, modifying, 178

RP (Responsible Person) resource record, RFC 1183, 198

RRs. *See* resource records

RRsets
defined, 163
ordering, 276
values, 277
TTL, 164

RSA Data Security RFC 1321, 288

RT (Route Through) resource record, RFC 1183, 198

RTT (Round Trip Time), 215
format, 104

S

SANS Institute Web site, 142

scalability
BIND 9, 228, 238-239
DNS, 8

scanning interfaces (BIND), 247

Schneir, Bruce, *Applied Cryptography: Protocols, Algorithms, and Source Code in C, 2nd Edition*, 287

scripts
named, writing, 224
named-bootconf, 210
ndc, writing, 225

searches, OS resolvers, 32

secondary servers, RFC 2182, 49

secure_zone (BIND 4), 217

security, 141
bad servers, 146
BIND, 23, 142-144
BIND 9, 228
BIND versions, hiding, 152-153
blackholing, 146
DNS information, 155-158
DNSSEC, 153
enhancements
DNSSEC, 240
TSIG, 239-240
keys, 166
mailing lists, 141
resource usage, 147-148
resources, 142
TSIGS, 153
zone transfers, 149-150
zones, 172

Security Focus (Bugtraq) Web site, 141

seeding dynamic zones, 167

semicolon (;)
comments, 259
listing multiple servers, 50

serial numbers
editing, 101
slave servers, 101-102
SOA records, 101

serial-queries option, 249

@server dig command-line term, 86

server statement, 282
  syntax, 282
severity clause, 263
servers
  adding resolving, 160
  bad, security, 146
  cache, 184
  debugging, 263
  DHCP
    DNS update clients,
      168
    dynamic updates, 174
  DNS
    determining amount
      internally, 68
    myths about, 67-68
    updates, 164
  lame, 62, 94, 100
  master, 12
    defined, 164
  multiple, listing, 50
  recursive, 213
  resources, limits, 273-274
  secondary, RFC 2182, 49
  slave, 12, 80
    adding, 49-50
    data, 101
    defined, 164
    serial numbers,
      101-102
    setting up, 184
    updating, 55, 171
  stealth, 50
  Web, moving, 54-55
Service Locator (SRV)
  resource record, RFC
  2052, 199

setting up
  chroot environment,
    223-224
  DNS
    domains, 34-41
    networks, 34-41
  nameservers, 80
  slave servers, 184
  stub zones, 182
  working named configu-
    ration, 222
severity (BIND logs), 63
shell scripting
  dig, 192
  DNS, 191
  nslookup, 192
Shell-style comments
  (BIND), 259
SIG (Signature) resource
  record, RFC 2065, 202
signals, ncd, 241-242
Signature (SIG) resource
  record, RFC 2065, 202
SINK (The Kitchen Sink
  Record) resource
  record, 202
sizes, caches, 234
slash, slash (//), C++-style
  comments, 258
slash, star (/*), C-style
  comments, 258
slave servers, 12, 80
  adding, 49-50
  data, 101
  defined, 164
  NOTIFY, updating, 171
  serial number, 101-102
  setting up, 184
  updating, 55

slave zones, 25
slaves, connecting to
  masters, 175
snooper (network
  traffic), 99
SOA (Start of Authority)
  resource record
  DNS, 53
  extended outages, 69
  RFC 1035, 198-199
  serial numbers, 101
  stub query, 182
  TTL, 37
software. *See* tools
sorting
  addresses, 215
    BIND, 243-244
    BIND 4, 214
    BIND 8, 214
  resource records, 245,
    275-276
sortlist directive, 214
sortlists, 243
  addresses, 244
split DNS, 155
  firewalls, 158-160
spoofing, 142
  BIND, 142-144
src directory (BIND), 220
SRV (Service Locator)
  resource record, RFC
  2052, 199
Stahl, M.
  "DOD Internet Host
    Table Specification", 288
  RFC 953, 292
  RFC 1032, 288, 292

star, slash (*/), C-style comments, 258

Start of Authority resource record. *See* **SOA**

starting BIND, ndc command, 26-27

statements
  acl
    ACLs, 281
    syntax, 280
  BIND 8, 258
  controls, 283
    syntax, 283
  include, 283
  key, 281
    syntax, 281
  logging, 98, 106, 263
    categories, 265-266
    channels, 263-265
    clauses, 263
    configurations, 262
    syntax, 261
  options
    Boolean statement, 268-273
    pathnames, 268
    periodic task intervals, 274
    resource limits, 273-274
    syntax, 266-267
  server, 282
    syntax, 282
  topology, 274-275
  trusted-keys, 281-282
  zone
    classes, 279
    options, 279-280
    syntax, 277-278
    zone types, 278-279

statistics (BIND), 250-252

status, ndc, 242-243

STDs (Internet Standard), 288

stealth servers, 50

Stevens, Richard W., *UNIX Network Programming,* **287**

structures, tree (DNS), 20

stub queries
  NS, 182
  SOA, 182

stub zones
  root zones, combining, 183
  setting up, 182

subdomains, 9, 47

switches, -F, 136. *See also* **options**

synchronous UNIX resolvers, 193

syslog clause, 263

Syslog logging facility (BIND), 64

T

-t <query-type> dig option, 89

-T <time> dig option, 89

task intervals, periodic, 274

tc flags, 91

tcp wrappers, 100

tcpdump network traffic, 99

tcplist option, 214

telnet, testing DNS connections, 99

testing
  BIND, 26-29
  connections (DNS), 99
  nsupdate, 170

Text Information (TXT) resource record, RFC 1035, 200

Thompson, S., RFC 1886, 289

time, logging, 264

TLDs (top-level domains)
  DNS hierarchy, 7
  ISPs, establishing, 75
  owners, finding, 76

tools
  command-line, nsupdate, 168
  dig, 85
  maintenance
    h2n, 132-133
    mkrdns, 134-135
    Webmin, 133
  quality control
    dnswalk, 136-137
    DOC (Domain Obscenity Control), 137-138
    nslint, 138-139
    nsping, 139
  Web
    DigIt, 132
    Internet Query tools, 132
    ZoneCheck, 132
  whois, -h option, 77-79

Topolcic, C.
RFC 1367, 292
RFC 1467, 292

topology
BIND, 244
statement, 274-275

traceroute, diagnosing network congestion, 98

traffic
BIND, 176
networks, 99

trafshow (network traffic), 99

transaction signature. *See* TSIG

transfer-source option, 248

transferring zones, 56, 107-108, 213-214
BIND, 247-250
incremental, 249-250
limiting, 214
manual, 249
NOTIFY request, 55-56
options, 248-249
security, 149-150

transfers-in option, 248

treat-cr-as-space option, 253

tree structure (DNS), 20

troubleshooting
DNS
network conditions, 98
resources, 97
domain delegation
DigIt, 99
dnswalk, 99
DOC, 99

errors, 106-130
reverse lookups, 100

trusted keys statement, 281-282

TSIG (transaction signature), 165
authentication, 166
BIND 9 security enhancement, 239-240
security, 153
updates, 165
HMAC-MD5, 165
Web site, 165

TTL
caching, 34
messages, bad, 139
RRsets, 164
SOA, 37
values, 36

$TTL zone, 102

tuning
lame-ttl, 277
max-ncache-ttl, 277
min-roots, 277

turning off recursion, 14-15

TXT (Text Information) resource record, RFC 1035, 200

U

UDP packets, 98

UNIX (BIND), 22

***UNIX Network Programming* by Richard W. Stevens, 188, 287**

UNIX resolvers, 31
configuring, 32-33
gethostbyaddr API call, 187-188
gethostbyname API call, 187-188
synchronous, 193

updates
DNS servers, 164
dynamic, DHCP servers, 174
TSIG, 165
HMAC-MD5, 165
zones, 217
actions, 169
prerequisites, 169
primary masters, 164
reverse zones, 55, 171
usage (resources)
security, 147-148
viewing, 147-148

USAGE line (BIND statistics), 251

V

values
ordering RRsets, 277
quoting, 104
resource limits, 273-274
TTL, 36

Van Oorschot, Paul C., *Handbook of Applied Cryptography,* **287**

vanishing domain, 99

Vanstone, Scott A., *Handbook of Applied Cryptography*

variables, makefile command, 221-222

versions (BIND), hiding, 152-153

viewing resource usage, 147-148

views, BIND 9, 234-235

Vixie, P.
RFC 1996, 289
RFC 2010, 289
RFC 2052, 289
RFC 2136, 290
RFC 2182, 290

W

Web servers, moving housing services, 54-55

Web sites
ASC, 22
Ask Mr. DNS, 97
AUS-CERT advisory, 145
BIND, 219
ISC, 22
configuration files listings, 1
CPAN, 190
Deja.com, 131
Demon, 132
DNS Resource Directory, 131
DNS Tricks and Tips, 97
DNScache library, 194
DNSRD, 97
dnswalk, 136
DOC, 137
Eddie, 59
GNU adns, 193
GNUs textutils package, 220
IANA, 76

ISC, 172, 219
ISC PGP, 220
log files, 106
Net::DNS, 190
nslint, 138
nsping, 139
Parnassus, 191
SANS Institute, 142
Security Focus (Bugtraq), 141
TSIG, 165
Webmin, 133
ZoneCheck Web tool, 132

Web tools
DigIt, 132
Internet Query tools, 132
ZoneCheck, 132

Webmin
maintenance tools, 133
Web site, 133

Well Known Service (WKS) resource record, RFC 1035, 205

whois database, 76-77
help command, 77

whois tool
-h option, 77-79
LinePro, 78-79

wildcard resource records, 60
errors, 62
querying, 61
restrictions, 61

WKS (Well Known Service) resource record, RFC 1035, 205

working named configuration, setting up, 222

Wright, R., RFC 2219, 290

writing scripts (named), 224
ndc, 225

X-Z

-x <dotted.address> dig option, 88

X.400 (PX) resource record, RFC 2163, 198

X25 (X25 Routing Information) resource record, RFC 1183, 200

xfrnets directive, 214

XSTATS line (BIND statistics), 251

Zaw-Sing Su, RFC 830, 291

zone statement
classes, 279
options, 279-280
syntax, 277-278
zone types, 278-279

zone/206.6.177 (reverse zone), 45

zone/walrus.bv, 43-44

ZoneCheck Web tool, 132
Web site, 132

zones, 34
access control lists (BIND 4), 217
BIND, 247-250
incremental, 249-250
limiting, 214
manual, 249
security, 149-150

BIND 4, configuring, 212
changes, NOTIFY exten-
   sion, 50-51
data mistakes, 104-105
distributing, 11
domains, 10
duplicating, 11
dynamic, seeding, 167
editing, 168
expiring, 36
files, 106
forward, 34-41
inspecting, 40
maintaining, 165-168
master, 25
NOTIFY request, trans-
   ferring, 55-56
reverse, 11, 41-42
   examining, 42
   finding owners, 76
   updating, 171
   zone/206.6.177, 45
securing, 172
slave, 25
stub and root, combining,
   183
subdomain, 47
transfers, 56, 167-168,
   213-214
   DNS, 12
   options, 248-249
$TTL, 102
types of, zone statement,
   278-279
updates, 217
   actions, 169
   prerequisites, 169
zone/walrus.bv, 43-44

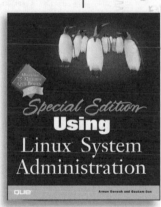